# Neighborhood Defenders

Since the collapse of the housing market in 2008, demand for housing has consistently outpaced supply in many US communities. The
failure to construct sufficient housing – especially affordable housing – in desirable communities and neighborhoods comes with significant social, economic, and environmental costs. This book examines
how local participatory land use institutions amplify the power of
entrenched interests and privileged homeowners. The book draws on
sweeping data to examine the dominance of land use politics by 'neighborhood defenders' – individuals who oppose new housing projects
far more strongly than their broader communities and who are likely
to be privileged on a variety of dimensions. Neighborhood defenders
participate disproportionately and take advantage of land use regulations to restrict the construction of multifamily housing. The result is
diminished housing stock and higher housing costs, with participatory
institutions perversely reproducing inequality.

Katherine Levine Einstein is Assistant Professor of Political Science and
Faculty Fellow at the Initiative on Cities at Boston University.

David M. Glick is Associate Professor of Political Science and Faculty
Fellow at the Initiative on Cities at Boston University.

Maxwell Palmer is Assistant Professor of Political Science, Faculty Fellow at the Initiative on Cities, and Junior Faculty Fellow at the Hariri
Institute for Computing at Boston University.

# Neighborhood Defenders

## Participatory Politics and America's Housing Crisis

KATHERINE LEVINE EINSTEIN
*Boston University*

DAVID M. GLICK
*Boston University*

MAXWELL PALMER
*Boston University*

CAMBRIDGE
UNIVERSITY PRESS

# CAMBRIDGE
## UNIVERSITY PRESS

University Printing House, Cambridge CB2 8BS, United Kingdom

One Liberty Plaza, 20th Floor, New York, NY 10006, USA

477 Williamstown Road, Port Melbourne, VIC 3207, Australia

314–321, 3rd Floor, Plot 3, Splendor Forum, Jasola District Centre,
New Delhi – 110025, India

79 Anson Road, #06–04/06, Singapore 079906

Cambridge University Press is part of the University of Cambridge.

It furthers the University's mission by disseminating knowledge in the pursuit of
education, learning, and research at the highest international levels of excellence.

www.cambridge.org
Information on this title: www.cambridge.org/9781108477277
DOI: 10.1017/9781108769495

© Cambridge University Press 2020

First published 2020

*A catalogue record for this publication is available from the British Library.*

*Library of Congress Cataloging-in-Publication Data*
Names: Einstein, Katherine Levine, author.
Title: Neighborhood defenders : participatory politics and America's
housing crisis / Katherine Levine Einstein, David M. Glick, Maxwell Palmer.
Description: First. | New York : Cambridge university press, 2019. |
Includes bibliographical references and index.
Identifiers: LCCN 2019029333 (print) | LCCN 2019029334 (ebook) |
ISBN 9781108477277 (hardback) | ISBN 9781108769495 (epub)
Subjects: LCSH: Housing – United States. | Neighborhoods – United States. |
Social change – United States. | Community organization – United States. |
Community power – United States. | Gentrification – United States.
Classification: LCC HD7293 .E48 2019 (print) | LCC HD7293 (ebook) |
DDC 363.50973–dc23
LC record available at https://lccn.loc.gov/2019029333
LC ebook record available at https://lccn.loc.gov/2019029334

ISBN 978-1-108-47727-7 Hardback
ISBN 978-1-108-70851-7 Paperback

*We dedicate this book to our children, Elise and Ezra, Henry, and Jacob and Noah. May they grow up in a world with enough housing for all.*

# Contents

# Figures

# Tables

# Acknowledgments

We are grateful to the vibrant intellectual community we have found at Boston University's political science department. Taylor Boas, Dino Christenson, Doug Kriner, David Mayers, Cathie Martin, Spencer Piston, Gina Sapiro, and Graham Wilson all provided helpful feedback on our research and the book publishing process. We especially appreciate Cathie and Spencer for telling us that what we thought was an article was, in fact, a book-length project.

This book would not have been possible without the generous support of Boston University's Initiative on Cities, especially Katharine Lusk, Stacy Fox, and Graham Wilson. Their funding helped us support much of the data collection for this book. Their partnership on the Menino Survey of Mayors provided invaluable national-level data for this project. They have generously promoted our work, allowing us to connect with interested policy makers and nonprofits. We also appreciate Citigroup and the Rockefeller Foundation's long-standing financial support of the Menino Survey of Mayors.

This book also benefited enormously from detailed feedback from the broader political science community. Conversations with and comments from Sarah Anzia, Justin de Benedictis-Kessner, Ryan Enos, Mike Hankinson, Alex Hertel-Fernandez, Mirya Holman, Vlad Kogan, Jeremy Levine, Megan Mullin, Clayton Nall, Joe Ornstein, Alex Sahn, Jessica Trounstine, and Chris Warshaw helped shape this book. Steve Ansolabehere and Jennifer Hochschild offered invaluable advice on the book publishing process. Joe Ornstein generously provided instrumental data on home ownership.

We had the opportunity to present this work at a variety of academic workshops. We are grateful to comments from participants at the American Political Science Association New Faces in Urban Politics Workshop; Brown University Political Geography and Inequality Conference; University of Wisconsin-Milwaukee Department of Political Science Workshop; University of Michigan Women's Political Science Caucus Workshop; University of Massachusetts Boston Department of Public Policy Workshop; and Vanderbilt Local Political Economy Conference.

One of the most exciting parts of this project for us has been the enthusiasm we received from outside of academia, in both the government and nonprofit sectors. We appreciate the comments we received from members of the government and community at presentations at the Citizens Housing and Planning Association (CHAPA), a Government Accountability Office seminar, CoUrbanize, and A Better Cambridge. We are especially grateful to Karin Brandt, Rachel Heller, Dana LeWinter, and Sara Matasci, who helped connect our research with practitioners. Linda Jason was instrumental in linking us with valuable research resources.

While we preserve their confidentiality by not listing them by name here, we are thankful for the numerous elected and appointed city officials, housing lawyers, developers, and housing advocates who so generously gave us their time, allowing us to interview them for this book project. Their comments shaped our research and pushed us to think about the many complicated trade-offs inherent in housing policy.

An outstanding team of undergraduate and graduate research assistants made the data collection for this book possible. We thank Luisa Godinez Puig, Sarah Sklar, Nick Henninger, Elizabeth Champion, Tara Martin-Chen, and Lianne O'Reilly. Sarah Sklar's able management of our undergraduate research team is especially appreciated.

We are deeply grateful to our editor Sara Doskow for her seamless oversight of the publication process. Seamless is not an adjective often applied to academic peer review, but Sara's guidance and transparency are so appreciated. We also thank this book's anonymous reviewers, who provided us with detailed and thoughtful comments.

Finally, we thank our spouses, David Einstein, Jessica Blankshain, and Cori Palmer, and parents, Marta and Marc Levine, Terry and Leonard Glick, and Nina and Geoff Palmer, for their love, support, and patience as we wrote this manuscript. Without them, this book would not have been possible. We especially appreciate David and Marc for reading drafts of our work. Our children, Elise and Ezra Einstein, Henry Glick, and Jacob and Noah Palmer, did not help with the writing of this book, but they made the times we were not writing so much brighter. It is to them that we dedicate this book.

# 1

# Introduction

On October 18, 2016, the Cambridge, Massachusetts Planning Board met, as they do every two weeks, to consider applications for new residential and commercial developments. Among other proposals, they examined an application from a developer who sought to convert a commercial warehouse on Regent Street into four residential units. After representatives for the developer made their presentation, members of the city's planning board asked a variety of fairly mundane questions about the building's structure, focusing on the dimension of the basement windows and the location of bike parking, among other things. The planning board then turned the proceedings over to the public. In most locations, public input is mandated for development proposals that are of a sufficient scale or require exceptions to current land use regulations (Schleicher 2013).[1]

While the planning board members initially asked fairly neutral and technocratic questions, the members of the public attending the meeting were considerably more pointed. The first speaker, a resident of Regent Street, observed:[2]

There are a variety of concerns among various neighbors, but I'll just speak to mine which are the density. I feel is very high. ... I feel that having four

---

[1] In case studies of zoning codes in six institutionally disparate cities, we found that all solicited public input at multiple stages of the zoning process. Even in famously unzoned Houston, Texas, projects presented before the Planning Commission receive public comment.

[2] All of these meeting minutes include the names and addresses of the individuals who participated in these meetings. To preserve the privacy of these individuals, we do not refer to them by name in this book.

units in that building with one parking space each is insufficient and that's my objection.

The next speaker – a resident of Regent Street for more than thirty years – came prepared with handouts:

I've done a little research and this is all information from the property database in Cambridge. ... We're in Zone B, my understanding is that there's a 2500 ... minimum square foot requirement per dwelling. And I think this development is very non-compliant and that's my objection. ... My main objection is to the density that is non-conforming.

The third speaker had lived on the street a whopping eighty years, and had perhaps the most pressing concerns:

We had a great problem, our house was leaning and it was leaning very badly. ... We had to have work done. It's cost us over $100,000 to have this work done. My concern is that ... demolition is going to affect all the work we've done. And not only my house but the house right next to it is having a lot of problems. We don't know what's causing the houses to sink. ... That's our biggest concern. Of course, the parking and all of that, too, that goes with it.

Another six neighbors spoke afterward. All strongly opposed the proposed four-unit development.

Cambridge law mandates that planning board officials take these concerns into account. The chair of the planning board stated this requirement:

The Board shall evaluate the impact of increased numbers of dwelling units above that normally permitted in the district on the demand for on-street parking by residents and visitors to the proposed buildings. ... In reaching a determination, the Board may require the applicant to provide elements of a parking analysis as set forth. ... The Board shall [also] evaluate the impact on residential neighbors of the new housing use and any other proposed use as it may affect privacy. ... The Board shall consider among other factors the potential negative impacts of the new activity on abutters as a result of the location, orientation, and use of the structures and its yards as proposed ... *And then, finally, community outreach. The Planning Board shall consider what reasonable efforts have been made to address the concerns raised by abutters and neighbors to the project site.* (emphasis added)

Another planning board member weighed neighborhood concerns heavily:

This board member would find it very, very difficult tonight ... in light of the input we've gotten from abutters and my review of the documents, to make findings in affirmative. ... It seems like there is the potential to engage in a more detailed conversation with the community to see whether ... the developer can assuage the primary concerns of parking, of density, and the issue of settlement. . . . I would also include the potential . . . for the Board to ask for a parking analysis or a traffic analysis.

A third board member built on these concerns: "In addition to what [the preceding board member] said, I would also request some sort of geotech engineering study done. More than one person mentioned houses sinking based on water." Other members of the Cambridge Planning Board largely echoed these concerns, similarly rooting them in neighbors' stated objections at the meeting.

In one of the country's most liberal cities – one facing rapidly increasing housing costs and frequent bidding wars over limited housing options – a group of neighbors uniformly opposed the development of new housing. Prior to hearing from community members, the Cambridge Planning Board indicated little opposition to the project. The picture was starkly different after the public comment period. The board members agreed that the concerns raised by the participating neighbors were valid, and suggested a variety of measures. In response, the developer undertook additional parking and geotech studies – each of which can cost upwards of $10,000 – and then returned to the planning board three months later in January 2017. When he returned, the developer not only brought completed parking and geotech studies; he also altered his proposal in a number of ways in an attempt to mollify neighbors' concerns. The developer said: "A number of the neighbors thought that four units was too many and asked whether we could actually consider having a successful project with only three, and we've come to a resolution that we are going to do that."

The developer also agreed to increase the number of parking spaces from one to two per unit. The planning board was impressed by these changes. The chair of the planning board observed: "Reasonable efforts have been taken to address concerns raised by abutters and neighbors. And I think quite substantial efforts have been taken to address those concerns."

His views were echoed by the rest of the planning board.

The demands of six individuals resulted in the developer commissioning two additional and highly costly studies. These studies took time and required an additional planning board meeting. Such delay requires the developer to pay additional property taxes and maintenance costs on the property. Even more importantly, these six neighbors reduced the number of units in the building, essentially replacing that space with additional parking for cars. Obviously, these costs and delays are not ideal for the developer who has to settle for a presumably less profitable project. Whether or not the developer and his bottom line deserve concern and sympathy, this process reduced the supply of housing in a city that desperately needs it. Moreover, the developer ended up constructing fewer units with more parking on the same parcel of land; to turn a profit, he will likely make each unit more expensive.

Building four very expensive condos (per the initial proposal) instead of three *even more* expensive condos would not have materially affected working-, middle-, and even upper-class people's ability to afford to live in the Boston metropolitan area. All that happened is that one well-to-do individual or family was denied one potential choice property, and one real estate developer was forced to accept less than his ideal profit margin.

However, when repeated over and over again – whenever a developer wants to build a new set of townhouses or a homeowner wants to add an accessory apartment – this process has a marked influence on housing availability. Individuals, empowered by local political institutions like planning and zoning boards, shape whether, and how, housing is constructed.

In this book, we analyze and unpack the participatory politics of housing. We present a new theory and new data connecting land use regulations and the individuals that use them. We show how local institutions, designed to enhance participation, actually empower an unrepresentative group of residents – who we call neighborhood defenders – to stop the construction of new housing.

*Neighborhood Defenders* is fundamentally about the people who participate in local housing politics and the institutions in which they participate. It centers on the motivated residents who show up at meetings to oppose new housing and zoning changes. These individuals use their privileged status as current members of a community to prevent new housing, and thus close its doors to prospective new members.

Many point, correctly, to the role of zoning in drastically shaping local housing markets. But, we cannot simply focus on regulations in isolation from the ways they are used and enforced. Projects are not necessarily stopped by zoning codes alone. They are often delayed, stopped, or altered by interested residents using local land use institutions. Indeed, delay, in particular, is critical and largely under-studied. Time is a valuable resource. Rules and participatory opportunities enable a small group of otherwise limited residents to marshal it to their advantage.

Similarly, many observers have worried about Not in My Backyard (NIMBY) sentiments – the natural psychological tendency to endorse something in theory, but not when it is proposed next door. Analyzing

NIMBY-type attitudes toward new housing alone is also insufficient. Such views, without institutions that empower them, would have a much more limited impact. We study who acts on these attitudes by participating in local housing politics (and, just as importantly, who does not).

*Neighborhood Defenders* is simultaneously a substantive book about housing policy, and a political science book about local institutions, resident participation, and political inequality. Using a variety of methods and data, we investigate the politics undergirding the housing shortage. Specifically, we ask how regulations and political participation interact to shape where, how much, and what type of housing is built.

## RISING HOUSING COSTS

Since the collapse of the housing market in 2008, demand for housing has consistently outpaced supply. In 2015, one million American households competed for 620,000 new units of housing, a shortfall of 430,000 units (Goodman and Pendall 2016). Bidding wars are commonplace in many of the nation's hottest housing markets, especially in more affordable segments such as condominiums, townhouses, and smaller starter homes. In Oakland, California, 84 percent of offers written by Redfin agents – a national online real estate agency – faced bidding wars. Over two-thirds of Redfin offers in Los Angeles, Denver, Seattle, and San Francisco similarly competed against other bids. These bidding contests are disproportionately clustered in the most affordable segments of the market: nationally, 55 percent of offers in the $200,000 to $400,000 range and 60 percent of offers in the $400,000 to $600,000 range faced bidding wars (Carlyle 2016).

In 2017, the median home price in San Francisco was $1.29 million. A 20 percent down payment for such a home is $180,000 – almost $100,000 more than the median household income in the city. Median earners would similarly fall short in New York and Boston, where the median home prices were $637,000 and $585,000, respectively (Martin 2017).

Even turning to rental markets offers scant relief. The median one-bedroom apartment in San Francisco cost $3,300 per month in 2017 (Zillow 2017). The annual cost of $39,000 equals 45 percent of the annual earnings of the city's median household. Housing analysts consider an individual to be housing cost burdened if they spend 30 percent or more of their income on housing. To put this in context, these data suggest that the median family in San Francisco would be cost burdened if it rented the median one-bedroom apartment – a much smaller housing unit than what a typical family would target. These prices place homeownership, and even reasonable commutes, out of reach of many middle-income residents. Indeed, high housing costs spurred the US Department of Housing and Urban Development (HUD) to label San Francisco families of four earning at or below $105,350 low income, qualifying families with six-figure salaries for subsidized housing (de Guzman 2017).

While San Francisco's market is extreme, an individual or family earning $80,000 – well above the national median of $55,000 – would be similarly cost burdened renting a median one-bedroom apartment in multiple coastal housing markets including Washington, DC, Los Angeles, New York, and Boston. Again, this is a striking statistic. These are not individuals attempting to tap into the luxury market or rent five-bedroom units. A person earning $80,000 would be cost burdened renting an average one-bedroom apartment in these communities.

These problems are not limited to coastal markets. Housing in cities across the country is priced too high for middle-income individuals and families. Such households have to spend more than 30 percent of their income to obtain an average two-bedroom apartment in a diverse set of cities, including Charlotte, NC, and Minneapolis, MN. The picture in Minneapolis is especially stark – the median Minneapolis household would need to spend half of its income to afford the $2,195 average rent for a two-bedroom apartment (Zillow 2017).

The picture is even bleaker for low-income individuals and families. There is not a single county in the country in which a minimum-wage earner can afford an average two-bedroom rental (National Low Income Housing Coalition 2017). The majority of poor renting families spend *half* of their income on housing (Desmond 2016). Lotteries for government-subsidized housing illustrate the extraordinary pressure faced by very low-income renters. In 2017, nearly 6,000 people applied for 239 subsidized apartments near North Station in Boston (Logan 2017). A 95-unit affordable housing development in downtown San Francisco drew 6,580 applicants (Badger and Kang 2017). When Baltimore's Section 8 housing voucher wait list opened in 2014, 74,000 applicants vied for a spot on the wait list. The Housing Authority of Baltimore City then selected 25,000 applicants *for the wait list*. Of these individuals, less than 9,000 are likely to receive vouchers. The wait list is presently closed until 2020 (Wenger 2014).

City leaders nationwide see housing affordability as a crisis. During the summer of 2017, as part of the nationally representative Menino Survey of Mayors, we asked mayors across the country about housing, amid a myriad of other topics.[3] Over half of the mayors we surveyed cited high housing costs as one of the top three reasons that residents left their cities. Housing was the most frequently mentioned policy area – more so than other highly salient policies and concerns like jobs, schools, taxes, or public safety (see Figure 1.1). Housing costs were chief concern for mayors of rich and poor cities alike. Furthermore, only 13 percent of mayors believed that their cities' housing stock was a good match for the needs of their constituents. In a subsequent survey, we asked mayors how many housing units their cities needed to add in the next ten years. On average, mayors said they needed a 16 percent increase in housing units. Achieving this goal over the next ten years would require the rate at which units are permitted and constructed in the average city to more than quadruple.

What's more, mayors largely want to change the *type* of housing their cities were building. On average, mayors would like the share of new multifamily housing to be thirty-three percentage points higher than what currently exists in their cities. Achieving such a goal would likely require substantial change in many neighborhoods, including the

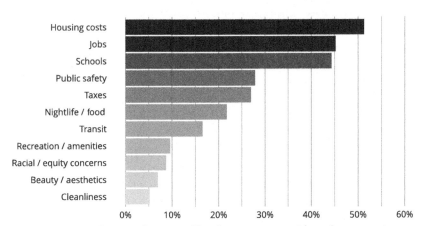

FIGURE 1.1: Survey of mayors: Top three reasons residents leave my city

[3] All survey of mayors results come from the 2017 and 2018 Menino Survey of Mayors. The survey is a nationally representative survey mayors of cities over 75,000. For more details on survey methodology and results, see the full research reports at www.surveyofmayors.com (Einstein, Glick, and Palmer 2018; Einstein et al. 2019).

construction of multifamily housing in neighborhoods mostly made up of single-family homes.

## COSTS OF THE HOUSING CRISIS

The failure to construct sufficient housing comes with significant social, economic, and environmental costs. Perhaps most seriously, the lack of affordable housing in areas with high social mobility could have a profound negative impact on many children's life opportunities (Chetty, Herdren, and Katz 2016). Multiple studies have linked housing instability with serious health problems. Public health researcher and physician Megan Sandel highlights the critical role of housing accessibility: "People talk a lot about health, education, or jobs, but they don't often pivot back to housing or where people live. A stable home is the foundation to thrive" (Butera 2018). She (along with her collaborators) surveyed more than twenty thousand low-income families at five urban medical centers nationwide. They found that 34 percent of surveyed families with children four and under experienced some form of housing instability, such as falling behind on rent, moving twice in the past year, and homelessness. These young children were 20 percent more likely to be hospitalized and 25 percent more likely to experience a developmental delay. Older children were three times more likely to experience a depressive episode (Butera 2018; Sandel et al. 2018). Sociologists Matthew Desmond and Rachel Tolbert Kimbro study the effects of eviction – a consequence of high housing costs, among other factors – on mothers. They find negative effects across multiple arenas. Women who were evicted were more likely to experience depression and parenting stress, and reported worse health outcomes for themselves and their children (Desmond and Kimbro 2015).

Housing access also strongly shapes educational opportunities and outcomes. Economist Jonathan Rothwell demonstrates that housing is more expensive in higher scoring school districts. Indeed, home values are $205,000 higher in neighborhoods with high-scoring schools. When translated into annual housing costs, this means that it is $11,000 more expensive each year to access housing in high-scoring school districts. While there is a robust debate among scholars about the precise impact of schooling on life outcomes, a large strand of research finds that higher quality schools increase the likelihood of economic success later in life (Rothwell 2018).

In addition, the Obama White House identified unaffordable housing as a key obstacle to equitable job access, arguing that "the growing severity of undersupplied housing markets is jeopardizing housing affordability for working families, increasing income inequality by reducing less-skilled workers' access to high-wage labor markets, and stifling GDP growth by driving labor migration away from the most productive regions" (White House 2016). Job seekers who would like to move to pursue better opportunities may be unable to do so because of high housing costs in places with more dynamic economies. Moreover, by impeding potential employees from moving, high housing costs may also be stagnating economic growth in many communities (Herkenhoff, Ohanian, and Prescott 2017). Removing impediments to the construction of new housing could increase city median GDP by 10 percent (Hsieh and Moretti 2015).

Many of these negative social, economic, and political costs of the housing crisis are disproportionately felt in communities of color. Housing availability has a profound effect on residential segregation. Land use restrictions that reduce the availability of multifamily housing are in many cases explicitly designed to exclude residents of color (Rothstein 2017; Trounstine 2018). Inadequate housing thus may prevent people of color from accessing communities with the highest quality public resources and services.

What's more, the insufficient construction of new housing may spur gentrification by pushing more development (and affluent home buyers) into communities of color that lack the resources to mobilize against development. We explore this political process in greater depth in subsequent chapters.

## INCREASING THE HOUSING SUPPLY

In this book, we focus on one major contributor to America's housing crisis: the housing supply. Most economists believe that, to address rising housing costs in many cities, we need to build more housing – especially higher-density, multifamily housing. While there are, of course, a myriad of reasons why American cities are experiencing a housing crisis, one common factor driving rising housing prices across the country is the well-understood dynamics of supply and demand (Quigley and Rosenthal 2005; Glaeser, Gyourko, and Saks 2005; Gyourko, Saiz, and Summers 2008; Glaeser and Ward 2009; Glaeser 2011; Gyourko and Molloy 2014; Goodman and Pendall 2016).

In addition to addressing housing affordability, more housing could also have a multitude of indirect environmental and economic benefits. Indeed, building more housing is integral to increasing the *density* of urban and suburban neighborhoods. Greater density – especially in conjunction with well-planned mass transit networks – would reduce car commuting and allow for the greater preservation of remaining urban green space (Glaeser 2011). The Environmental Protection Agency officially endorses such dense transit-oriented developments as critical to reducing the roughly 16 percent of US greenhouse gas emissions that come from cars and light-duty trucks (Environmental Protection Agency 2017). It suggests that this type of planning has "important consequences for the environment, including air and water quality, climate change, and open space preservation. How communities develop also affects how convenient and appealing public transportation, bicycling, and walking are for their residents."

Increased density also comes with economic benefits in the form of agglomeration economies. Individuals and businesses benefit from being close together. Greater density facilitates the exchange of information between residents and businesses. It also reduces the costs of production and permits greater specialization (Glaeser 2011; Schleicher 2013).

While the dynamics vary between housing markets, we are not building enough housing in the cities and neighborhoods where it is most needed. What's more, we are failing virtually everywhere to build enough of the type of housing – dense, multifamily homes – needed to sustainably house low- and middle-income individuals and families, young workers, and the elderly, among others. The most acute housing supply problems are concentrated in the hottest housing markets located disproportionately along the nation's coasts. But, a broader set of housing markets – including many not typically thought to be the epicenter of housing politics – are failing to build sufficiently, especially in their most desirable neighborhoods, in part because of the political processes highlighted in this book.

## POLITICS OF LAND USE

Despite the seeming consensus around building more housing, the housing shortage and affordability crisis persists. Why, if most informed observers believe that we need more housing, are most cities failing to keep pace with growing housing demand? Explanations of America's housing shortage tend to fall into one of two main categories: (1) zoning is too restrictive and (2) homeowners (and perhaps even renters) strongly oppose development in their communities. By considering land use institutions and the people who use them separately, these frameworks – while helpful – fail to fully capture how institutions and behavior jointly have created a nationwide housing shortage.

## Housing Regulations

A multitude of studies on the economics of housing construction can be boiled down into one simple and powerful statement: regulations prevent the construction of new housing (Quigley and Rosenthal 2005; Glaeser, Gyourko, and Saks 2005; Gyourko, Saiz, and Summers 2008; Glaeser and Ward 2009; Glaeser 2011; Gyourko and Molloy 2014; Goodman and Pendall 2016). By outright forbidding multifamily apartment buildings across wide swaths of city neighborhoods, local zoning codes in this account are the key culprit behind a nationwide housing shortage.

While there is significant variation across cities, jurisdictions across the country typically impose extra restrictions on the development of anything other than single-family homes on substantial lots. They do so using a wide array of laws and regulations. These laws encompass virtually all elements of the development of new housing, including, but not limited to the minimum size of the plot on which housing can be built, the size of the buffer zone separating a home from wetlands and vernal pools, the minimum distance separating a home and the street, and the number of units a septic system can legally accommodate. While zoning and land use have long been central to local government power (Burns 1994; Dreier, Mollenkopf, and Swanstrom 2004; Trounstine 2018), land use restrictions have become notably more restrictive in many regions of the United States over the past four decades (Glaeser, Gyourko, and Saks 2005; Glaeser and Ward 2009; Schleicher 2013).

These restrictions have been particularly acute in the most economically productive regions of the country (Glaeser 2011; Schleicher 2013). Economist Paul Krugman divides the country into two regions – Flatland and the Zoned Zone: "In Flatland, which occupies the middle of the country, it's easy to build houses. When the demand for houses rises, Flatland metropolitan areas, which don't really have traditional downtowns, just sprawl some more. As a result, housing prices are basically determined by the cost of construction."

The housing market, Krugman argues, operates quite differently in the Zoned Zone:

In the Zoned Zone, which lies along the coasts, a combination of high population density and land-use restrictions – hence "zoned" – makes it hard to build new houses. So when people become willing to spend more on houses, say because of a fall in mortgage rates, some houses get built, but the prices of existing houses also go up. And if people think that prices will continue to rise, they become willing to spend even more, driving prices still higher. (Krugman 2005)

This stark divide between coast and heartland is overly simplistic. While Houston, Texas, is famously unzoned, it restricts land use via a variety of regulations, including minimum lot-size requirements for single-family homes, minimum parking requirements, and restrictions on the construction of townhouses (Lewyn 2005; Schleicher 2013). Moreover, we find evidence in this book that, even in the so-called Flatland, neighborhood residents are able to take advantage of zoning regulations to restrict housing development in their cities' most highly desirable neighborhoods. Nonetheless, the impact of land use regulations is certainly felt more sharply in some communities than it is in others.

Much of the zoning reform movement is built around this focus on land use regulations. Take the example of Charlottesville, Virginia, where officials have described the area's limited housing supply as a "housing crisis" and "chronic disease." The city's senior planner, Brian Haluska, worries that the city's zoning restrictions make keeping pace with supply impossible: "I don't know that new construction can put much of a dent in the demand at all." With 55 percent of the city's land zoned for single-family homes, Haluska believes that the city is largely "built-out." Developers agree, with one noting: "You just cannot get your hands on buildable lots" (Castro 2018).

The solution, according to the city's affordable housing advocates and developers, is to upzone: take neighborhoods currently zoned for low-density development (like single-family homes) and legally allow higher density housing (like apartment buildings). Lyle Solla-Yates, a member of the Charlottesville Planning Commission and affordable housing advocate, agrees that upzoning is key. He points to the racial origin of earlier zoning decisions ("It's white supremacy – sorry – it's a bummer") and argues that "upzoning to allow more housing" is the only solution to the "housing crisis" (Castro 2018). Solla-Yates and other Charlottesville officials are hardly alone in their view that upzoning would make a significant dent in the housing crisis. Vox's Matthew Yglesias has tirelessly endorsed upzoning to the point where he acknowledges, "I've been tedious on this subject." He supports upzoning everywhere to "raise real wages" by decreasing housing costs in expensive metropolitan areas; such a reduction would permit more people to move to these communities, live there comfortably, and participate and contribute to agglomeration economies (Yglesias 2013).

## Public Opposition to New Housing

On the behavioral side, a second strand of research centers on public opinion about new housing. These researchers argue that the public exhibits NIMBY attitudes (Dear 1992; Fischel 2001; Marble and Nall 2017; Hankinson 2018). In these accounts, economic self-interest drives opposition. Homeowners fear a loss in their home values (Fischel 2001) or a decrease in the quality of their local public goods, like schools and parks (Trounstine 2018). Even renters may oppose the construction of new housing out of economic fears – at least in high-cost cities. Recent experimental evidence suggests that renters in expensive communities associate new development in their neighborhoods with increasing rents (Hankinson 2018). According to this research, even in more liberal places – where we might otherwise expect high levels of support for new housing – the public will oppose new projects when they are proposed "in their backyard." In these accounts, mass public opposition to new housing is a central driver of the housing crisis.

A battle over affordable housing in Cedar Rapids, Iowa, is emblematic. Developers of the Crestwood Ridge Apartments proposed constructing forty-five units of housing, of which forty-one were subsidized, in northwest Cedar Rapids. Neighbors opposed the proposal, collecting more than one thousand signatures to stop the project. One worried: "I've lost I don't know how many mailboxes. People drive too fast down the hill and they lose control and end up in my yard. It's just not a safe place for an apartment building." Others expressed concerns over flooding and a lack of walkability for incoming residents. Some residents were adamant that their concerns had nothing to do with race or class: "We would have felt the same way if they were building luxury apartments." Another asserted: "We attempted as neighbors to never focus on the fact that the complex was lower income. It's too big a structure on too small a piece of land." Other comments suggested racial overtones and outright racism. One woman declared at a public hearing: "I will not live with drug dealers. If you like them so much, why don't you live with them?"

Another worried about Crestwood children entering her yard: "I don't want those little monkeys climbing up my trees" (Kirk 2017).

While the project was eventually approved by one vote after a lengthy battle, government officials and affordable housing advocates say that the experience taught them that community dialogues and persuasion are key to promulgating affordable housing. The Iowa Finance Authority – which offered $8 million dollars in tax credits for Crestwood Ridge – is holding conversations in other towns in Iowa to better understand how to collaborate with residents affected by new housing. The authority's chief programs officer Carolann Jensen said: "The push for housing has to be a grassroots effort. It has to be community driven" (Kirk 2017).

Indeed, a nationwide social movement, Yes in My Backyard (YIMBY), has been built in part around the presumption that persuasion and counteraction of NIMBYs is key to constructing more housing. Sonjia Trauss, a movement leader in San Francisco, described the problem: "There's people moving here every day. I saw it, I was one of them." The message she heard from NIMBYs, however, was: "You are ruining San Francisco. You are ruining the Bay Area. Go home." By testifying at public hearings, YIMBYs might outweigh messaging from NIMBYs that typically dominate these venues (Murphy 2017). Multiple prominent intellectuals agree that NIMBY sentiments are a significant contributor to crushing housing costs in many cities. Urban studies researcher and CityLab writer Richard Florida issued among the more forceful critiques of NIMBYs, who he refers to as New Urban Luddites:

> Over the past several years, a growing chorus of urban economists have decried the way that NIMBY sentiment ... keeps urban housing prices unnecessarily high. Traditionally, the presence of NIMBYs was a sign of a healthy community: These were concerned residents who were motivated to keep "bad" things, like prisons or waste treatment plants, out of their neighborhoods. But NIMBYism has grown substantially over time, and it now erupts in opposition to all manner of new development. The behavior isn't just selfish, it's destructive. By limiting density and clustering, NIMBYs hold back the urban innovation that powers growth. (Florida 2017)

Vox's Timothy Lee writes about the consequences of NIMBYism in Silicon Valley: "Technology companies in the region have ... faced resistance from not-in-my-backyard (NIMBY) advocates. The result: not only is the Valley failing to deal effectively with growing congestion and soaring housing costs, these myopic local policies could end up hampering the country's most important driver of economic growth" (Lee 2015).

## The Intersection of Zoning and Neighborhood Defense

These accounts reflect important components of housing politics. But, by failing to jointly consider regulations and the people that use them, they miss important insights about the power of land use institutions and the political inequalities they engender. Land use regulations gain their power, in part, from the people who use them to their advantage. Likewise, NIMBY attitudes without institutions that amplify them would have more muted effects than they currently do.

One central – and underappreciated – facet of land use regulations is that they provide opportunities for neighborhoods and individual residents to voice their views on land use and proposed housing developments. A multitude of land use regulations require developments above a certain size to receive special permits. Similarly, anytime a development seeks an exemption from existing zoning codes, it must receive a variance from the local zoning board. These procedures trigger public meetings, in which members of the public are invited to share their views on proposed developments in front of their community's planning and zoning boards.

There are potentially good reasons to enable those most directly affected by change to have a strong say in whether it happens. As we discuss further in the next chapter, enhanced neighborhood participation ostensibly acts as a check against developer excess. But, rather than empowering under-represented interests, these institutions could, in fact, be amplifying the voices of a small group of unrepresentative individuals with a strong interest in restricting the development of new housing – like the Cambridge neighbors discussed at the opening of this chapter. We call these individuals *neighborhood defenders*, a term we unpack in greater depth in Chapter 2. The political activities of these neighborhood defenders may help explain why changes in land use regulations may not yield immediate impact on housing production, as one recent study in Chicago found (Freemark 2019).

Most economics-centered accounts of the housing shortage fail to fully explore how land use regulations of all types – and the special permitting process – create opportunities for individuals or small groups to inhibit development. Moreover, these studies fail to consider that it is often ordinary people who directly and indirectly invoke regulations in a variety of ways. These individuals play a critical role by amplifying the impact of land use regulations. Where defenders are present and active, housing proposals are far more likely to face the politics of delay. Citizen participants use land use regulations to buttress lawsuits, demands for parking and traffic studies, and other claims that constrain housing development. Without these motivated individuals, land use regulations certainly can have some impact, but building, even in highly regulated places, is easier without myriad public hearings and years of legal battles.

Meanwhile, research on public opinion ignores which people are most politically relevant to housing politics. Nationally (or locally) representative samples do not attend local planning and zoning board meetings to provide comments on local housing developments. We know virtually nothing about the individuals who actually attend these meetings or how they might use land use regulations to stymie development. Those who show up to participate might be very different than those surveyed in public opinion studies. Because participatory institutions and land use regulations empower these individuals, their voices are far more consequential. We show that these individuals are unrepresentative on two key dimensions. Relative to their broader communities, they are (1) socioeconomically advantaged and (2) overwhelmingly opposed to the construction of new housing. Moreover, even very small numbers of them can have a profound influence. Land use institutions empower one person, or a small group of people, to have a very large impact. Surveys do not tell us who these individuals are and what motivates them.

## Senior Housing in LaGrange, New York

Ongoing efforts to construct senior housing in LaGrange, New York – a small town of 15,000 located 85 miles north of New York City – help illustrate this process, and underscore its reach beyond major metropolitan areas. In November 2017, a developer appeared before the LaGrange, New York, Planning Board to present his senior housing project. He proposed building 120 densely packed single family homes for seniors. The chairman of the planning board instructed the developer that this hearing was for public comment on the State Environmental Quality Review. The issues discussed in the hearing were wide-ranging, and the developer would be required to respond to all of the concerns:

We have to look at anything that can affect ... water, traffic, sewer, and others that might affect anything, not only nature, but the environment, meaning community. ... The applicant will not conduct back and forth discussion. He will respond to the comments in writing to the Planning Board. Comments and concerns will be mitigated.

The chair of the committee informed the public that its concerns would be taken seriously: "When you give us your comments about SEQR, we can make sure that those particular issues are looked at and mitigated, but that is all we can do according to the law. We can't stop it, we can't say no ... but we can say there has to be concrete reason and data to back everything up."

Indeed, the chair highlighted one of the central features of land use institutions: they may not necessarily permit residents to completely block projects, but they offer ample opportunity to impose delays.

One neighborhood resident expressed concerns about the septic system and water table. The meeting minutes recorded: "He said there is a high water table. He said ... the surface water will be funneled to the lake, which would add [to] the pressure of the water coming onto his property. He asked if there was a study done." The chair replied that there would indeed be a water study that would evaluate those concerns.

Another neighbor expressed broader concerns about how this proposed senior housing development would affect her community:

We the people of this community will not let the character of our community be compromised or mutilated in such a fashion. There is no need for 105 3-bedroom units that only opens up the doors to seniors' adult children moving in with their children in tow should there be a divorce or loss of job. ... Traffic on 376 ... was a study done? 376 is overloaded already. Would you put a light there? OR do we have to wait for the required number of fatalities before doing so. ... What about the horrendous drainage problem behind me? I see no provisions in your blue print for the water that comes from the top of Caudie Drive. ... What does the Fire Department say about handling this ridiculous amount of homes should a catastrophe arise?

Her concerns raised the possibility of a number of additional reviews, including traffic, water, and safety studies.

Other neighbors discussed the wildlife. The LaGrange meeting minutes detailed the conversation: a woman "talked about Blanding turtles by the pond with babies." The chair seemed especially interested in concerns about wildlife, asking "what color they were." The neighbor replied, according to the minutes, that "they really have no color; they are not like a painter turtle or a box or snapping turtle."

As other neighbors expressed similar concerns, members of the planning board indicated that the developer would need to either mitigate or respond to all of the public comments, either via additional studies or significant modifications to the proposal. They outlined a number of issues they found especially problematic, including insufficient access for emergency medical services, dangerous traffic, and wildlife. They decided to continue public discussion to a December meeting, which was similarly rancorous. Each of these meetings offered additional opportunities for the public to impose costs on the developer simply by delaying the project and requiring additional studies.

What's more, this hearing was merely the first in a series of hurdles the project needed to clear prior to starting construction. As part of the environmental review process, there have been at least two public hearings as of this writing. Moreover, after the LaGrange Planning Board offers its approval, the project then goes before the Town Board, where it faces additional review. At all stages of the process, the public has the opportunity to comment, and the developer is required to respond to and mitigate public concerns.

Importantly, the individuals empowered to delay this development do not necessarily comprise a representative selection of the community. Indeed, the small group of twenty residents that spoke passionately about the senior housing development may differ markedly in their personal characteristics and views – something we evaluate more rigorously in Chapter 5. Such political inequities would indicate that the ostensibly democratizing impetus behind neighborhood meetings – as a check against developer excess – has been seriously undermined.

The language that LaGrange residents use to combat the construction of senior housing is remarkably similar to that employed by residents in places like Cambridge, Massachusetts, and San Francisco, California, where affordable housing crises have been more widely documented in the media. Unlike these economic centers, LaGrange is not a community facing massive growth pressures; its population grew by less than one thousand between 2000 and 2016. Moreover, 15 percent of its population is older than sixty-five, making senior housing an obvious area of need. As one journalist put it: "The next crisis facing the Hudson Valley isn't an economic one – or not entirely, anyway. Rather, we're headed for a social emergency caused by the aging of the baby boom generation. Namely: housing for elders. Or a lack thereof" (Schaerlaeckens 2013). One Massachusetts housing lawyer we interviewed suggested that senior housing generally spurs the least opposition. People "are not threatened by seniors. [They] are worried about demand on schools." A Massachusetts town official similarly observed that seniors are viewed positively because "traffic impacts are less." Even much-needed senior housing in a relatively low-growth community can spur community residents to engage in the politics of delay. Neighborhod defenders not only drive up housing costs – they prevent communities from flexibly responding to residents' housing needs.

## METHODOLOGICAL APPROACH

To more systematically evaluate the participatory politics of housing policy, we amass a wide array of quantitative and qualitative data to investigate whether land use rules and other institutions shape housing outputs, empower small groups, and exacerbate political inequality. Some of the data come from national-level sources. We use evidence from a national survey of mayors that we conducted (Einstein, Glick, and Palmer 2018). Moreover, we analyze case studies of housing regulations and developments across all regions of the United States. The bulk of this book's empirical evidence, however, comes from Massachusetts. Massachusetts has outstanding and unique data on land use regulations courtesy of a multiyear data collection effort by the Rappaport Center for the Study of Greater Boston (Pioneer Institute for Public Policy Research and Rappaport Institute for Greater Boston 2005; Glaeser and Ward 2009); we discuss these data in greater depth in Chapter 3. Moreover, Massachusetts's unique open meeting laws mean that the state has extraordinarily detailed planning and zoning board meeting minutes, which allow us to measure who attends local meetings concerning housing development and zoning. We investigate these data in Chapters 4, 5, and 6. Throughout, we consider the strengths and limitations of Massachusetts as a case and, when possible, supplement our analyses of Massachusetts data with case studies from other parts of the country. While much of our evidence comes from Massachusetts, we are writing about the politics of land use regulations across the country.

Chapter 2 develops our theory; it highlights how land use regulations and participatory inequalities come together to constrain the supply of new housing. Chapter 3 uses land use regulation and housing permitting data to (1) clearly describe how land use regulations operate and (2) statistically link their proliferation with a diminished housing supply. Chapters 4, 5, and 6 turn to public hearings and members of the public.[4] Chapter 4 illustrates the connection between these land use regulations

---

[4] Some of the materials in Chapters 5 and 6 are featured in our article in *Perspectives on Politics* (Einstein, Palmer, and Glick 2019).

and public hearings; it documents what types of projects lead to hearings across a multitude of regulatory contexts and juxtaposes the concerns members of the public raise with the ostensible reasons for holding the meeting in the first place. It shows that land use regulations provide members of the public an opportunity to comment on a wide range of issues on proposals large and small. In Chapter 5, we combine a novel data set of all resident participants in planning and zoning board meetings in Massachusetts with the state voter file to describe the demographic and attitudinal attributes of meeting attendees. We demonstrate that these individuals are overwhelmingly opposed to housing proposals and demographically unrepresentative of their broader communities across a number of important domains. Chapter 6 then explores how these individuals stymie housing development using a mix of quantitative analysis of meeting minutes and in-depth case studies. Finally, Chapter 7 concludes by investigating the consequences of the participatory politics of housing in less advantaged communities; it explores gentrification in these places, and how these market pressures and political inequalities have rendered coalition-building around housing extraordinarily difficult.

## IMPLICATIONS FOR INSTITUTIONAL DESIGN

The meetings surrounding land use central to this book may seem modest in scope compared to some of the most pressing policy challenges of the day. But, control over land use is perhaps the most important power that local governments wield (Logan and Molotch 1987; Mullin 2009; Trounstine 2018). It shapes crucial social, economic, environmental, and political outcomes. It dominates and divides local politics. It even does so in smaller communities that have less traditionally been the subject of study in urban politics (Oliver, Ha, and Callen 2012).

Moreover, housing policy is an area that touches on many other facets of individuals' lives. Housing access dictates the quality of individuals' local public goods, from schools to sewers (Trounstine 2018). It affects the jobs that are available to them, and the likelihood that they will be victimized by crime (Sampson 2012). It shapes important physical and mental health outcomes (Sampson 2012). Where one lives affects political participation (Gay 2012) and the quality of political representation (Dreier, Mollenkopf, and Swanstrom 2004; Flavin and Franko 2019). Relative neighborhood deprivation is passed on from generation to generation. If parents are unable to obtain housing in a desirable community, the same is apt to be true of their children (Sharkey 2013). While the data in this book center on housing, in doing so, they touch on virtually all facets of individuals' economic, political, and social lives.

Beyond the study of local politics, this book represents a new way to study political participation. A multitude of political science studies focus on inequalities within the realm of voting. A similarly voluminous body of scholarship uses public opinion surveys to explore how and why individuals participate in politics. Smaller literatures explore protest activity and use more limited case studies to illuminate neighborhood meeting dynamics. This book is unique in that it directly and systematically observes participants in neighborhood-level institutions. Moreover, it blends a rich literature in institutions with scholarship on political behavior to show how they can interact to yield important policy outcomes. Institutions, behavior, and policy in this context align in a way that is detrimental to democratic governance and equitable service provision.

This book also adds to a nascent body of scholarship exploring the institutional importance of *delay*. The institutional capacity to create delay may be critically important in shaping policy outcomes. Recent political science research focused on the US Senate shows that even the right to delay, but not veto, the enactment of policies can reshape the policy agenda (Fong and Krehbiel 2018). We show that unrepresentative members of the public can use the institutional power to delay to enormous effect in a critically important local policy arena.

This book also illustrates the powerful reach of incumbency. Social scientists have long recognized that incumbents hold powerful advantages in a wide variety of contexts. Incumbent politicians are more likely to win elections (e.g., Erikson 1971; Gelman and King 1990; Cox and Katz 1996), in part due to financial advantages (Fouirnaies and Hall 2014). Incumbent firms may be able to lobby for regulations that keep new competitors out of their markets (e.g., Djankov et al. 2002; Klapper, Laeven, and Rajan 2006). Whether competing for votes or market share, already holding power advantages incumbents over new entrants, who have to overcome these advantages to succeed. Neighborhood defenders, in our account, are a form of incumbent. As we show in the ensuing chapters, neighborhood defenders are advantaged members of their community via their racial backgrounds and homeowner status. They use this advantage – their incumbency in their neighborhoods – to exclude other prospective residents. As current residents, they are able to support candidates in local elections and endorse policies in local meetings that maintain their advantages over newcomers.

Finally, this book contributes to important debates about empowerment and democracy at the local and national levels. In addition to housing policy, a wide array of federal government programs emphasize and encourage neighborhood involvement (Stone and Stoker 2015) – a trend we describe in greater detail in Chapter 2. This celebration of the neighborhood could serve as a check against powerful interests, such as developers. It may permit the amplification of underrepresented groups and allow for the mediation of competing interests (Dahl 1961; Berry, Portney, and Thomson 1993; Fung 2006; Michels and Graaf 2010; Stone and Stoker 2015). Neighborhood institutions may also provide venues for deliberative democracy, in which decision makers engage in authentic deliberation with one another (Gutmann and Thompson 2012). Such a vision of neighborhood-level empowerment is consistent with research that finds that political efficacy is higher in smaller jurisdictions (Oliver 2001; Lassen and Serritzlew 2011).

However, participatory politics could distort democracy if the individuals who attend neighborhood meetings are not representative of their broader communities (Mansbridge 1980; Fainstein 2010). Indeed, political theorist and urban planner Susan Fainstein's (2010) theory of the "just city" articulates "equity" and "democracy" as important, but separate, aims that may at times come into conflict. In his book *Democracy More or Less*, political scientist Bruce Cain (2015) worried that efforts at democratizing governance at both the local and national levels may have perverse consequences: "Being responsive to the crowd that shows up exacerbates a tendency in representative government to be more attentive to those defending concentrated benefits and costs than the more dispersed interests of the general public" (61). The motivating nature of concentrated costs, in particular, is central to our story of distorted democracy in housing politics.

Such distortionary consequences abound generally in national-level political reforms. In response to participatory inequalities in voting, some policy makers and advocates have pursued a variety of initiatives designed to facilitate registration, offer more early voting, and shorten lines at polling places, for example. These policies may, however, have unanticipated consequences. In some cases, they may exacerbate the very inequities they attempt to solve. Political scientist Adam Berinksy (2005) finds that reforms designed to facilitate voting actually *increase* socioeconomic inequalities in turnout; political scientist Daniel de Kadt (2017) uncovers a similar phenomenon in South Africa. Political scientists Barry Burden, David Canon, Kenneth Mayer, and Donald Moynihan

(2013) discover that, while Election Day registration has a positive effect on overall turnout, early voting appears to decrease turnout in isolation.

Enhancing resident participation may engender governance challenges beyond just enabling an unrepresentative group outsized say. These participatory reforms may also reduce the flexibility that political officials have to tackle challenging, long-term policy questions. Making proceedings public may decrease local officials' ability to make policy tradeoffs that allow for long-term interlocal partnerships (Mullin 2009; Cain 2015). Once a meeting is made accessible to the public, it becomes politically unappealing to seemingly ignore said public during meeting proceedings.

By exploring who participates in neighborhood-level meetings surrounding housing, and how these individuals participate, our book makes an important contribution to studies of neighborhood-level empowerment, participatory government, and deliberative democracy. Moreover, it adds to scholarship exploring how best to redress significant political inequalities. Institutions designed to empower underrepresented groups may distort political influence in ways that shape critically important policy outcomes.

# 2

# Neighborhood Defenders and the Power of Delay

St. Aidan's Catholic Church – built in 1911 – sat in the middle of a relatively dense and highly desirable residential area in Brookline, Massachusetts. It was, among other things, President John F. Kennedy's childhood church and the site of his baptism. In 1999, the Archdiocese of Boston merged the shrinking parish with one across town and sought to redevelop the land to create new housing. About one year after closing the church, the diocese was working on a plan to raze the structure and build a 6-story, 140-unit residential building, with 92 affordable units and 48 market – rate units (Kiley 2004). Roughly three years after St. Aidan's closed, in response to neighborhood concerns, the town and developer proposed preserving the church building and converting the rest of the site into 74 units, of which 58 would be affordable housing and 16 sold at market rates (Giordano 2002). The intervening decade featured a multitude of rancorous public hearings, lawsuits, studies, and costly alterations. About eight years later, the permitting process resolved and work began in earnest. In June 2010 – after almost eleven years of battling with project opponents in the community – Cardinal Sean O'Malley, Congressman Barney Frank, local officials, and others celebrated the completion of a 59-unit, mixed-income development on the site, with 50 affordable units and 9 luxury condominiums (Hilliard 2010). Despite almost uniform agreement from town officials that the redevelopment of St. Aidan's Church into dense, multifamily housing was desirable – and a relatively favorable regulatory environment in Brookline – it took eleven years and multiple alterations for a project to come to fruition.

In the St. Aidan's case, as in many similar episodes across the country, a developer (in this instance the diocese and its partners) tried to increase the density of housing in a desirable location.[1] A group of motivated neighborhood defenders participated in the development process and raised a variety of concerns about the project. They used every regulatory tool at their disposal to slow down, alter, and stop the development. While they ultimately were unable to stop the development, their participation had a dramatic impact on the housing produced. The project ultimately took eleven years to complete, and the final version included nearly 60 percent fewer housing units than the original proposal.

In this chapter, we outline a theory illustrating how land use regulations and inequalities in political participation interact to diminish the supply of housing. Motivated neighborhood defenders use participatory institutions and land use regulations to stop, stall, and shrink proposals for new housing. They are even able to do this in places with relatively few regulations, so long as there are zoning and planning board meetings to participate in, and *some* land use regulations that allow them to validly contest developments. Notably, even if regulations do not allow them to outright *stop* a project, neighborhood defenders can use regulations to *delay* housing – a surprisingly powerful alternative that often provides negotiating leverage.

We first outline land use institutions and describe how they provide opportunities for residents to delay unwanted developments. We also provide greater historical context into the origins of these participatory forums. We then introduce neighborhood defenders and explore what motivates them to participate. We combine these insights on political participation and land use institutions to outline our theory of participatory politics. We then use the case of the redevelopment of St. Aidan's Church to illustrate the process and conclude by outlining the empirical evidence we marshal to support our theory in subsequent chapters.

## LAND USE REGULATIONS IN THE UNITED STATES

In order for neighbors to affect proposed housing developments, the regulatory context must permit such community influence. While there is

---

[1] While the Archdiocese of Boston is a nonprofit organization, the Catholic Church at this time – and especially after sex abuse scandals and subsequent lawsuits in the mid-2000s – was cash-strapped and eager to maximize earnings on its real estate dealings while also increasing the supply of affordable housing (Paulson 2004).

significant variation in the building permitting process across the United States, in most cities and towns it begins with a planning or zoning board. Some developments are permitted by right; after a review and approval by the planning or zoning board, these projects can go straight to construction without public review.

For many projects – some large, some mundane – the process is considerably more involved. Projects above a certain size typically require *special permits*. Similarly, any project that requires an exemption from existing land use regulations – a *variance* – must go through the planning or zoning board. (Chapter 4 outlines in far greater detail which types of proposals trigger public review.) These boards generally have the authority to grant or deny variances or special permits for construction that is not allowed by right. In some places, these decisions can then be appealed to another board or even the city council itself. At each stage of the process, one or more public meetings are held in which the board hears presentations from the developer, as well as views from interested members of the community.

These institutions introduce many different opportunities for neighbors to delay projects that they oppose. These include simply raising concerns, threatening lawsuits, or trying to involve additional regulatory boards. A project that might have been otherwise approved in the absence of neighborhood objections may instead require repeated public hearings. For example, neighbors can raise concerns at an initial planning board meeting that force developers to undertake a particular study. When the results of the study are presented at a future meeting months later, they can challenge the results of the study or raise an entirely new concern requiring a different kind of study. One developer we interviewed told us about an affordable housing development where neighbors' concerns about traffic and safety resulted in four sequential traffic studies of the same streets, all producing the same results, at a total cost of $100,000 and more than a year of delay. In the same project, the developer spent another year negotiating with a group of neighbors and the town over the development. When they finally reached an agreement and sought to move forward with the permit process, a separate group of neighbors, who had not been previously involved in the process, raised new objections, causing further delay.

When developers are granted permits by local planning boards, neighbors have further avenues to delay or attempt to stop projects. Perhaps most prominently, neighbors can turn to the courts to challenge building permits. They can sue developers and the town boards that grant permits.

They can claim that developments violate the town zoning codes or that the town boards incorrectly interpreted bylaws or used improper procedures. While long lawsuits and trials are costly to the neighbors, simply filing a lawsuit is inexpensive, and even the most frivolous lawsuit adds significant delay (and imposes legal costs) while developers work to get it dismissed.

Lawsuits can also be a useful mechanism for preventing development by running out the clock on issued building permits. In some jurisdictions, a building permit is valid only if construction begins within one year (or another specific time period) after it is granted. If neighbors are able to use lawsuits to delay the start of construction for more than a year, the permit may expire, forcing the developer to restart the process. Neighbors can then use this opportunity to demand updated studies, by arguing that traffic, the environment, or other conditions may have changed. New residents, or previously disinterested neighbors, can also become involved in the process, introducing new objections and disrupting previously negotiated agreements.

In some cases, other regulatory boards can delay or prevent developments before the developer applies for a permit. Environmental commissions, for example, may review projects for their impact on the surrounding environment and wildlife. Neighbors can raise environmental concerns before these commissions, resulting in lengthy studies. Take the case of the California Environmental Quality Act (CEQA), which requires state and local agencies to carefully consider the environmental impacts of proposed new developments, including housing projects. In part, the law aims to protect low-income communities of color from predatory developers. In practice, the law is used by homeowners in wealthier, whiter communities to file lawsuits that stop or delay new housing (Hernandez 2018), suggesting that the groups most likely to utilize these land use institutions may not be representative of their broader communities or those individuals most deleteriously affected by poor environmental conditions.

## The Power of Delay

The ability to delay is a powerful force in political disputes of all types. From the filibuster in the US Senate to filing a lawsuit to temporarily halt development, those with the power to prevent or slow something, either by threat or action, can force others to accommodate their preferences. For political actors, we often think of such an ability as "'negative power' – the consequences of an institutionalized ability to say no"

(Cameron 2000, 3). Negative power is dispersed throughout all levels of American politics. Presidents and governors (in most states) can veto laws or use the threat of a veto to force the legislature to modify them. Senators can use the filibuster to prevent legislation, either by denying a cloture vote or running out the clock in a time-limited session. Congressional committee chairs can tie up legislation in committees, bureaucrats can delay the implementation of laws, and courts can issue injunctions and delay rulings (Cameron 2000; Kagan 2003; Koger 2010; Mann and Ornstein 2013).

The power of delay establishes a bias in favor of the status quo (Epstein and O'Halloran 1995; Fernandez and Rodrik 1991; McKay 2012). The more points of potential delay in a political process, the more obstacles there are in effecting change. Any American government textbook documents all of the points where a bill can fail in the federal legislative process, preserving the status quo, but this pattern is replicated in state legislatures and city councils, as well as in bureaucracies and courts at all levels of government. The power to delay makes producing change harder than keeping things the same. In land use politics, local institutions grant neighbors the power to delay – and thus preserve the status quo – via participatory institutions.

## Movement toward Neighborhood Participation

The ability of neighbors to participate and impose delays in the planning and zoning process is not an accident. Participatory institutions were specifically created to empower neighborhood residents, in response to excessive developer power in many cities in the mid-twentieth century. Through the 1960s, the US government – dominated by business-led coalitions – bulldozed multiple low-income and working-class neighborhoods under the guise of urban renewal, largely replacing these communities with highways and other urban "mega-projects" (Altshuler and Luberoff 2003; Rae 2004; Schleicher 2013). Indeed, there are few communities in the United States that do not bear the scars of urban renewal and its lost neighborhoods. In New York City, Robert Moses presided over the construction of the Bronx Expressway, which uprooted thousands of people and eliminated the middle-class neighborhood of East Tremont (Ouroussoff 2007). As with virtually all housing policy, his decisions were disproportionately and intentionally consequential in communities of color. Robert Caro's (1974) definitive biography of Moses notes that he deliberately made the clearance on the Southern State Parkway's bridges low to prevent low-income people of color from traveling to Jones Beach by bus – a claim corroborated by an urban planner's recent analysis of bridge heights in New York City (Campanella 2017). His disinvestment in the New York subway system created massive service disruptions today – again, disruptions that disproportionately harm low-income communities of color (Finnegan 2018). Even as the federal government moved away from these policies, neighborhoods remained under siege from developer-dominated urban regimes (Logan and Molotch 1987). In response to these excesses, local institutions designed to constrain developers and empower neighborhood-level and environmental interests proliferated (Gerber and Phillips 2004; Glaeser and Ward 2009; Schleicher 2013).

Many policy makers and advocates for disadvantaged communities see neighborhood-level meetings as promising tools for redressing political inequalities. Almost half of U.S. mayors we surveyed identified neighborhood meetings as one of the top two ways they learn about their constituents' views (Einstein, Glick and LeBlanc 2017). The National League of Cities – a major interest group representing cities – also highlighted neighborhood meetings as a critical component of community engagement (Hoene, Kingsley, and Leighninger 2013).

Moreover, several federal administrations have made neighborhood-level participation a cornerstone of their antipoverty programs.[2] For President Jimmy Carter, neighborhoods and local control were central to his housing policy. Upon reauthorizing the Housing and Community Development Act in 1980, he highlighted the promise of the now-defunct Urban Development Action Grants (UDAG):

Our UDAG program . . . has been one of the most effective programs that I have ever seen in government, a program that has expanded tremendously, through a multiplication factor, the small investment of Federal funds and efforts and the enormous cooperation between local and State funds and particularly private investments, a minimum of paperwork, a minimum of delay, *a maximum of local participation and control.* (Carter 1980, emphasis added)

In his speech, Carter went on to emphasize the importance of working with *neighborhood* organizations:

I've just issued a memorandum to all agencies and departments in the Federal Government asking them to review every Federal program which affects neighborhood and community-based organizations to make sure that the cooperation

---

[2] The examples here come from Democratic presidential administrations because those administrations have typically made the expansion of federal urban policy programs part of their platforms. Republican administrations, in contrast, have largely overseen the retrenchment of federal urban spending (Dreier, Mollenkopf, and Swanstrom 2004).

is at a maximum level and to make sure that any impediments to the close working relationship or partnership between Federal Government and all of its agencies and neighborhood-based organizations are absolutely removed ... I've also established a liaison for this purpose, to neighborhoods and community-based organizations, within the White House itself. (Carter 1980)

For Carter, amplifying neighborhood voices was critical to ensuring effective and responsive federal urban policy.

The Empowerment Zones and Enterprise Community Initiative, launched in 1994 under the Clinton administration, similarly encouraged neighborhood involvement in the allocation of federal urban spending. As part of the grant-awarding process, neighborhoods themselves developed economic and community development plans (Rich and Stoker 2014; Stone and Stoker 2015). This neighborhood participation is formalized through community boards. The West Philadelphia Empowerment Zone, for example, formed a Community Trust Board "comprised of community representatives and other experts. The community-driven model is guided by the principle that the successful revitalization of designated neighborhoods depends on a strong working partnership among residents, community organizations, local businesses, and local government. The process is successful because it allows residents to determine priorities for their neighborhood and then allocate funds for program implementation" (City of Philadelphia 2012).

President Obama perhaps most explicitly endorsed neighborhood-based policy programming with his administration's Neighborhood Revitalization Initiative, an interagency collaborative effort. Multiple programs fell under the initiative's umbrella, including Choice Neighborhoods, Promise Neighborhoods, Byrne Criminal Justice Innovation, Community Health Centers, and Behavioral Health Services. A memorandum from the Department of Housing and Urban Development described Obama's grassroots, place-centered policy approach:

The Initiative's strategy ... reflects an awareness of the limits of Federal programs; indeed, the difficult process of solving interconnected problems in distressed neighborhoods has always happened at the local level, with dedicated, inventive leaders and practitioners adapting their tactics to changing conditions, rewriting rigorous community plans to target their efforts and diligently managing ... those plans to achieve their vision. President Obama recognized this fundamental truth in his speech to the nation's mayors on June 21, 2008, affirming that "in this country, change comes not from the top-down, but from the bottom-up," and that "the change we seek ... will not come from government alone." (White House 2011)

One guiding principle for all of the programs under the initiative's auspices was formalized neighborhood planning: "Agencies in the Initiative will create incentives for local communities to develop plans, build organizational capacity, and establish accountability mechanisms to ensure that revitalization activities have the best prospects for success" (White House 2016). In all of these programmatic initiatives, neighborhood participation was officially requested, incentivized, and used in the dispersal of federal funds.

Local government bureaucrats are similarly enthusiastic about neighborhood participation. Indeed, it is a cornerstone of contemporary urban planning syllabi and textbooks. Frequently used urban planning course readings discuss the importance of empowered participation and neighborhood control (Arnstein 1969; Fung 2006; Brabham 2009). While these readings critically evaluate different forms of resident participation, and whether participatory forums have been implemented appropriately, most take as a given that more opportunities for participation will yield a more just planning process.

On its face, encouraging neighborhood participation is laudable. It makes sense that the people who live in a neighborhood best know which streets need repaving, which paths children traverse on the way to school, and what housing is most dilapidated. Democratic theorists believe that neighborhood-based participation can help provide voice to underrepresented groups, mediate competing interests, enhance resident efficacy, and are integral to a thriving democracy (Dahl 1961; Berry, Portney, and Thomson 1993; Fung 2006; Michels and Graaf 2010).

Given business interests' historic dominance of urban regimes (Logan and Molotch 1987; Stone 1989), such neighborhood participation could serve as a valuable and equalizing check on private interests. As political scientist Clarence Stone (1989) notes in his seminal work *Regime Politics*, "governmental conduct is constrained by the need to promote investment activity in an economic arena dominated by private ownership. This political economy insight is the foundation for a theory of urban regimes" (7). He underscores that this reality makes business' participation in government both inevitable and necessary: "Although the nature of business involvement extends from the direct and extensive to the indirect and limited, the economic role of businesses *and the resources they control* are too important for these enterprises to be left out completely" (7). In Stone's account, the demands of urban policy making make private interests integral to governing. Institutions that aggressively promote neighborhood-level interests may, then, be the only realistic means of balancing the influence of residents and businesses.

These institutions may also offer opportunities for deliberative democracy, in which interlocutors formally discuss a political or policy decision to achieve consensus (Gutmann and Thompson 2012). Because such discussions tend to work better in smaller groups, the local level may offer the greatest potential to benefit from such institutions (Oliver 2001; Lassen and Serritzlew 2011). Moreover, they may serve as a valuable staunch against tyranny of the majority, particularly for people of color. Civil rights legal scholar Lani Guinier (1994) writes, "In a racially divided society, majority rule may be perceived as majority tyranny" (3). She instead advocates for institutions that follow the "principle of taking turns" (3), allowing minority groups to have sufficient bargaining power such that groups have "equal opportunity to influence legislative outcomes regardless of race" (14). Institutions that allow for neighborhood-level veto may enhance the voice of otherwise marginalized people of color in important development decisions.

This rosy picture of neighborhood governance starts to look quite different, though, if it turns out that the local Community Trust Board is actually captured by a small, advantaged group with intense preferences. A small group could redirect federal resources selfishly for their own benefit. Or, even if guided by high-minded principles, the small group's wishes – despite good intent – may not reflect actual community needs (Mansbridge 1980; Fiorina 1998; Cain 2015). As the next section shows, there is good reason to suspect that participatory land use forums may be captured by a demographically and attitudinally unrepresentative group inclined to employ these institutions to their own advantage.

NEIGHBORHOOD DEFENDERS

Land use regulations in and of themselves can directly constrain the construction of new housing by forbidding it, or indirectly, by creating multiple hurdles to development. Our theoretical framework suggests that their impact is amplified when residents participate in the land use process and use these regulations to slow down or stop development in their neighborhoods. This requires actual people to show up and oppose the construction of new housing.

The concentrated costs of housing development make the existence of opponents inevitable. Let's return to the four-unit building proposal in Cambridge that opened this book. The benefits of such a housing development will be almost imperceptible. While cities with housing shortages need to construct more housing to mitigate rising costs, the marginal benefit of an additional four units is minimal. Residents across the city will not notice a change in the cost of their housing as a consequence of these additional condominiums.

In contrast, neighbors of this proposed four-unit project acutely feel the downsides – concerns that were ardently voiced in the meeting described in first pages of this book. Indeed, in their minds, it threatens their ability to peacefully enjoy their homes, their broader sense of community, and their property values. It is this desire to protect their community and property that leads us to term these individuals *neighborhood defenders*.

Most immediately, the development will be disruptive to their daily lives. Neighbors will hear construction noise, potentially for months on end. If each new unit brings one to two cars to the neighborhood, they may see street parking options dwindle. The views from their windows may change. They may face new privacy concerns if, say, a roof deck provides a view onto their property.

Neighborhood defenders also may have deep economic concerns about a proposed development. An individual's residence is often their single largest financial asset. Consequently, neighbors are especially concerned about changes that could lower property values (Fischel 2001; Trounstine 2018). The same factor that drives many scholars and policy advocates to support the construction of new housing – that increased housing supply reduces housing prices – is a decided negative in the minds of many homeowners whose wealth is derived from higher home values. Moreover, even if a project is unlikely to have a marked impact on community housing prices – indeed, the marginal impact of any single housing development on neighborhood housing values is, for the most part, insignificant – neighbors may perceive that a project will diminish their home values.

In addition, neighborhood defenders see a more inchoate threat to their sense of community. Sociologist Jeremy Levine spent four years studying redevelopment politics in Boston. He found that poor residents at public meetings gained the appearance of power and status by referencing and policing membership in the "community." While he finds that government officials coopted discussions of community to disempower these disadvantaged neighborhood residents – a result that we will return to in our final chapter's discussion of gentrification – we believe that this community orientation will be particularly motivating for individuals of all economic backgrounds (Levine 2017).

Housing developments – even small ones – provoke anxiety about one's community because they comprise rapid and highly visible changes. One housing lawyer we interviewed said, "Human instinct is to be adverse to change and like things the way they are and see other people as intruding, making things more dense, more traffic, more problems." His insight is backed by a wealth of research suggesting that rapid changes are especially psychologically salient (Green, Strolovitch, and Wong 1998; Hopkins 2010; Enos 2016).

This anxiety could be compounded by class- or race-based concerns. Depending on the composition of the neighborhood's current housing stock, the residents of these four new units may be demographically quite different than current neighborhood residents. Longtime residents living in single-family houses may feel anxiety about the identities of newcomers residing in new one-bedroom apartments (Tighe 2010). The affordable housing development in Cedar Rapids from Chapter 1 illustrates the potency of these forces in contemporary politics. Political scientist Jessica Trounstine amasses a wide array of historical data to show that racial prejudice and the desire to maintain clearly demarcated race-based boundaries are key drivers of attitudes towards land use policy (Trounstine 2018).

### Neighborhood Defenders versus NIMBY

Our conceptualization of neighborhood defenders is related to, but distinct from, NIMBYism. The very name NIMBY – Not in *My* Backyard – connotes concerns about individual self-interest, whether it is worries about property values or encounters with individuals who differ demographically from oneself. These motivations clearly matter. This focus on individual self-interest, though, misses the community-centric orientation of many neighborhood defenders. As Levine (2017) notes, individuals have community boundaries and concerns in mind when they evaluate proposed developments. In Cedar Rapids, multiple neighbors framed their critiques as "our concerns," conceiving of them as neighborhood – rather than individual – worries. The LaGrange, New York, hearing from Chapter 1 featured one neighbor worried about *neighborhood* drainage, traffic, and fire safety problems as well as broader questions of *neighborhood* character. Several other LaGrange neighbors mentioned the wildlife – an important member of the "community" for some residents.

Worries about turtles scarcely fit in with a NIMBY framework focused on individual self-interest and property values.

The image that scholars and policy makers conjure when they use the language of NIMBYism is starkly discordant with neighbors' self-perceptions as being motivated by external concerns related to community preservation. Conceiving of opponents to new housing as NIMBYs paints an entire group of people as selfish and worried about their own individual welfare at the expense of others. In contrast, many neighborhood defenders see themselves as attending public meetings on behalf of their communities, eager to police their community's boundaries and, in some cases, share their expertise. The ways that neighbors crusade for their communities is varied. Some "community" worries – like those that label children of color "monkeys" – are driven by racism and abhorrent. Other community-oriented claims, such as concerns about crumbling building foundations or community flooding, are more sympathetic. The term *neighborhood defenders* better encapsulates the varied reasons – some unacceptable, some relatable – that foment opposition to housing developments. It still incorporates the narrow self-interested concerns about home values and the desire to hoard public goods that motivate many neighborhood defenders. But it better fits neighbors' self-conception as community-oriented.

This distinction has important implications for how we understand and address the housing crisis. First, it offers a better explanation for the political power of these individuals. Concerns framed narrowly around selfish economic interest seem unlikely to motivate large neighborhood movements or sway zoning and planning board members. In contrast, a community orientation based around defending one's neighborhood seems both unifying to a broader swath of the population and more appealing to political elites. No one wants to be known as a politician who caves in NIMBYs – or, indeed, as a NIMBY themselves. In contrast, it is much easier to understand how both ordinary people and elites might become (or listen to) neighborhood defenders. Second, it helps illuminate why these views are so hard to change (Marble and Nall 2017). People who oppose housing largely do not think they are being selfish; they believe they are community-minded neighborhood defenders.

## Neighborhood Defenders and Battles Over Integration

We are not the first scholars to refer to neighborhood defenders or neighborhood defense. Multiple historical accounts of white flight into suburban communities have used this terminology to describe the behavior of whites seeking to preserve their property values and control over local public goods in the face of potential neighborhood racial or class integration (Self 2003; Kruse 2005; Trounstine 2018). Our conceptualization of neighborhood defense certainly shares a great deal with these prior iterations. Many neighborhood defenders in our account are motivated by a fierce need for control over local public goods and a desire to maintain their property values. Some are, as Chapter 6 shows, quite explicitly driven by class- and race-based animus.

Others in our account see themselves as representing broader community concerns that are not so directly tied with local government services or property values. They worry about wildlife and children's safety while walking to school. Some neighborhood defenders citing these wildlife concerns, for example, may believe more local flora and fauna improve their property values. Others may not care at all about wildlife, but know that such concerns hold weight with local zoning and planning board officials, and thus serve as a means to an end. Some, though, genuinely see rare local birds as a neighborhood concern and an asset to their communities worthy of defense. We incorporate these broader community-based concerns – not just classist and racist impulses – into our account of neighborhood defense.

## Dominance of Neighborhood Defenders

Opponents of new housing, then, appear to have strong motivations to make their voices heard. What about supporters? The concentrated costs and diffuse benefits of housing mean there are fewer ardent supporters than opponents. Indeed, few individuals are motivated to spend multiple hours at a public zoning board hearing by the marginal decrease in citywide housing costs that four units of housing might produce.

Moreover, support is likely to be less motivating than equally intense opposition. Prospect theory suggests that losses have a greater impact on behavior than equivalently sized gains (Kahneman and Tversky 1979). In other words, those individuals who fear a loss of community or diminished property values will be more inclined to show up then individuals facing identical gains in community or property values.

Finally, at least some of the individuals most likely to benefit from a new housing development – potential new residents – live outside the jurisdiction in which the development is proposed. In contrast, virtually all of those experiencing the costs of new housing already reside in that jurisdiction. Relative to supporters, then, housing development opponents are more likely to (1) be informed about developments happening in their community, and (2) be able to target their own appointed or elected officials in voicing their views about housing. Both information (Lassen 2005) and efficacy (Shingles 1981; Finkel 1985) are positively associated with political participation.

Even in places where residents generally support the construction of additional housing (and worry about rising housing costs), the voices disproportionately heard at local housing meetings will likely be those of opponents. While developers' interests overlap to some extent with other housing supporters', community-based housing proponents are largely missing from these proceedings.

## Socioeconomically Advantaged Voices

Neighborhood defenders are also likely to be demographically unrepresentative of their broader communities. Canonical political science research suggests that three critical variables predict an individual's likelihood of participating in the political process: resources, engagement, and recruitment. Take the example of voting, the subject of hundreds of political behavior studies. An individual is more apt to vote if she has the time and financial *resources* to take time off of work to go to a polling place and cast a ballot. Moreover, individuals who are *interested* and *engaged* in politics are more inclined to vote. Finally, individuals who are *recruited* – whether by friends, neighbors, or organized political groups – are more likely to cast a ballot. All of these factors are tightly correlated with an individual's socioeconomic status. One is more likely to have the resources, be interested in politics, and be asked to participate in politics if one is wealthier, all else equal. Consequently, socioeconomically advantaged individuals are more likely to vote, make political donations, and contact government officials, among other forms of political participation (Verba, Schlozman, and Brady 1995; Schlozman, Verba, and Brady 2012).

These forces should operate in even greater force when applied to participation in public meetings on housing developments. Attending a two-hour public meeting on local housing clearly requires a significant outlay of time. Moreover, individuals are more likely to attend such a meeting if they are interested in the subject matter. Not only are public meetings long – they entail discussions of the minutiae of septic systems and building setbacks. Only a person passionately engaged about a particular housing proposal (or a housing politics researcher!) would eagerly sit through such a proceeding. Finally, recruitment is especially critical; an individual will probably be more inclined to attend a meeting if their neighbor or neighborhood association asks them to do so, for example. Such recruitment provides social pressure *and* provides an individual with valuable political information – namely, about the housing development and meeting time – that they might not have otherwise had. We therefore anticipate that housing meeting attendees will *not* be representative of the general population of their communities. Rather, they will comprise a socioeconomically advantaged sample of the general population. This creates inequality on two dimensions: the demographics and attitudes of meeting participants.

## Homeownership

Homeownership should prove especially motivating to neighborhood defenders. As we noted previously, a desire to protect one's home value and exclusive access to public goods spurs homeowners to oppose new development. The same factors that predispose homeowners to oppose new projects should also lead them to participate at a far higher rate than renters. What's more, homeowners are, on average, less mobile than renters; they are more likely to have lived in their communities for a long period of time and to plan to continue to live in their communities for a longer time horizon (DiPasquale and Glaeser 1999). This long-term investment in the community should lead to greater participation in local government proceedings. Homeowners may also have greater bureaucratic knowledge about their communities, providing them with the civic skills necessary for political participation (Oliver, Ha, and Callen 2012).

Regulatory institutions exacerbate these disparities by disproportionately recruiting homeowners to participate in planning and zoning board proceedings. While the details vary between localities, when a development necessitates a public hearing, nearby residents are formally alerted via abutter notifications. These notices are like a bat signal for neighborhood defenders. They inform neighbors that there is a potential change coming, outline it, and provide information on how neighbors can participate in the process. While abutter notifications serve an important purpose – providing information on proposed development and inviting public participation – they target a distinct and nonrepresentative population. All potentially concerned residents are not individually invited to participate in the planning meetings and process. Developers are required to notify direct and nearby neighbors – defined as being within a certain number of feet of a property – in advance of public meetings. Moreover, the set of abutters is not defined as the residents of these neighboring properties, but the property owners.[3] Renters may also have strong views about changes to their neighborhoods; they might favor additional housing to provide them more options, or oppose it due to concerns about gentrification and displacement (Hankinson 2018). Local governments, however, do not prioritize or solicit their views in the planning process. Unlike landowners, renters may not know about changes to their neighborhood until after official decisions have been made. The official solicitation for meetings thus likely contributes to a bias in favor of homeowner attendance.

Indeed, the abutter solicitation process is part of a broader movement among some local jurisdictions to promote the political rights of homeowners. Special district governments provide a variety of important services in many communities, including water, utilities, and transportation (Berry 2009). In some places, participation in elections for these governments is determined by property ownership rather than residence in a community. Landowners sometimes do not need to even live in a district to vote there. What's more, owning more land can directly enhance one's political power; some jurisdictions allocate voting rights based on size and value of a parcel of land. These franchise restrictions have been upheld by the Supreme Court (Mullin 2009).

## White Voices

Lower levels of homeownership and income in communities of color mean that these forces will also likely decrease participation in public meetings among people of color. Indeed, local politics is generally a low turnout affair, and the voices of communities of color are especially underrepresented in these electoral contests (Hajnal 2010; Hajnal and Trounstine 2010). A number of additional factors may further depress Latino participation, including language and citizenship barriers, a lack of racial group consciousness (Masuoka 2008; Barreto 2010), and a failure of party and political organizations to adequately recruit Latino voters (Barreto and Collingwood 2015). In the most recent presidential

---

[3] The term "abutter" is used in Massachusetts. Other states may use terms such as "adjacent landowner" or "adjoining landowner," which makes explicit the importance of ownership, rather than residence.

election, Latino voter turnout was over twenty percentage points lower than that of whites and blacks (Krogstad and Lopez 2016). Survey analyses of neighborhood meetings find especially low participation among socioeconomically disadvantaged Latinos (Berry, Portney, and Thomson 1993).

The picture is less clear for black people. Better community organization and recruitment (Verba, Schlozman, and Brady 1995; Schlozman, Verba, and Brady 2012) and strong group identity (Dawson 1995) amplify turnout in the black community. This should lead, at a minimum, black turnout to exceed that of Latinos at participatory land use forums.

But the racially biased history of zoning and land use in the United States may depress minority participation in these venues. American cities and towns have a long and sordid history of using land use institutions to de jure and de facto exclude people of color (Rothstein 2017; Trounstine 2018). In the early part of the twentieth century, many local governments enacted racial zoning ordinances that expressly prohibited members from select minority groups, primarily immigrants and African Americans. Baltimore's ordinance was the first in 1910. Mayor J. Barry Mahool championed the policy that "Blacks should be quarantined in isolated slums in order to reduce the incidents of civil disturbance, to prevent the spread of communicable disease into nearby White neighborhoods, and to protect property values among the White majority" (Silver 1997). Multiple cities across the country adopted Baltimore's approach in the subsequent decade before the Supreme Court declared such regulations unconstitutional in its 1917 decision *Buchanan* v. *Warley*, arguing that the ordinances interfered with property owners' rights (Nodjimbadem 2017; Rothstein 2017).

After 1917, cities were no longer able to maintain explicitly racial zoning laws. Nonetheless, many hired legal experts to help them design legally defensible racial zoning plans. H. L. Pollard, a Los Angeles land use attorney, noted, "Racial hatred played no small part in bringing to the front some of the early districting ordinances that were sustained by the United States Supreme Court, thus giving us our first zoning decisions"(Silver 1997). Birmingham, Alabama, provides one such example. In 1925 – eight years after *Buchanan* – the city passed a comprehensive zoning ordinance "to protect the property holders against manufacturing plants and corner grocery stores which tend to spring up promiscuously about the city and to restrict the negroes to certain districts." Atlanta's initial attempt at comprehensive zoning in 1922 failed to pass court muster after assigning racial groups to particular zones. A rewritten version of the plan still allowed the city to pursue its goal of "controlled segregation" (Silver 1997). The federal government actively encouraged these efforts. Richard Rothstein, a research fellow at the Economic Policy Institute, describes the role that Secretary of Commerce (and future present) Herbert Hoover played:

> In the 1920s, Secretary of Commerce Herbert Hoover organized an advisory committee on zoning, whose job was to persuade every jurisdiction to adopt the ordinance that would keep low-income families out of middle-class neighborhoods. The Supreme Court couldn't explicitly mention race, but the evidence is clear that the [Commerce Department's] motivation was racial. Jurisdictions began to adopt zoning ordinances that were exclusive on economics, but the true purpose was, in part, to exclude African-Americans. (Nodjimbadem 2017).

These so-called economic ordinances include banning the construction of apartment buildings in the suburbs and forcing single-family homes to have large setbacks on multiple acres (Nodjimbadem 2017). Despite the close linkages between these ostensibly economic regulations and racial exclusion, the Supreme Court upheld them in 1926. Justice George Sutherland justified the court's decision: "Very often the apartment house is a mere parasite, constructed in order to take advantage of the open spaces and attractive surroundings created by the residential character of the district." He went so far as to describe apartment buildings as being "very near to ... nuisances" (Rothstein 2017, pp. 52–53).

Exclusionary zoning persists today. Communities across the United States still either outright ban the construction of apartment buildings or create requirements – such as minimum lot size requirements – that are so onerous that multifamily units are effectively banned (Winkler 2017). Such zoning decisions both contribute to racial segregation (Trounstine 2018) and exacerbate growing class segregation (Rothwell and Massey 2013).

Zoning thus originated, in large part, out of an intentional desire to segregate people of color from whites. It succeeded. People of color may consequently feel less trust in institutions that have policed their presence and excluded them from accessing high-quality public goods. This lack of trust and efficacy may further diminish minorities' propensity to attend planning and zoning board meetings.

A rich array of political science research shows that policy choices can have a profound effect on political behavior. Some policies – like Social Security and the GI Bill – increase participation by providing beneficiaries with the resources, interest, and sense of efficacy integral to democratic engagement (Campbell 2005; Metter 2007; though see Katznelson 2005). In other cases, policies depress participation by reducing individuals' resources and trust in government. Research on the political effects of Medicaid (Michener 2018) and the American carceral state (Weaver and Lerman 2010; Soss and Weaver 2017; White 2019) find that these policies can spur stark decreases in democratic participation, in large part because policy recipients mistrust that a system that has treated them punitively will respond to their preferences. While America's land use institutions differ from these policies in a myriad of important ways, the racist origins and racially disparate impacts of America's land use policy may similarly serve to depress participation among people of color.

## A THEORY OF PARTICIPATORY POLITICS

This inequality in participation matters. The depressive impact of land use regulations on the housing supply will be more deeply felt in places (both cities and neighborhoods) that are socioeconomically advantaged. Such places are, on average, more likely to be home to neighborhood defenders who oppose construction by making their voices heard at planning and zoning board meetings and other proceedings. Using participatory institutions and land use regulations, these individuals will limit the amount of new housing available in their communities. This has real social and political consequences. The cities, towns, and neighborhoods with the highest quality public goods will be the least likely to supply adequate housing for potential new residents.

The two-by-two grid in Figure 2.1 illustrates the relationship we propose between neighborhood participation and housing regulations. The rows identify levels of land use regulations, while the columns identify levels of neighborhood participation. Economists have, thus far, mainly compared the two rows, and have viewed the two cells in each row as conceptually indistinguishable. In their account, streamlining or eliminating land use regulations would dramatically increase development.

This story, however, ignores the role that community members might play in shaping housing development in their neighborhoods, as depicted in the columns. High levels of political participation might limit the construction of new housing even in lightly regulated communities. In low-regulation communities, participation-minded neighbors opposed to new housing might take advantage of limited existing zoning codes to, at a minimum delay the construction of new housing (top right). In

**Neighborhood Participation**

| | | Low | High |
|---|---|---|---|
| **Regulations** | Low | New Development, Gentrification | Limited (and Delayed) Development |
| | High | Limited Development, Some Gentrification | Little or No Development |

FIGURE 2.1: Effects of the relationship between regulations and participation

more restrictive locales, this high level of participation might translate into virtually no development (bottom right). We expect to see the most development in places with low levels of regulations, *and* low levels of neighborhood participation (top left). It is not simply regulations themselves that matter, but whether there are individuals inclined and able to use them to stymie new housing.

Similarly, accounts centered on public opinion implicitly assume that these opinions matter because regulations empower them. These studies do not, however, distinguish between different regulatory frameworks. This leads them to miss variations in the public's ability to influence housing policy. They also miss how few neighborhood defenders are needed to exercise considerable power. Effective opposition to housing does not require majority public opinion or participation; a few motivated individuals alone are sufficient.

Moreover, the failure to explore the intersection between land use institutions and neighborhood activism has caused scholars to miss how their confluence can also lead to gentrification and displacement. If neighborhood participation in land use decision-making is fiercer in more advantaged places, our theory has important implications for the gentrification of low-income communities. Low participation communities – which we predict are less advantaged – experience more development in our account. This means that, in cities desperate for more housing, like New York City, Boston, and San Francisco, low-income communities will be disproportionately targeted for development. The intersection of participatory inequities and regulatory institutions may be partially fueling the displacement of low-income individuals and families. This book primarily focuses on the right-hand side of Figure 2.1. We study places where participants are able to employ land use regulations to delay or prevent development. In the concluding chapter, we return, however, to these low-income communities facing gentrification. We explore the painful economic and social costs to the families living in these places, and outline how their experiences make coalition building for housing reform especially difficult.

Indeed, the failure to recognize joint the effects of participation and institutions – and their implications for gentrification – poses a formidable obstacle to building effective and lasting coalitions to reform housing policy. One of the central critiques of the YIMBY movement is that its members have failed to adequately recognize the crisis in lower-income communities. Miriam Zuk, the director of UC Berkeley's Center for Community Innovation says that the YIMBY movement acknowledges one crisis – the one squeezing moderate- and upper-income families. This one, she believes, can be addressed by increasing the supply of housing. The second – that facing low-income families – is largely ignored by YIMBYs. Zuk argues: "There's no reason to think that everybody's going to be better off if we just build a lot more housing. There's no reason to believe that if we just let the market do its thing and let development happen, the housing problems for low-income housing would be solved" (Murphy 2017). This fissure between relatively advantaged YIMBYs and affordable housing advocates was a key factor in the demise of SB 827, a California bill that proposed increasing density in neighborhoods near transit stops (Dillon 2018*b*). We return to a more detailed discussion of these political divides in the final chapter.

In short, previous research has missed several critical components of the politics of housing. Institutional accounts have failed to consider the people who participate and how they actually interact with land use institutions. Consequently, the power to delay has not received sufficient attention. Moreover, while the contours of NIMBYism are fairly well understood, we know virtually nothing about the identities of the neighborhood defenders, and *how* they use these regulations to obstruct and delay housing developments.

## ST. AIDAN'S CHURCH

The arduous path to construct housing on the site of St. Aidan's Church helps make these theoretical arguments more concrete. The shrinking of the proposal both in terms of its magnitude (more than halving the number of units) and in its radicalness (from razing the church to preserving it) illustrates the dynamics of participation and delay. A relatively small number of private individuals can delay, block, or alter housing proposals.

In many ways, the Brookline, Massachusetts, neighborhood in which St. Aidan's was located is an ideal site for development. The neighborhood features several tall apartment buildings (including one across the street from the site), brownstones, triple-deckers (three-unit condominium buildings common in New England), and very expensive single-family homes on relatively modest lots. This was not a neighborhood comprised solely of single-family homes on large plots of land. Moreover, there was unusually strong support for the project from virtually every level of government, as well as powerful private actors. The Archdiocese of Boston, the town (which pledged millions of dollars), and federal officials, including Senator Ted Kennedy and Congressman Barney Frank, among others, strongly endorsed the project. Perhaps most importantly, the regulatory environment was favorable. Brookline has fewer land use regulations than most other towns in Eastern Massachusetts (Pioneer Institute for Public Policy Research and Rappaport Institute for Greater Boston 2005). Moreover, the developers used a state zoning law called Chapter 40B, which allows developers proposing affordable housing in expensive Massachusetts cities to bypass certain local zoning laws. This site was, in many regulatory and contextual respects, a best-case scenario for the construction of new housing.

What's more, the town of Brookline desperately needed more housing – a fact that largely explained strong elite support for the development. In 1999 (as today), the town was one the priciest in Massachusetts. Properties the size of St. Aidan's rarely come on the market in towns as developed as Brookline. *The Boston Globe* highlighted the extraordinary nature of the parcel: "A dense Brookline rarely comes upon public property that it can use for affordable housing. Instead, it must rely on the good graces of institutions in transition, like the archdiocese" (Scharfenberg 2001*a*). The initial proposal of 140 units (of which 92 would be affordable) would help address a serious housing crunch.

But a forceful and active group of neighborhood defenders willing to avail themselves of the limited land use tools available proved formidable. *The Boston Globe* noted, in early 1999, the rapidly brewing conflict between state and city officials worried about increasing real estate prices and neighborhood defenders bent on stopping the construction of more housing: "The obstacles are foreboding: a raging real estate market, an increasingly crowded town and a resurgence in neighborhood activism around traffic, parking, open space, and historic preservation rather than affordable housing"(Scharfenberg 2001*a*). David Trietch, a member of the Brookline Housing Opportunities Task Force, worried about the inherent conflict between two town-level movements:

One is a growing movement around the need for affordable housing. The other is a growing sense of neighborhood empowerment. Neighborhoods are organizing and flexing their political muscle. There is going to come a point in the next year where these two movements converge, and the town is going to have to figure out how to balance the push for affordable housing with a respect for neighborhood empowerment. (Scharfenberg 2001*a*).

St. Aidan's would prove to be a protracted battle for these competing town interests.

### Historic Preservation

Even in a relatively lenient regulatory context, neighborhood defenders had a number of land use tools at their disposal. First, the building was old and had a strong connection with the Kennedy family; this allowed neighbors to avail themselves of appeals to historic preservation. A local Town Meeting member, argued, "This is a beautiful church with beautiful grounds, and it's got historic value. . . . My feeling is, if they try to put in affordable housing, they will destroy the inside because developers will have to cut corners" (Scharfenberg 2001*a*).

This "highly organized campaign" of "some neighbors" pursued a warrant article at Town Meeting (the town legislative body composed of resident participants) to get St. Aidan's designated as a "local historic district," which would block redevelopment (Scharfenberg 2001*b*). Strikingly, the neighbors, and not the church, sought to preserve St. Aidan's. Reverend Jack Ahern of St. Mary's, the parish that absorbed St. Aidan's, vocally opposed the preservation efforts. "This is probably the only instance in Massachusetts where the [church] owner is against a preservation effort, and it's proceeding anyway."

The push for historic preservation succeeded in delaying the project. By the summer of 2001 – two years after the closing of the parish – the archdiocese had not made any tangible progress toward building. The organized opponents, however, had already made substantial progress toward stopping, or at least altering, the redevelopment efforts. In May 2001, the Town Meeting passed a resolution asking the preservation commission to study granting St. Aidan's "historic district" status. The Town Meeting's decision directly contradicted the preferences of the town's Board of Selectmen (the town's executive body), which, along with the archdiocese, opposed the resolution (Scharfenberg 2001*b*). This defeat forced the Board of Selectmen to create a committee to study the "adaptive re-use" of the church. This committee included representatives from the neighborhood and town commissions. By the fall of 2001, the project's opponents had successfully pushed for and achieved a special committee and a broader conversation around reuse. Just as importantly, they had ensured that *for more than two years*, no construction would take place on the St. Aidan's property.

By October 2001, the archdiocese had moderated its proposal. It agreed to reduce the number of housing units to 120 – down from 140 – and to keep the church facade. Reverend Ahern argued that this was a significant concession on the part of the church: "We could not continue the present plan while retaining the whole building. ... While housing units could theoretically be built within the existing structure, the cost of such a plan would prohibit them from being targeted to low-income families" (Warner 2001). The neighborhood defenders were not swayed. A longtime parishioner, invoking President Kennedy, said: "I think it's terrible ..., here is our only Irish Catholic president, and he is not getting any recognition from his church" (Warner 2001).

## An Appeal to the Vatican

Unsatisfied with the church's new proposals, fourteen neighbors opened up an unusual legal front. They hired a Canon Lawyer to appeal to the Vatican and challenge the Archdiocese of Boston's permission to sell St. Aidan's (Warner 2002c). While certainly an atypical tactic in housing wars, this new legal approach highlights the time and resources neighborhood defenders were willing to expend to fight the proposal, and the range of land use and legal tools they planned to use to accomplish their goals. Moreover, it lluminates the socioeconomic advantages of these neighborhood defenders. As one planning official we interviewed put it, in Brookline many people "are rich enough to sue."

In the face of forceful opposition, the diocese continued making design concessions. By late April, the diocese fully reversed its position on razing the church. According to Reverend Ahern, "in order to head off a proposal to make the building a local historic district," a downsized plan would have repurposed the church building as market rate residences while knocking down the rectory and garages (Warner 2002a). The number of units proposed continued to decline. The diocese now suggested 62 low- and moderate-income units and 29 to 59 market-rate units (91 to 122 total). This new plan to preserve the entire church building did not mollify the opposition. In mid June 2002, an active neighborhood opponent and member of the town's review team stated that the evolving proposal was "too much development for the area" (Warner 2002*b*).

By August 2002, the church and town further reduced the scope of the proposal. The project would now consist of 16 market rate condominiums (with a starting price of $1.1 million) and 58 subsidized units – a stark decline from the 140 units in the initial plan. Opponents were still not satisfied, worrying about their "fragile" and "endangered" neighborhood, where incursions from apartment buildings and the "buildings of ever-expanding Boston University" have diminished available open space (Giordano 2002).

## The Million Dollar Tree

Moreover, the neighborhood defenders had found their next regulatory angle: an old and very large tree. *The Boston Globe* noted that, at public hearings in fall and winter of 2002: "neighbors have spoken passionately ... and even submitted poems about [the tree] to the zoning board" (Giordano 2002). Letters to the editor in *The Boston Globe* highlighted the beloved tree. One *seven-year-old* asked for "the church to stay like it is" and raised concerns about the streets "becoming busier," with "more accidents," and worrying that his bike shortcut under the tree will be blocked by the new development (Mears 2002). Another letter writer underscored the tree, among other factors:

> The scale and density of the proposed St. Aidan's project is totally inappropriate and represents a real disservice to this congested neighborhood. Obliteration of the forecourt with *its magnificent, irreplaceable copper beech tree* (emphasis added) is unacceptable. Affordable housing is absolutely necessary in Brookline, but the archdiocese has another, larger, abandoned site in Brookline. Build there, put a civilized number of units at Saint Aidan's and preserve the church and surrounding green space for community use. (Davidson 2002)

Not all neighbors opposed the development. One resident from a neighboring section of Boston (which abuts Brookline) wrote: "what Brookline desperately needs to preserve is its own integrity and continue its tradition as a diverse community is affordable housing. Any development of the St. Aidan's property must create as many units of reasonably priced housing as possible while respecting the overall tenor of the neighborhood" (Epstein 2002).

The diocese appeared incredulous at the new line of arguments about the tree. Lisa Alberghini, Executive Vice President of the church's planning office, explicitly cast support for the tree as arguments against affordable housing: "it's a very nice tree … but if it comes down to housing ten more families in need or keeping the tree, I'm going to vote for the 10 families in need "(Giordano 2002).

Strong neighborhood support for the tree, however, led to extraordinary concessions in 2003 – leading town officials to label the copper beech as "the million dollar tree."4 The new proposal kept the tree, and reorganized the entire site to preserve more open space – eliminating thirty housing units in the process. The project now featured nine high-end, market-rate condominiums in the old church building, fifty affordable units, and a reduction of twenty thousand feet of building space (Samburg 2004).

## Continuing Legal Challenges

Despite the church's concessions and strong town political and financial support – Brookline committed $4.5 million in public funds (Boston Globe Editorial Board 2005) – the project continued to experience massive delays. Some of this was due to construction complications, such as increases in material expenses and changes in available financing, that inevitably lead to delays in projects of this scale (Knudson 2005). These rising costs, however, offered neighbors an opportunity to impose further delays. Responding to increased expenses, the church sought more money from the town and asked to change some of the affordable units to market-rate ones. These, and other changes, both motivated and sustained resistance, and provided opportunities for neighborhood defenders to continue their opposition (Knudson 2005).

One such avenue was an additional lawsuit. In September 2005, a group of seventy-five residents filed a lawsuit in county court challenging recent changes to the project's design and additional financial commitments from the town. The lawsuit argued that the developer violated the prior agreement by both shifting some units slated to be affordable back to market price and demanding an additional $1 million town contribution to help offset increased costs. Town officials were apoplectic about mounting delays. Robert Allen, chair of the Board of Selectmen, was blunt: "I am extremely frustrated and disappointed that this is the route they chose. This was a huge chunk of affordable housing for Brookline. We won't see a lot of [projects this size in town] in our lifetime" (Knudson 2005).

---

4 Authors' interview with local planning officials.

One year later – a year in which construction was stalled – the town and seventy-five plaintiffs settled the lawsuit. It was now August 2006 – two years after the town and residents had ostensibly reached an agreement on a fifty-nine-unit plan. The lawsuit resulted in modest aesthetic changes and a pledge (ultimately unfulfilled) to "try to eliminate the fifth story" from the affordable apartment part of the complex (Stickgold 2006). The main effect of the lawsuit was to delay the project.

The next year consisted of a new round of public meetings and, due to delays, reopening the construction bidding process. Finally, in the summer of 2007, the *Boston Globe* could report that the development "where John F. Kennedy was baptized might finally, after more than six years of public debate and a court settlement, break ground this fall"(Downs 2007). The town explicitly acknowledged the profound impact neighborhood defenders had on the project. Housing Advisory Chairman Roger Blood said, "This could have been a much larger 40B project, but we have saved open space, the historic St. Aidan's church building, and a treasured beech tree, put parking underground, and gotten 36 affordable units, or more than 60 percent of the total" (Downs 2007).

### Fifty-Nine New Housing Units

In 2010 – eleven years after the project's initial proposal – fifty-nine units opened for new residents. The final project included nine luxury condominiums, twenty affordable rental units, and thirty units available for purchase by first-time home buyers. In some ways, the project was a success. Fifty-nine new housing units – most of which were affordable – were built in the middle of a desirable and established neighborhood featuring top-notch schools and public services. Ultimately, many of the opponents were satisfied and accepting of the ultimate compromises. One of the most active opponents said, after the final lawsuit resolved, that neighbors "realized we'd gone as far as we could go," credited the town's building commissioner, and concluded that "everybody felt we all got something out of it" (Hilliard 2010). Of course, "it" was a years-long project featuring multiple regulatory obstacles imposed by neighborhood defenders. Battles over historic districts, trees, and open space would not have happened were it not for the vociferous objections of neighborhood defenders. A very valuable parcel of land consequently went unused for over a decade. The project was far more costly due to the numerous delays and reduction in the number of total housing units. Perhaps most importantly, 60 percent less total housing (and 46 percent less affordable housing) was built. At the end of the whole process, the town ended up with fifty-nine additional housing units. The neighbors protected a historic church building, kept the scale of the new construction relatively modest, and preserved open space and a grand old beech tree. Meanwhile, five hundred people submitted their names to get on the list for twenty new affordable apartments (Hilliard 2010).

### Neighborhood Defenders and Defense Tactics

The behavior and power of neighborhood defenders in slowing and shrinking the redevelopment of St. Aidan's are emblematic of our theory. These neighborhood defenders were active, advantaged, and overwhelmingly opposed to the construction of new housing. Indeed, they included individuals willing to use their money and expertise to sue the Vatican and the Town of Brookline, cite regulations on historic preservation and trees, and write letters to the editor – all in the name of stopping development. There were no neighborhood countersuits in support of the project and few letters to the editor from neighbors endorsing the endeavor.

What's more, even in a relatively relaxed regulatory context, there were still a variety of institutional tools at neighborhood defenders' disposal. Historic and environmental regulations (as well as the somewhat unusual circumstance of Vatican involvement in church redevelopment) provided ample grounds for neighborhood defenders to contest the project. Moreover, neighborhood defenders could use these tools in a variety of ways. They could highlight concerns in public meetings, as grounds for lawsuits, or as parts of media campaigns.

While neighbors' aim might be to stop a development, they can accomplish a similarly powerful goal: delay. Costly delays spurred a series of significant concessions in which the church dramatically reduced the scope of its proposal. Neighborhood defenders empowered by land use institutions engaged in the politics of delay and decreased the production of housing in a high-cost community desperate for more housing.

## EMPIRICAL EVIDENCE

Illustrating our theory more systematically requires marshaling multiple, interwoven pieces of evidence. First, in our account, land use institutions should create opportunities for delay. In places with more opportunities for delay, we should anticipate (1) the pursuit of more delaying tactics (like lawsuits) and (2) less housing construction. Chapter 3 combines data on land use regulations, building permits, and the redevelopment of former Catholic Church properties to illustrate that more regulations of all types – and thus more opportunities for delay – diminish the supply of housing. Chapter 4 connects regulations to meetings; it shows how projects trigger meetings and describes the concerns raised about these projects. Notably, the issues meeting participants highlight do not necessarily correspond with the regulatory reasons for holding a meeting in the first place. Chapter 6 links regulations with lawsuits.

Second, we expect participation in land use politics to be higher among socioeconomically advantaged individuals – thus rendering land use regulations more potent in highly advantaged cities, towns, and neighborhoods. We also anticipate that these individuals will be overwhelmingly opposed to the construction of new housing. Chapter 5 features novel data on *all* resident participants in planning and zoning board meetings across a two-year period. By merging these data with several statewide databases, we can learn valuable demographic data about these individuals, including age, gender, homeownership status, and race. We show that neighborhood defenders are unrepresentative of their broader communities across a variety of dimensions. They are also disproportionately opposed to the construction of new housing – far more than what mass attitudes in their communities would indicate. We confirm these insights from meeting minutes with a mix of survey evidence, case studies, and elite interviews.

Third, we expect that these advantaged and oppositional individuals will use land use institutions – both the participatory venues and the regulations limiting development – to stymie housing development. Chapter 6 shows how sophisticated neighborhood defenders use participatory forums to raise community concerns that can be explicitly or implicitly linked with land use regulations. These concerns carry, in some cases, racist and classist sentiments. This chapter marshals a variety of data types including quantitative analyses of meeting minutes and lawsuits, archival evidence from meeting minutes, and elite interviews.

Finally, our theory suggests that less advantaged – and therefore less participatory – communities will be more vulnerable to gentrification pressures in high housing demand cities. We explore these phenomena in Chapter 7, and consider how gentrification pressures have hampered coalition-building surrounding housing policy. This chapter features a mix of quantitative analysis of housing permitting data and archival and interview evidence.

## CAVEATS

While we have amassed a wide variety of data to bolster our claims, this study – as with virtually all social scientific inquiries – comes with limitations. Identifying causes is challenging. In an ideal world, we would find circumstances in which regulations or neighborhood defenders were randomly assigned to particular communities, either by historical accident or as some sort of policy experiment. While our analysis of the redevelopment of Catholic Church properties in Chapter 3 comes closest to a natural experiment, the reality is that regulations and people are not located randomly. Regulations are the consequence of deliberate decisions on the parts of local officials to restrict access to their communities and people – including neighborhood defenders – certainly do not choose their homes on a random basis. To address this, we amass a variety of different types of evidence, control for confounders when possible, and rely on strong theory to drive our empirical predictions. Cumulatively, these data present a compelling narrative consistent with our theory.

First, because we are investigating regulations as they occur in the real world, we cannot control which ones vary and which ones do not. In our analysis, we uncover substantial differences in the regulatory environments across cities and towns. Local governments have wildly different requirements about what parcel shapes require special permits, when a development's proximity to wetlands requires a hearing in front of the zoning board, and the minimum acreage on which an apartment building can be built. There is *not*, however, variation in the existence of public planning and zoning board hearings at which neighborhood defenders can speak. These participatory institutions exist in every local government we study. Thus, we are unable to measure whether eliminating or restricting such institutions would shape the production of housing. Institutional configurations have a potent impact on the composition of the electorate (Bridges 1997; Trounstine 2008; Mullin 2009), the political strength of real estate interests in land use decisions (Lubbell, Feiock, and Ramirez 2005, 2009), and neighborhood meeting participation (Berry, Portney, and Thomson 1993), among other policy arenas. Variations in how these participatory institutions are promulgated – whether they are neighborhood- or city-level, for example – could certainly shape who shows up and how these individuals affect housing policy outcomes.

What we can show is how the propensity of neighborhood defenders to participate in land use politics and use available institutional tools shapes the housing supply. While opportunities to participate do not vary, people's inclination to do so varies enormously.

We similarly do not investigate what predicts variations in land use regulations. Jessica Trounstine (2018) and Richard Rothstein (2017) have both provided trenchant historical analyses illustrating that contemporary land use regulations emerged out of a multi-decade effort on the part of local governments (and their advantaged residents) to exclude people of color and low-income individuals and families from their communities' boundaries. In part, because this ground has been so ably covered by others, we do not outline these historic origins in great detail here. We do, however, return to the role of race as motivator for neighborhood defense in Chapters 5 and 6.

Second, we cannot directly observe the causal effect of neighborhood defender commentary at planning and zoning board meetings on project outcomes. Neighborhood defenders do not randomly attend meetings; they instead respond to particular kinds of projects. An analysis that correlated negative commentary at neighborhood meetings with project outcomes would not be able to adjudicate whether (1) neighborhood defenders influenced zoning board officials, (2) the kinds of projects that attract neighborhood defenders are also concerning to local officials, or (3) developers in some cases were able to anticipate neighborhood defender complaints and avoid them. We instead rely on a mix of quantitative data consistent with our theoretical predictions and detailed historical case studies and interviews where we are able to more directly observe the process by which neighborhood defenders diminish the supply of new housing.

Third, much of our empirical data comes from one state: Massachusetts. Massachusetts is the only state where scholars have systematically measured land use regulations, allowing for the kinds of analyses featured in Chapters 3 and 4. The Pioneer Institute for Public Policy Research and Rappaport Institute for Greater Boston (2005) spent years collecting extraordinarily detailed data on dozens of land use regulations across more than one hundred cities and towns in Greater Boston. No other area features near this level of detail on land use institutions. What's more, it is also the only state where open meeting laws mandate detailed planning and zoning board minutes that allow us to merge participants in meetings with other databases. We show in Chapter 3 that Massachusetts cities and towns provide enormous variation in demographic and institutional contexts, allowing us to make generalizable claims about the impact of land use regulations and participation on the construction of new housing.

Moreover, we investigated zoning codes in six cities – Charleston, South Carolina; Charlotte, North Carolina; Los Angeles, California; Milwaukee, Wisconsin; Phoenix, Arizona; and San Francisco, California – to determine whether public input is similarly solicited in other locales. These six cities are all demographically and institutionally distinct from many of the Massachusetts communities featured in our statistical analyses. There are certainly important procedural differences across different cities: in some places, for example, the city council reviews proposed development plans, while in other communities, appointed boards are primarily responsible for development decisions. Some cities require developers to meet with neighbors in advance of public hearings, while others simply mandate abutter notifications.

Importantly, however, these cities share two important facets with Massachusetts land use politics. The first is that the process by which these communities permit multifamily housing is similarly laborious. Projects typically must go through multiple reviews, frequently with different governing bodies; indeed, in several cities, developers must first present to a neighborhood meeting before a public hearing in front of the planning commission. Should the project pass this first stage, it then faces a third set of public hearings before the city council. The second commonality across these disparate institutional settings is that all of these cities feature *public* hearings – in many cases, multiple public hearings across different public bodies. Like the housing politics in Massachusetts that we thoroughly empirically document in the ensuing chapters, land use rules across an array of locales encourage and privilege the voices of neighboring residents in housing construction.

Nonetheless, Massachusetts is institutionally and demographically distinct from other places. It is much whiter than the country as a whole. Moreover, its local governments are highly fragmented and have unusually strong powers over land use. Whenever possible, our empirical chapters expand the focus of our book beyond Massachusetts. They feature evidence from a national survey of mayors, interviews with local elites in other cities, and case studies of developments in other communities. While the empirics of this book are geographically clustered, the concepts are nationally generalizable. Indeed, we have presented this work to local policy and planning official hailing from across the United States, as well as several global officials; these policy makers collectively found the empirics of this work reflective of their local communities.

Fourth, this book centers primarily on the interactions between the regulatory framework, developers, and neighborhood defenders. Notably absent are variations in the preferences of city or town officials. We show that, as in the case of the redevelopment of St. Aidan's Church, even when town officials are uniformly favorable towards a development, neighborhood defenders inclined toward participation can use land use regulations to delay and alter a development. Moreover, with most planning and zoning board officials serving on a part-time or voluntary basis, there is good reason to expect that they will be particularly responsive to neighborhood defenders' entreaties. Bruce Cain (2015) considers this point in his broader exploration of open meeting laws and public participation in local governance: "Many local boards consist of part-time and volunteer members. Unlike professional politicians, they are not used to being criticized and are more easily flustered by vocal, angry critics" (61).

Throughout the book, we use a survey of local officials and elite interviews to explore how local politicians perceive the politics of land use. We do not, however, systematically explore how variations in local elite behavior shape the construction of new housing. We consider in our conclusion elite coalition-building strategies for promulgating housing reform.

Fifth, this is a book about the construction of market-rate and affordable housing. There are certainly some political dynamics that are unique to specific segments of the housing market; building luxury condominiums naturally involves a different politics than the development of affordable housing. Our interest in this book is unveiling obstacles to the construction of all housing types in the places that need it. Investigating the politics of market-rate housing, then, is in many respects a tougher test of our theoretical predictions. Units that target the bottom of the market and offer subsidized options provide valuable neighborhood access to groups that may differ markedly in their economic status and racial and ethnic backgrounds from current residents. By tapping into antipoor and antiminority prejudice, affordable housing proposals frequently elicit strong opposition from neighborhood residents (Pendall 1999; Tighe 2010; Trounstine 2016). The political processes we describe in this book impede the construction of all types of housing. Their effects on affordable housing are likely even more severe.

Finally, the projects featured in this book are the ones that are actually proposed in front of planning and zoning boards – not all possible developments. These proposals reflect both developer and local government preferences. Developers will only propose projects that they believe they can plausibly build, and that they believe will yield a profit. Local officials will, in many cases, only allow proposals before land use boards that pass some kind of internal quality review. In many respects, we should expect these selection processes to lead to less public opposition to development; the public is only commenting on those projects that the developer believes will survive public review, and that the local government has – at least in some communities – deemed of sufficiently high quality to be worthy of the full review process. This makes the strong opposition to the proposed housing featured in this book all the more striking.

3

# Land Use Regulations and Multifamily Housing Development

In Waltham, Massachusetts, a developer seeking to build a three-family home would first need to acquire a 6,000 square foot lot. If she purchases a lot in one of Waltham's multifamily zones, her project is exempt from the lengthy and contentious public review introduced in the previous two chapters. The process is considerably different in Waltham's northern neighbor, Lexington. First, the developer would need to purchase a plot of land more than two-and-a-half times as large as she would in Waltham: 15,500 square feet. Moreover, regardless of where her plot is located, her proposed development would require a special permit, and would consequently necessitate public review – potentially over the course of multiple meetings. Indeed, *all multifamily developments* in Lexington – from townhouses to large apartment complexes – require a special permit. These differences reflect broader variations between Lexington and Waltham's land use institutions. Overall, Waltham has 17 different types of regulations on housing development, compared with Lexington's 34.[1]

These regulations affect the construction of new housing in two separate ways. First, they outright prohibit certain forms of development. Second, any form of housing requiring a special permit or variance – a one-time exception from existing regulations – has to go through a lengthy hearing process. The provision of special permits and variances offers municipal officials and residents substantial control over what is constructed, and opportunities to modify developers' plans to

---

[1] Housing regulations are based on the Pioneer Institute for Public Policy Research and Rappaport Institute for Greater Boston (2005) database, discussed as follows.

fit town and neighborhood preferences. Because zoning and planning board meetings feature public input, these applications for special permits and variances provide the public with a substantial voice in the housing construction process. Towns with more regulations require more special permits or variances for housing development. Each additional regulation creates opportunities for town authorities to deny permits or variances, and *chances for neighbors* to voice opposition or make additional requests for information, studies, and project changes. Chapters 4 and 6 feature neighborhood defenders citing regulations regarding issues like parking and wetlands as reasons to either outright deny a development or, at a minimum, require further study prior to approval.

Lexington's thirty-four housing regulations appear to be limiting the construction of multifamily housing. In relatively unregulated Waltham, 65 percent of permitted units between 2000 and 2015 were for multifamily housing, and 35 percent were for single-family homes. Over the same time period, 94 percent of the permitted units in Lexington were for single-family homes, and only 6 percent were for units in multifamily buildings.

In this chapter we build on the argument developed in Chapter 2 using data on town building regulations and housing permits. While there is a substantial body of research – situated primarily in economics – finding that more restrictive land use policies prevent localities from keeping pace with rising demand for housing (Quigley and Rosenthal 2005; Glaeser, Gyourko, and Saks 2005; Gyourko, Saiz, and Summers 2008; Glaeser and Ward 2009; Glaeser 2011; Gyourko and Molloy 2014; Fischel 2015), little of this research examines the effects of different types of regulations. Here, we show that there is a negative relationship between *a variety* of town zoning regulations and the permitting of multifamily housing. The more highly regulated the town, the less multifamily housing gets built. Furthermore, we show that different types of regulations, including regulations ostensibly unrelated to density, reduce the construction of multifamily housing. We then use the special case of Catholic Church redevelopments as a natural experiment to show that the previously examined relationships are not just correlations; zoning and land use regulations reduce the construction of multifamily housing.

## Measuring Land Use Regulations

Due to their complexity, systematic data on land use and zoning regulations are scarce. Municipal land use codes are often opaque and lengthy, featuring hundreds of pages of detail on layers of local regulations. Most research on the effects of such policies has required scholars to make tradeoffs between breadth and depth, either examining a few individual places or using high-level data that can miss important variation. For example, economists Joseph Gyourko, Albert Saiz, and Anita Summers (2008) use surveys of local officials to provide relatively cursory information about land use policy in a large number of cities. One important exception to this dearth of detailed zoning data is metropolitan Boston. In the early 2000s a team of researchers at the Pioneer Institute for Public Policy Research and the Rappaport Institute for Greater Boston at the Harvard Kennedy School undertook a massive data collection effort to assemble a comprehensive data set of local housing regulations in the greater Boston area (Pioneer Institute for Public Policy Research and Rappaport Institute for Greater Boston 2005; Glaeser and Ward 2009). Because of our interest in better understanding the mechanisms underlying land use institutions, we use these data to analyze Boston area communities in depth rather than attempting comparisons across a wider geographic area. Our results here are applicable to communities across the United States. The types of regulations that we analyze are not unique to the Boston area, but used by local governments nationwide.

The depth of the Boston data is extraordinary. The Local Housing Regulation Database (hereafter LHRD) features regulatory data on 187 cities and towns located within 50 miles of Boston. For each community, coders tracked *all* regulations that could have an impact on housing development and could be measured objectively. Using a combination of surveys of local officials and city and town regulatory codes, researchers assembled information on 119 zoning, subdivision, wetland, and septic regulations (Pioneer Institute for Public Policy Research and Rappaport Institute for Greater Boston 2005). No other data source on housing regulation comes close to offering this level of detail about land use institutions. The depth and breadth of regulations covered means that we can disaggregate between less obviously density limiting land use regulations, like parcel shape restrictions, and more explicitly density-targeting regulations like direct restrictions on multifamily housing.

On top of data quality, metropolitan Boston also represents an excellent case because of its extraordinary variation in land use institutions across otherwise demographically similar places. Unlike some parts of the United States, the relatively compact Boston metro area is divided into hundreds of autonomous cities and towns. As our introductory example of Waltham and Lexington illustrated, the large number of towns in metro Boston offers many opportunities to observe different regulatory configurations in places that are within miles of each other and similar in many other ways, like demography, economy, and topography. Figure 3.1 maps the towns in the data set, shaded by the number of

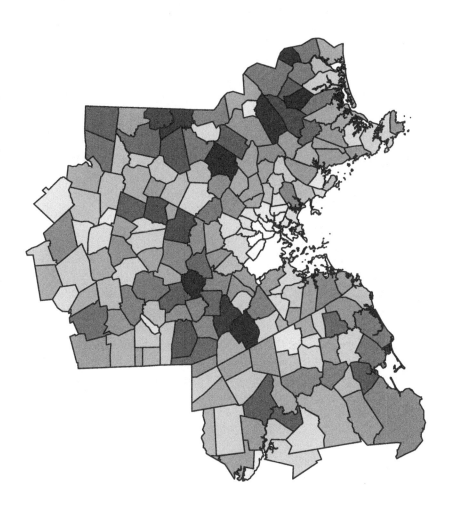

# Regulations

10    20    30    40    50

FIGURE 3.1: Map of sample towns by number of housing regulations

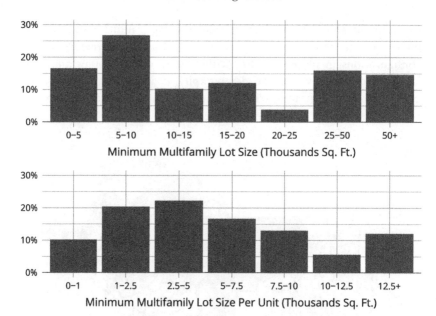

FIGURE 3.2: Distributions of lot size regulations

housing regulations. The darker the shading, the greater the number of regulations in the town.[2]

Figure 3.2 plots the full distribution of two key land use regulations: (1) the minimum lot size required for multifamily housing, and (2) the minimum lot size per unit.[3] The variation in regulations across municipalities is striking. For example, Cambridge's minimum lot size for multifamily housing is 900 square feet – in contrast with Weston's whopping 240,000. While we might expect substantial differences between relatively large and diverse Cambridge (which is adjacent to Boston), and small and homogenous Weston (about fifteen miles away), we also observe variation between cities that are demographically similar. Groton

---

[2] Notably, our sample does not include the city of Boston itself, which does not operate under the same state zoning law (Chapter 40A) as all other state municipalities. There is consequently not one large city – which often have very distinct political structures and climates (Judd and Swanstrom 1994; Oliver, Ha, and Callen 2012) – driving our results. Importantly, we do have a sizable number of midsized and diverse cities in our sample, including Cambridge, Worcester, Lawrence, and Lowell, among others.

[3] Some of the towns in the sample do not specify a minimum lot size or minimum lot size per unit, and are excluded from the plot. These towns either prohibit multifamily housing or use other regulations to define acceptable lot size, such as cluster development regulations.

and Marblehead are both small, homogenous, and affluent towns, but they exhibit markedly different regulatory environments. Groton has a median income of $117,000, and is 94 percent white. Marblehead has a median income of $103,000 and is 95 percent white.[4] However, Groton requires an eighty thousand square foot lot to build multifamily housing, while Marblehead requires only five thousand square feet. Between 2000 and 2015, the share of permitted units in buildings with at least five housing units was substantially higher in Marblehead (26.4 percent) than in Groton (18.6 percent).

We code each regulation in the LHRD using a binary scale where a regulation is coded "1" if it is a potential impediment to multifamily housing and "0" if the regulation is not an impediment or is not used in the town.[5] For example, some towns regulate the construction of mixed-use developments. We code such regulations as "0" if the town does not regulate mixed-use development or if it is allowed in some zones by right, and as "1" if it is not permitted or only allowed with a special permit. We then count the number of restrictive regulations in each town, in total and by type of regulation. While this coding and method of aggregation is approximate, we believe that it captures the overall level of restrictive housing regulations by town. Some towns may rely more on some types of regulations than others, and there are significant variations in the strength of particular types of regulations across towns. By coding them all using a binary scale, we weigh all regulations equally, and variations in regulatory strength across towns will average out by using all available regulations. As this coding is imperfect, we also present more granular data for select regulations in the analysis as follows.

Overall, we include eighty-three regulations across nine categories in our analysis. Table 3.1 presents summary statistics for each category. The median town has twenty-nine potentially restrictive regulations on housing development and five regulations on multifamily housing in particular. Some towns have a larger number of regulations in certain categories but fewer in others. For example, the town of Peabody has sixteen different regulations pertaining to wetlands, but no regulations on growth, inclusionary zoning, or septic systems. Plympton has eight

---

[4] 2015 American Community Survey, five-year estimates. US Census Bureau.
[5] We focus on multifamily housing in this analysis, rather than all housing, because of the broad consensus that increasing density in metropolitan areas is essential to addressing the housing crisis and affordable housing. However, we recognize that zoning regulations may also reduce the supply of single-family homes (large lot size requirements, for example, reduce density even in single-family neighborhoods).

TABLE 3.1 *Summary statistics for zoning regulations*

| Category | N | Median | Min. | Max. |
| --- | --- | --- | --- | --- |
| Cluster regulations | 6 | 2 | 0 | 6 |
| Growth regulations | 6 | 0 | 0 | 5 |
| Inclusionary regulations | 5 | 1 | 0 | 5 |
| Multifamily regulations | 11 | 5 | 1 | 8 |
| Parcel shape regulations | 8 | 3 | 0 | 7 |
| Senior housing regulations | 4 | 2 | 0 | 4 |
| Septic regulations | 17 | 3 | 0 | 10 |
| Subdivision regulations | 10 | 5 | 1 | 9 |
| Wetlands regulations | 16 | 7 | 0 | 16 |
| All regulations | 83 | 29 | 6 | 52 |

different regulations on multifamily housing (tied with five other towns for the most in this category), but no regulations on growth or wetlands, and only one regulation in the cluster development and inclusive zoning categories.

## Measuring Multifamily Development

To assess the relationship between housing regulations and multifamily housing, we need a town-level measure of multifamily housing development. Following economists Edward Glaeser and Bryce Ward (2009), we use data on building permits from the US Census. Each year the Census Bureau conducts the Building Permits Survey (BPS), which collects data on building permits for privately-owned residential buildings. The Census Bureau collects these data directly from the permit-issuing places, which is the city or town in Massachusetts. The BPS data includes the number of buildings and units in buildings with one unit, two units, three to four units, and five or more units. We combine all of the multifamily units into a single category.[6] We pool data from the 2000 to 2015 BPS to measure the share of single and multifamily housing constructed in each town. We use this time period for two reasons. First, the long time span ensures that any single anomalous year does not substantially affect the results. Second, Glaeser and Ward (2009) find that zoning regulations are stable, so we should expect the same general regulatory environment

[6] In the appendix we provide additional analysis that distinguish between units in smaller buildings (two to four units) and larger buildings (five or more units).

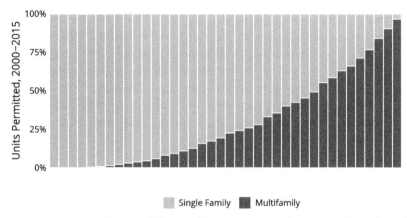

FIGURE 3.3: Distribution of shares of housing permits by town and number of units. Each bar corresponds to five towns.

across this time period. In our analyses, we measure multifamily housing permits as the percentage of units that are located in multiunit buildings during this time period.[7]

As with the regulation data, there is substantial variation in unit types permitted across towns. Figure 3.3 plots the distribution of permits across town by the share of total permits for each category. Each bar corresponds to five towns. At the far left, there are twenty towns that only issued permits for single-family housing. Some of these towns prohibit all multifamily housing. Most, however, technically allow some multi-family housing, at least in some neighborhoods; they simply did not issue permits for any such buildings.[8] On the right are towns where the vast majority of permits issued were for multifamily housing developments

---

[7] These analyses generally follow those in Glaeser and Ward (2009), which also use permitting as a dependent variable; we, however, use share of single-family and multifamily permitted units – rather than a log of total permitted units – as our key dependent variables. In the appendix we repeat our analysis with different measurements of multifamily housing: (1) the share of permitted buildings (rather than units) of each type, and (2) the log of total permitted units, as in Glaeser and Ward (2009).

[8] We are unable to observe all requests for building permits, only building permits issued. It is likely that no multifamily housing permits were requested in any of these towns. This may be due to lack of demand for multifamily housing, but also due to developers choosing not to attempt development in these towns. In our interviews with developers, several mentioned that they would not attempt to build in specific towns, not because the town regulations prohibited the development, but because the regulations and approval process was so onerous and contentious in some places that they would rather pursue projects elsewhere.

with at least five units. The highest share is in Chelsea, where more than 99 percent of permitted units were in multifamily buildings, and only four single-family homes received permits across the entire period. In the median town, 80 percent of the permits issued were for single-family housing and 20 percent were for multifamily housing. In short, there is stunning variation between cities and towns in the extent to which they construct high-density housing. Some places almost exclusively build multifamily housing. Others build none.

### Regulations Reduce Multifamily Housing

We anticipate that the accumulation of housing regulations reduces multifamily housing development. Each additional regulation creates a new potential barrier to development. Because these regulations frequently trigger public review, they create multiple points at which members of the community can object to proposed housing projects; this both increases costs for developers and blocks or delays new housing. Moreover, we predict that the effect of regulations on multifamily housing is not restricted to multifamily housing regulations alone, but also applies to other regulations that are not specific to multifamily housing. Indeed, as we saw in the introduction, neighbors can raise all sorts of concerns at public meetings – from traffic to turtles – to stymie unwanted development. Figure 3.4 illustrates this relationship for Waltham, Lexington, and some neighboring towns – all similarly sized inner-ring suburbs of Boston. Towns with fewer housing regulations, such as Watertown, Arlington, and Medford, issued a larger share of housing permits for multifamily housing than towns with more regulations, such as Needham and Lexington.

Simple plots of the number of regulations and the share of total permits issued to multifamily housing reveal a consistent pattern: highly regulated places are constructing less multifamily housing. Figure 3.5 plots the share of multifamily housing permits by the number of regulations in each town, where towns are classified as having a "low" or "high" number of regulations in each category.[9] Overall, we find that

---

[9] Appendix Table A.1 presents OLS results, as well as models using other methods of defining the amount of multifamily housing constructed. We find statistically significant negative relationships between the total number of regulations and multifamily housing permits, as well as between the number of growth, multifamily, parcel shape, senior, or septic system regulations and the multifamily housing permit share.

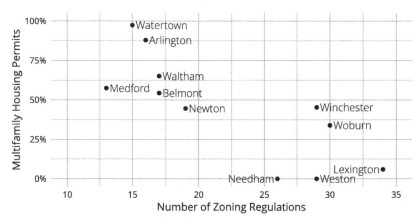

FIGURE 3.4: Proportion of multifamily housing permits, 2000–2015, for selected towns

each additional regulation is associated with a roughly one percentage point decrease in the multifamily permits. Moving from the median level of regulations, twenty-nine, to the maximum, fifty-two, decreases the share of multifamily permits by twenty-one percentage points. This pattern holds even when we disaggregate by a number of regulation types: growth, multifamily, parcel shape, senior housing, and septic regulations all are associated with decreases in multifamily permitting. However, the number of inclusionary zoning regulations, wetland regulations, subdivision regulations, and cluster developer regulations are not.

Unsurprisingly, regulations that explicitly target multifamily housing have the largest negative relationship with multifamily permitting. Each additional multifamily housing regulation is associated with a decrease in multifamily unit permits of four to nine percentage points. Moving from the median level of multifamily regulations, five, to the maximum, eight, decreases multifamily unit permits by a striking twenty percentage points. To further illustrate this relationship, Figure 3.6 plots the share of multifamily unit permits by town for four different kinds of multifamily regulations: new construction of buildings with three or more units, townhouses, mixed-use developments, and converting single-family homes to multifamily housing. The regulations are coded in the LHRD using three categories: "Not Permitted," "Special Permit Only," and "Some by Right."[10] In the first case, the town forbids multifamily

---

[10] For the 3+ unit Buildings category, the LHRD coding is more complex and includes cluster zoning as well. We include "by cluster/planned development only" with the "Special Permit Only" category.

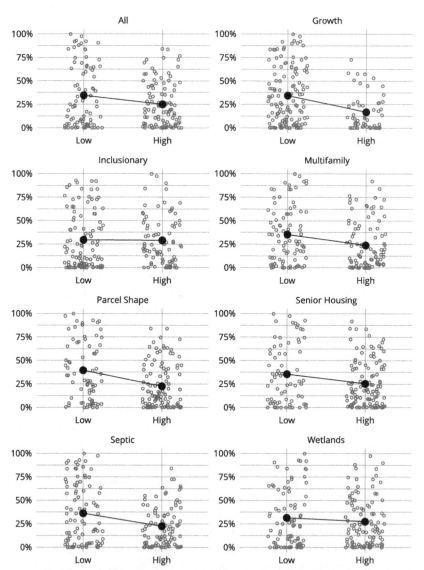

FIGURE 3.5: Multifamily housing permit share by number of housing regulations

housing.[11] In the second, the town only allows multifamily housing with a special permit. Typically, this means that the development must be approved by the town's planning or zoning board – and thus go through a lengthy review process and public hearings. In the third case, some zones of the town allow such development by right, with no public meetings necessary. However, this category does not mean that all such developments are allowed by right; there may be many zones within the municipality that still require a special permit.

Figure 3.6 shows that more flexible regulations increase the share of multifamily housing unit permits. For example, the share of multifamily unit permits is twelve percentage points higher in towns that allow special permits for mixed-use buildings compared to those that prohibit them, and twenty-four percentage points higher when mixed-use development is allowed in some zones by right. The figure shows the relationship between the share of multifamily housing permitted of all types and regulations on specific types of multifamily housing. For all four categories of regulations, the increase in the level of multifamily unit permits

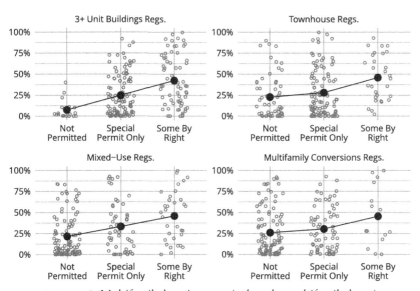

FIGURE 3.6: Multifamily housing permit share by multifamily housing regulations

---

[11] In some cases, such housing may still be constructed, by using state-level regulations that allow for town-level regulations to be bypassed.

between towns where such development is not allowed and towns where it is allowed in some zones by right is statistically significant.[12]

While the negative relationship between multifamily zoning regulations and multifamily housing permitting may seem obvious, we also find similar relationships between other types of regulations and the construction of multifamily housing – in arenas like frontage requirements and septic systems that are not explicitly about housing density. With the exception of senior housing regulations, these negative effects persist *even when we control for multifamily housing regulations.* In other words, we do not find a negative relationship between septic regulations and the permitting of multifamily housing simply because septic regulations are highly correlated with multifamily regulations.

For example, Figure 3.7 divides towns by whether they have a bylaw that imposes constraints on lot shape and prevents oddly shaped lots. As in Figure 3.6, which looked at differences across multifamily regulations, we see that towns that regulate parcel shapes have a lower share of multifamily unit permits than those that do not. We cannot empirically demonstrate with these town-level analyses whether neighbors are using these types of regulations to delay development or render it more costly; but, the negative relationship between a multitude of regulation types – not just multifamily limits – and the production of multifamily housing suggests that regulations in general provide opportunities to impose costs, alterations, and delays on housing development.

Interestingly, one type of regulation designed to promote the provision of multifamily and affordable housing – inclusionary zoning – appears to

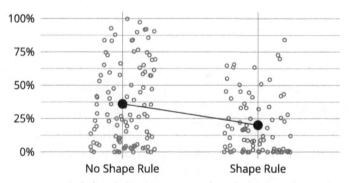

FIGURE 3.7: Multifamily housing permit share by shape rule regulation

[12] For the 3+ Unit Buildings and Mixed-Use regulations, the difference between "Special Permit Only" towns and "Not Permitted" towns is positive and statistically significant as well.

have little impact on permitting. Indeed, there is no relationship between inclusionary zoning rules and housing permits. At least in Massachusetts, these measures appear to be ineffective at promoting greater affordability via increased housing density, perhaps in part because multifamily housing still faces potent public scrutiny in these regulatory regimes.

## CATHOLIC CHURCH REDEVELOPMENTS AS A NATURAL EXPERIMENT

We have shown thus far that zoning regulations are linked with a lower supply of multifamily housing. Because zoning regulations are not randomly assigned to different communities, however, we cannot say for certain that regulations *caused* this diminished supply. Perhaps most problematically, housing regulations might cause certain types of properties to become available. If fewer properties are available in more highly regulated communities, it would lead us to observe a negative relationship between regulations and multifamily housing; the central driver of this relationship, though, would be the *availability of property*, not necessarily the regulatory environment. Similarly, some towns have a reputation of being hostile to development, such that developers do not choose to pursue projects there. Since we only observe what is actually permitted, rather than either all proposed projects (or, ideally, all theoretically profitable projects that a developer could consider), this might bias our analyses.

To address these issues, we treat the redevelopment of former Catholic Church properties in the greater Boston area as a natural experiment. In an ideal experiment, we would be able to randomly assign regulations to towns and to randomly make comparable plots of land in each town available for development. We would then compare the housing developments in the parcels in towns with a high number of regulations to those in towns with a low number of regulations. While we cannot randomize either part of this ideal experiment, Catholic Church redevelopments offer pseudo-random assignment (Dunning 2012) of the second part: which parcels of land become available for development. Though this approach will not resolve all potential selection problems, it will help us identify the effects of regulations on housing supply by providing a large number of comparable properties across towns with very different regulatory contexts.[13]

---

[13] Glaeser and Ward (2009) argue that regulations are as-if-random across towns, such that we should not be concerned with selection effects involving different kinds of towns

The Roman Catholic Church is one of the world's largest landowners. The Archdiocese of Boston is both one of Boston's oldest institutions
and one of the largest dioceses in the United States (McEnery 2011). To
give a sense of the proportions, the Archdiocese of Boston is the fourth
largest in the United States behind only Los Angeles, New York, and
Chicago, which are all considerably larger cities. Because of its age and
size, the church owned (and owns) acres of valuable property in heavily developed Eastern Massachusetts. According to Forbes Magazine, in
2002, the archdiocese owned approximately $1.3 billion ($1.8 in current
dollars) worth of property (Schiffman 2002). Much of this real estate
was held in large plots and buildings that had not been available for
decades. As developer Richard Friedman said in a 2001 *Boston Globe*
article, "The truth is that in some instances, nonprofit institutions have
extremely valuable real estate because they have owned their properties
a long time and have resisted development pressure for a long time"
(Paulson 2001).

Due to declines in participation, the archdiocese was already con-
solidating parishes and selling some properties when the decades-long
sexual abuse scandal became public and the church agreed to an $85
million settlement in 2003 (Butterfield 2003). As a consequence of
the sexual abuse scandal, the Archdiocese of Boston was forced to
sell hundreds of properties across a wide array of communities in
Greater Boston. The redevelopment of these properties allows us to
evaluate the impact of regulations on development because the church
sold a number of prime (and similar) properties across Eastern Massachusetts in a relatively short period of time. While these properties
are not all identical as would be the case in an ideal natural experiment, they still offer many benefits for studying housing development.
Many of them are in very attractive locations that are part of the
fabric of existing communities and neighborhoods. They are not, for
example, abandoned, isolated, former industrial sites. They are also

choosing different kinds of regulations. Fischel (2015) suggests that the rapid spread
of zoning to communities of all types indicates the presence of zoning regulations are
not explained by density or "settlement patterns." However, Trounstine (2018) shows
that specific regulations were adopted later to segregate communities and maintain segregation, suggesting that zoning regulations should not be taken as if random. If the
Glaeser and Ward (2009) argument is accepted, then, coupled with the as-if-random
land availability of church developments, both regulations and land parcels are effectively randomized. If regulations are not random, then the as-if-random sale of church
properties is sufficient to maintain the validity of this analysis.

dispersed throughout Eastern Massachusetts. Moreover, to become housing (which the majority did) nearly all required moderate to major redevelopment.

Importantly, because these data are real properties and not experimental manipulations, they do exhibit more variation than what we would have in an ideal experiment. They feature a mix of former churches, schools, and housing for clergy, among other property uses. Moreover, the parcels also range in size from very small urban plots to large multibuilding campuses. We use a number of different analytical tactics to ensure that this variability does not bias our results.

We analyze church developments as a natural experiment in four different stages. First, we show that there is no relationship between what the Catholic Church sold for redevelopment and local zoning regulations. Second, we illustrate that properties in places with more housing regulations were less likely to be developed into housing (of any type) than properties in towns with fewer regulations. Third, we demonstrate that the type of housing is also dependent on zoning regulations; towns with more regulations built more single-family homes than townhouses or apartments and condominiums. Finally, we show that even when housing is built, the density of the housing is also reduced by additional zoning regulations. Overall, these analyses demonstrate that the church did not take zoning regulations into account when selling properties. But, once a property was selected for redevelopment, zoning regulations substantially reduced the density of the housing that replaced these former churches and schools.

## Where Church Properties Were Sold

The Archdiocese of Boston was one of the largest property owners in the Boston metro area. The archdiocese owned hundreds of churches, Catholic schools, cemeteries, and a wide variety of housing, as well as a large number of investment and commercial properties. To analyze the sale of church properties, we first sought to assemble a data set of every property owned by the church. This proved to be infeasible. In conversations with registrars of deeds and other officials, we discovered that the church holdings were so vast that not even the archdiocese itself had a definitive list. Locating all church properties was further complicated by the fact that many of these properties were acquired in the 1800s and early 1900s, with property owners' names listed inconsistently across records.

Accordingly, we developed two data sets to track church property ownership and redevelopments. The first is a profile of all churches in the diocese before the accelerated sell-off. We focused here on parishes rather than schools or other properties both because there are significantly more of them and the data were more readily available, complete, and comparable. We recreated the full set of 1999 parishes by combining the list of current parishes (Archdiocese of Boston 2018) with the list of closed or otherwise altered parishes. In total, we have a data set consisting of 348 church properties in 135 towns (excluding the City of Boston), of which 93 (27 percent) were closed.

These data reveal a consistent and important pattern explaining church closures: the more churches in the town, the more likely one or more would be closed. When there was only one church existing in the town, the church was likely to be spared.

Importantly, the church sold properties in towns that run the gamut in terms of population, wealth, and proximity to Boston. Controlling for the number of churches in a town, there are no strong relationships between where churches were sold and town-level conditions, including the number of regulations in the town, its proximity to Boston, household income, population, or support for multifamily housing development.[14] This result is critical for our natural experiment. There is no evidence of strategic selling based on the ease of redevelopment. Church properties simply became available based on the underlying distribution of church properties.

Our second data set consists of all properties (churches, schools, office buildings, land, etc.) that the diocese sold, and information about what these properties became. Our research team searched the records of seven Massachusetts registries of deeds to collect data on all Catholic Church property sales in them from 2004 to 2017.[15] These searches yielded 266 deeds on which the archdiocese was the seller. These properties were located in seventy-five cities and towns. In total, this dataset covers approximately forty-four million square feet of land sold for approximately $450 million. We downloaded and analyzed each deed to document aspects of the property and researched the ensuing redevelopment to determine each property's condition at sale, if it was developed,

---

[14] Appendix Table A.2 presents results from binomial regressions predicting the number of church closures by town.

[15] We search the registries of deeds for North and South Essex, North and South Middlesex, Suffolk, Norfolk, and Plymouth counties.

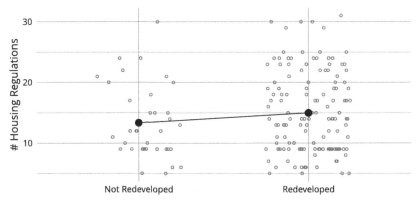

FIGURE 3.8: Church property redevelopment by number of town housing regulations. The one-regulation difference between properties that are and are not redeveloped is not statistically significant.

and what it ultimately became. These data enable us to learn: what properties were developed; which were developed into housing; what kinds of housing they became, and how many housing units were constructed.

Overall, we identified 177 distinct properties that were potential targets for redevelopment.[16] Of these properties, 80 percent were redeveloped.[17] Figure 3.8 plots properties by their development status and the number of housing regulations in their towns. We find no significant relationship between the number of regulations and whether a property was redeveloped.[18] Regulations are not preventing the redevelopment of these properties overall. Furthermore, the site's original use did not affect its likelihood of redevelopment. Whether a parcel was previously undeveloped land, a church, or housing had little to no connection to its ultimate use.

If we look only at those properties that were redeveloped, regulations appear to have a very small effect on whether the parcel became housing or something else, such as an office building or day care facility. Figure 3.9 illustrates this pattern by plotting each parcel by the type of redevelopment and number of regulations in the town. Eighty-two

[16] We excluded some properties, such as cemeteries, that could not be developed, as well as properties located in the city of Boston itself, where we lack land regulation data.

[17] Among the other 20 percent, some remained as churches for other denominations or were repurposed in other, nonresidential ways.

[18] Appendix Table A.3 reports logistic regression results predicting which properties get redeveloped based on a number of factors; only parcel size has a statistically significant effect on redevelopment (larger parcels are less likely to be redeveloped).

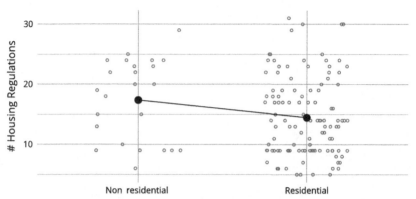

FIGURE 3.9: Church properties by redevelopment type and town housing regulations. Properties redeveloped into housing averaged three fewer town housing regulations than those that were redeveloped into nonresidential uses.

percent of the properties were redeveloped into housing. Properties that became housing were located in towns with an average of three fewer housing regulations than those that were redeveloped for other uses. However, this difference is only marginally significant. Overall, parcel redevelopment appears to be largely independent of zoning regulations. The majority of parcels were redeveloped, and the majority of those redeveloped became housing. When we control for other town-level factors, there is no effect of zoning regulations on development.[19]

## What Housing was Built?

Having shown that the regulatory context *did not* affect which properties were sold, or even which were redeveloped into housing, we now shift to showing that it *did* affect what type of housing, and how much of it, was built. Of the 116 parcels developed into housing, 47 percent became single-family housing, 17 percent became townhouses, and 36 percent became apartments or condominiums.[20] Figure 3.10 illustrates the effect of housing regulations on the type of housing that was built. Properties in towns with more regulations were more likely to become single-family

[19] See Appendix Table A.3, Model 2, for the full regression results.
[20] Some parcels were subdivided to develop multiple single-family homes. Parcels that were developed into a mix of housing types were credited with the most dense form of housing created (e.g., a site that mixed townhouses and single family homes counts as "townhouse" for this analysis.)

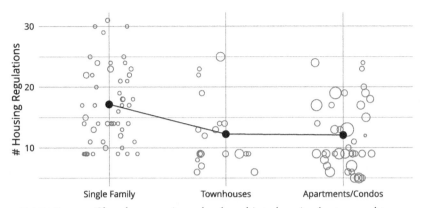

FIGURE 3.10: Church properties redeveloped into housing by type and town housing regulations. The average single-family development is built in a town with five more housing regulations than the average townhouse or apartment/condominium development. Circle size is proportional to the number of housing units in the development.

homes, while properties in towns with fewer regulations were more apt to become townhouses, apartments, or condominiums.[21]

As with our earlier analyses, the negative relationship between regulations and the production of multifamily housing is driven by a multitude of regulations – not just those directly limiting multifamily buildings. When we separate regulations into two simple categories – multifamily regulations and all other regulations – we find that *all types of regulations*, not simply limitations on multifamily housing, reduce multifamily housing. Figure 3.11 illustrates this pattern by plotting each development by the number of town regulations in each category. In towns with more regulations – even just counting non-multifamily limitations – we see a higher proportion of single-family homes. Similarly, in towns with fewer regulations *of all types*, we see the production of more townhouses, apartments, and condominiums.[22]

These regulations not only impact the number of units built – they shape the density of church redevelopments. Figure 3.12 plots the density of each development against the total number of housing regulations

---

[21] There is a statistically significant five-regulation (on average) difference between single-family properties and multifamily properties, but no difference between townhouses and apartments/condominiums. Appendix Table A.4 presents these results in a logistic regression with a full complement of statistical controls.

[22] These results hold regardless of the size of a parcel or the distance a parcel is from Boston (full analyses of these subsets are available in the appendix in Figure A.1).

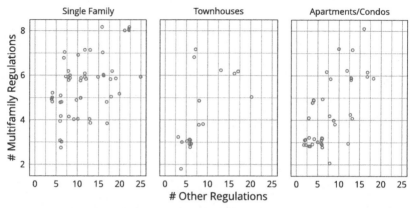

FIGURE 3.11: Type of housing developed by the number of multifamily and
other housing regulations in the town

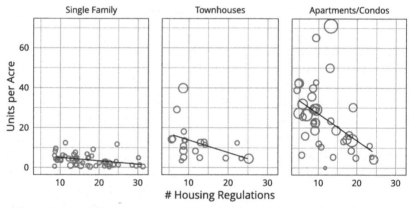

FIGURE 3.12: Density of housing redevelopments by housing type and town
housing regulations. Density of all housing types decrease with regulations.
Circle size is proportional to the number of housing units in the development.

in each town. Each property is represented by a bubble. The larger the
bubble, the higher the density (units per acre). Across all three categories
of housing, density decreases with regulations. Moreover, the impact of
regulations on density is greatest for multifamily housing, followed by
townhouses and single-family homes.[23]

---

[23] These results once again hold regardless of parcel size and distance from Boston (full
results are available in the appendix in Figure A.2).

## CONCLUSION

In this chapter, we ask whether local housing regulations *of all types* shape the provision multifamily housing construction. The share of permits for multifamily housing units decreases with additional regulations. Both regulations explicitly targeting multifamily housing and other land use restrictions – including regulations on parcel shape and septic systems – reduce the housing supply and the density of new housing.

The fact that other types of regulations – not just ones pertaining to multifamily housing – depress the construction of new housing suggests that *regulations that necessitate special permits or variances reduce the supply and density of housing.* The next chapter shows that these regulations, and their associated special permits and variances, require public meetings to review proposed developments. These meetings in turn offer opportunities for neighborhood defenders to obstruct or delay unwanted projects by bringing up a plethora of concerns they might have about a development.

# 4

# Land Use Regulations and Public Input

The previous chapter illustrated a tight link between the number of regulations – even those not directly tied to multifamily housing – and the construction of new housing. Places with more regulations issued fewer housing permits. In the ensuing chapters, we reveal that regulations derive their power in part by offering unrepresentative members of the public an opportunity to delay or stop the construction of new housing. Because the nature of these meetings disproportionately attracts advantaged opponents, these public forums are overwhelmingly weighted toward obstruction rather than production of new housing.

Central to all of these chapters is one integral institution: public meetings about proposed housing developments. Land use regulations frequently require developers to obtain *special permits* for projects of a certain scale. In other cases, developers must apply for *variances* – exemptions from existing land use regulations. Whenever a proposal requires a variance or a special permit, it appears before a public hearing of a city or town's planning or zoning board.

In the Cambridge, Massachusetts, case that opened this book, the developer's plans were open to public scrutiny in a planning board meeting because they required a special permit. In Cambridge, the conversion of nonresidential structures – in this case, a commercial warehouse – to residential use must comply with specific dimensional requirements. Given the age of Cambridge's building stock and the small lot sizes in the city, most city buildings do not comply with modern land use requirements. Thus, the developer – like many others proposing similar projects across the city – found himself before the Cambridge Planning

Board, presenting his plans before an audience of board members and city residents in order to receive a special permit. Moreover, even upon receiving said special permit – a process that required multiple meetings and additional studies – the developer's plans were still open to public scrutiny. He also had to go before the Board of Zoning Appeals – an entirely separate entity – in order to receive a variance from existing zoning, because (1) the building's floor area ratio – the ratio of the building's size to the plot of land it sits on – was not compliant with existing zoning and (2) the developer proposed "alter[ing] ... an existing non-conforming structure." Again, in a city where the bulk of housing predates modern land use requirements, the developer is hardly alone in seeking to modify a "non-conforming structure."

Indeed, this process helps highlight just how many proposals are reviewed under the auspices of these meetings. In Manhattan, 40 percent of buildings do not comply with modern zoning regulations (Bui, Chaban, and White 2016). To rebuild two out of every five buildings in Manhattan, developers would have to obtain special permits or variances from existing zoning. Old buildings are frequently built on lots that do not comport with modern dimensional requirements. They are often too big for the existing lot, and nothing economical could be rebuilt that complies with modern floor area ratio requirements. Some lots are oddly shaped, making it impossible to construct a building that is sufficiently set back from neighboring dwellings. In short, public meetings surrounding developments are not sporadic events limited to the most high-profile developments. They are embedded into the housing development process for many projects – some quite small or routine.

These meetings typically begin with a presentation from the developer's team, followed by questions from zoning or planning officials. Proceedings are then opened to the public. Local planning and zoning officials take these proceedings in their entirety into account in deciding to approve, deny, or stay an application to a subsequent hearing.

At first glance, these proceedings seem fairly technocratic and mundane. Indeed they often focus on subsections of the zoning code or the details of drainage plans. However, they are also political and influence the amount, makeup, and geographic distribution of housing in a community. When dominated by neighborhood defenders, these meetings pose potent obstacles to keeping pace with housing demands.

Despite their seeming prominence in the land use process, we have virtually no systematic evidence on why proposals end up in public meetings, who attends and speaks at these public hearings, and what is said.

This chapter, along with Chapters 5 and 6, takes up these questions, and illustrate how these forums constrain the supply of new housing.

This chapter asks why proposals end up in public meetings and what types of issues members of the public and zoning officials raise. It illustrates that these are not forums reserved for the largest and most controversial projects – developments come before planning and zoning boards for a variety of mundane reasons. Once these projects necessitate a public meeting, members of the public can and do raise any and all concerns – not just those directly pertaining to the regulations that spurred a meeting in the first place. The regulations described in the previous chapter provide the opportunities for neighborhood defenders to air their concerns and objections. What's more, they create openings for neighborhood defense against projects that are quite modest in scope.

This chapter thus provides the bridge between Chapter 3 and the remaining chapters of this book. It shows that land use regulations spur public hearings, typically via special permits or variances. Once triggered, these public hearings offer ample opportunity for neighborhood defenders to stop or delay unwanted developments. Land use regulations do not merely limit development by prohibiting certain types of projects – though that is certainly an important consequence of these policies. Rather, by requiring public review of a wide variety of proposals – some quite modest – they offer openings for neighborhood defenders to obstruct unwanted incursions in their communities. Neighborhood defense emerges not only against large, controversial projects; rather, we find neighborhood opposition – enabled and amplified by special permit and variance requests – to the modest and mundane.

## MEETING MINUTES

Unique public meeting recording and reporting requirements in Massachusetts allow us inside hundreds of public meetings across dozens of communities. The state's open meeting law requires public bodies to record government proceedings in depth, including both what was discussed and who participated. In some cases, localities post exact transcripts of what transpired. Moreover, Massachusetts provides extraordinary details about meeting participants: a majority of cities and towns in metropolitan Boston report the names and addresses of all members of the public who spoke at the meeting. We have found no other set of localities nationally where meeting minutes are comparably detailed.

We downloaded all available public hearing minutes for local planning and zoning boards. In all cities and towns, these are the two bodies responsible for reviewing any housing developments not permitted by right under local zoning code. Under Chapter 40A in Massachusetts, all public hearings for these bodies are announced in "a newspaper of general circulation in the city or town once in each of the two successive weeks, the first publication to be not less than fourteen days before the day of the hearing." Cities and towns are also required to post a notice "in a conspicuous place in the city or town hall" with similar advanced notice. Moreover, the city or town also must mail a notice of a public hearing to "parties of interest," which are defined as "the petitioner, abutters, owners of land directly opposite on any public or private street or way, and abutters to the abutters within three hundred feet of the property line of the petitioner as they appear on the most recent applicable tax list" (Commonwealth of Massachusetts 2017). We used all minutes that were posted on cities' and towns' websites. The example from Cambridge, Massachusetts, that opened this book came from such meeting minutes.

The public hearings covered a wide range of policy areas, ranging from the construction of large multifamily or mixed-use housing developments with hundreds of rental units to the addition of wireless communication towers. We focus on all hearings on housing developments featuring the construction of more than one unit of housing on a lot. Even within this more limited policy category, public meeting minutes exhibit enormous variation. Some of these projects are relatively small (e.g., a family seeking to add an accessory apartment), while others are expansive proposals from large professional development companies. Some meetings feature comments from one neighbor who shows up to support a friend in obtaining a variance from local zoning regulations. Others, in contrast, are filled with dozens of comments from residents with deep concerns about a proposed project.

In Table 4.1 we provide summary statistics about a variety of traits (mean, minimum, and maximum) for the ninety-seven cities and towns for which we have coded meeting comments. Our sample is, as would be expected in Eastern Massachusetts, relatively white (86 percent on average) and affluent. More important than these averages, however, is the wide *range* of communities represented in our data. For example, the sample has tremendous variation in terms of residential density (237 to nearly 17,000 people per square mile), housing prices ($200,000 to $1.2 million median housing value), population growth (0 percent

TABLE 4.1 *Traits of cities and towns for which we have participation data*

|  | Mean | Min | Max |
|---|---|---|---|
| Population | 25,772 | 4,427 | 183,382 |
| Population density | 1,976 | 237 | 16,880 |
| Population growth 2010–2015 | 5 | 0 | 11 |
| Median age | 42 | 24 | 53 |
| Percent over 65 | 15 | 9 | 28 |
| Percent white | 86 | 17 | 98 |
| Percent black | 2 | 0 | 15 |
| Percent hispanic | 5 | 0 | 76 |
| Median household income ($) | 97,650 | 34,852 | 19,9519 |
| Median house price ($) | 431,844 | 205,200 | 1,170,400 |
| Distance from boston (miles) | 24 | 4 | 43 |
| Observations | 97 | | |

to 11 percent from 2010 to 2015), and age (9 percent to 28 percent over 65).

From this broad database of meeting minutes, we assembled a novel data set of all citizen participants and comments made in planning and zoning board meetings between 2015 and 2017. We return to these data in Chapters 5 and 6 to better understand who participates in housing politics.

Before delving deeper into the resident participants themselves, we first want to understand at a basic level what triggers these meetings in the first place. What connects land use regulations to the public hearings that comprise the central set piece of this book?

To answer this question, we randomly selected one hundred proposals from our broader database.[1] For each project, we located the first time the proposal was commented on in a meeting.[2] We then determined whether it was the subject of a public meeting because of a request for a *special permit* or a *variance*.

---

[1] We collected data on a sample – rather than the entire data set – because of time constraints. The detailed nature of these meeting minutes was both a blessing and a curse. While they offered an incredible amount of data, they were also time-consuming to analyze, sometimes featuring hundreds of pages of transcripts. Indeed, each town recorded meeting minutes in a different format, making automated text analysis impractical.

[2] In some cases, the first appearance in minutes predated the three-year span for which we downloaded them. In these instances, we used the earliest appearance in our time span, such that for some projects, we picked up the conversation partway through a multi-meeting process.

Special permit requests occur when the developer is asking for a new property use – such a rezoning. They also frequently include waivers from existing land use regulations. In the Cambridge example that opened this chapter, the developer sought to transform a commercial warehouse into a residential dwelling; this change of use necessitated a special permit. He also sought a waiver from dimensional requirements. Similarly, when suburban developers propose converting empty lots into subdivisions, they typically must first secure a special permit, frequently accompanied by a waiver for road width requirements. When a project in our data necessitates a special permit, we recorded both the use (e.g., residential use in a previously commercial space) and any specific regulations from which the proposal needed waivers (e.g., dimensional requirements).

Variances are specific exceptions to general land use regulations. For example, when the Cambridge developer needed an *exemption* from the existing floor area ratio requirement, he asked the Cambridge Board of Zoning Appeals for a variance. In these cases, we simply recorded the reason for requesting a variance. So, in the case of the Cambridge development, we would note the floor area ratio requirement.

Finally, many of the meeting minutes provide an extraordinary level of detail. We are consequently able to code the reasons public commenters offered for supporting or opposing a project for these one hundred developments – and roughly half of all meeting minutes in subsequent chapters. These reasons encompassed a wide variety of topics, including parking, environmental concerns, traffic, density, affordability, noise, aesthetics/history, property values, and septic systems, among others.[3] A full codebook describing these categories and criteria for inclusion is included in Appendix B. The data in this chapter thus juxtapose the reasons that developers ended up in front of public boards and the content of public comments made at these meetings.

Our project database illuminates several key aspects of the housing politics process. First, it shows the frequency with which special permits and variances spur public meetings. It illustrates how the land use regulations highlighted in Chapter 3 lead to public hearings; by mandating special permits and variances for a wide swath of projects, they ensure that many development proposals, large and small, are subject to public scrutiny. Second, these data reveal what issues members of the public

---

[3] Intercoder reliability checks showed that coders agreed 100 percent of the time about whether a comment should be labeled support/oppose/neutral. They selected the same set of nineteen total topic categories 85 percent of the time.

raise at these hearings. Moreover, when juxtaposed against the issues that triggered these hearings in the first place, they show that the hearing process creates opportunities for neighborhood defenders to voice a myriad of objections – not just the narrow land use regulations that prompted the public hearing in the first place.

## PUBLIC MEETING TRIGGERS

The bulk of meetings – 75 percent – were triggered by special permit requests, while the remaining 25 percent focused on variances. Suburban efforts to redevelop empty plots of land comprised the majority (53 percent) of special permit requests. These subdivision requests varied in nature; some were for so-called cluster developments, in which developers propose densely-packed single-family homes and townhouses on an empty lot. Others were for more standard suburban subdivisions, with large single-family homes situated on large lots.

The special permit process typically features an overall plan review. This means that all public comments – at least in theory – are germane to the public proceedings. Once a project requires a special permit, it is open to any and all public concerns. The subsequent section shows that, indeed, once the public has the opportunity to comment on special permit projects, they offer a wide range of critiques.

What's more, we will show that comments on special permit hearings are not limited or focused on the topics raised in waiver requests. As part of the special permit request process, developers typically must also ask for waivers on issues like road design and setbacks. For example, 24 percent of special permit processes requested a waiver on road design, with another 24 percent asking for waivers on setbacks.[4]

In contrast, the variance process is (again, at least in theory) more narrowly focused on a small set of underlying regulatory issues. The most common variances centered on setbacks and buffers (48 percent), such as distance from the street or neighboring buildings; lot size (44 percent), the size of the parcel relative to the size of the structure; parcel shape, the

---

[4] Other specific reasons that triggered or featured in special permit public meetings were zoning designation (11 percent; a project of a different type than the zoning allows or one in a zone, such as a flood plain, that automatically required special review), earth movement (5 percent; a waiver for moving more earth than automatically allowed), and prior non-conforming use (5 percent; special permit review of projects that seek to replace existing buildings that are noncompliant).

dimensions of the lot (17 percent); and building height (13 percent). As in the special permit process, many of these projects were quite modest, featuring townhouses or small condominium buildings.

Resident comments at these variance request meetings should hew closely to the issues that triggered the variance in the first place. The next section shows that this is not the case. As with special permits, variance hearings open the door for neighborhood defenders to cite concerns that range far beyond the regulatory issues that prompted the public meeting in the first place.

## RESIDENT CONCERNS

The bulk of special permitting projects included requests for waivers on issues such as road design and setbacks. In contrast, the public discussions were often dominated by environmental, flooding, aesthetics, neighborhood character, and septic concerns. Fifty-four percent of these special permit project meetings featured at least one comment about the environment. Forty-nine percent include at least one comment about flooding, 42 percent about project aesthetics, 37 percent about traffic, and 32 percent about neighborhood character and water/septic concerns respectively. Other commonly invoked reasons in public comments were density (31 percent), procedural noncompliance (30 percent), and parking and safety (27 percent). Some of these comments are certainly pertinent to the project proposals; indeed, a new subdivision on an undeveloped plot of land may very well threaten area wetlands, for example. The connections in other cases, however, are likely more distant. Instead, they are the prototypical concerns that housing opponents tend to raise – worries about the character of a neighborhood, traffic, parking, and safety. In many instances – especially for relatively modest new streets featuring a handful of single-family homes – some of these issues appear tenuous.

The mismatch between the regulatory drivers of meetings and focus of the public comments comes into sharper relief in our analysis of meetings about variances. While the bulk of projects in our data require variance hearings due to concerns about setbacks, lot size, and dimensions, a whopping 68 percent of the meetings about variances featured comments about parking. Forty-one percent included comments on the proposal's design aesthetics, and 37 percent included comments about the proposal's fit with the "neighborhood character." Other frequently mentioned concerns include density (32 percent), safety (32 percent), traffic (27 percent), and environmental concerns. Some of these public concerns have connections to the regulatory issues at hand. For example, it makes sense to raise density as an issue for a project requesting a variance for lot size. In general, though, the links between the issues triggering the variance request and public comments are weak. Hearings about narrowly-defined variances opened the door to public comment about parking, neighborhood character, aesthetics, and a host of other neighborhood defender concerns.

In the case of both special permits and variances, then, zoning and planning officials hear from the public on a wide array of issues related to the development – not simply the narrow regulatory concerns that triggered public review in the first place. Once land use regulations necessitate public review of a housing proposal, neighborhood defenders use the opportunity to raise any and all concerns in an effort to stop or delay new housing.

## PROJECT PROFILES

To make this process more concrete, we turn now to the journey of four of the hundred proposals we studied. We selected a variety of project types – one apartment proposal (Westwood), one subdivision (North Reading), and two small (two to three units) multifamily housing plans (Newburyport and Lawrence). Two of the projects are special permit requests (Westwood and North Reading), and two are variance requests (Newburyport and Lawrence). Two generated many comments (Westwood and Newburyport), while two induced less participation (Lawrence and North Reading).[5] For each of these four proposals, we identify the reasons it ended up in a public meeting, the considerations members of the public raised in these meetings, and what became of it. These proposals offer a window into how proposals progress (if they do so), what types of public input these projects receive, and the variation in both the proposals and the scope of opposition to them.

### A Contentious Proposal for Sixteen (then Twelve)
### Apartments in Westwood

In 2015, developers in Westwood, Massachusetts (a suburb of Boston), proposed a three-story building featuring commercial space at street level

---

[5] We defined high commenting proposals as those in the ninetieth percentile of total comments. Medium-commenting proposals had around the median number of comments.

and sixteen apartments populating the top two stories. They planned to both renovate an existing structure and expand onto an adjoining lot. The proposal included "extensive exterior renovations," "facade improvements," and sixty-two parking spaces. In December 2015, the developers applied for a special permit under town's Flexible Multiple Use Overlay District. The proposal violated land use regulations in two ways that required a request for waivers on top of the special permit general review. First, the lot was 41,363 square feet, but the regulations required 43,560 for the structure. The developer consequently asked for a "dimensional waiver" for relief from the 2,198 square foot shortfall. Second, the developer also requested relief from the "buffer" requirement. The land use regulations called for a distance of 20 feet between buildings. The existing building they were repurposing was only 3 feet from the one behind it. Moreover, the proposal called for the new addition to also come close to the building behind it.

In addition to requesting these waivers, the developer reported the results of a traffic study, which concluded that the project would "meet safety standards and have a minimal impact on existing traffic conditions." The meeting also included the results of a fiscal impact study, which found that the assessed value of the final project would be 28 percent greater than the current value and that the apartments would likely rent for around $1,500 a month.

Relative to other projects we studied, the public was quite active at these meetings; the proposal generated roughly sixty public comments across all meetings for which we have records. Most of the comments opposed the development – a predilection we turn to in earnest in the next chapter. For now, we primarily focus on the *reasons* offered by commenters, and how closely they hewed to the regulatory issues at hand in the special permitting process. Roughly a quarter mentioned density and parking, while another fifth addressed aesthetics. Other frequently highlighted issues were pedestrian concerns (10 percent), the environment (8 percent), and traffic (8 percent). Many of these opponents offered broad critiques about the project and its impact on the neighborhood, calling it a "substantial detriment to neighbors." These worried residents noted that the area is "a village center, not an urban center," and expressed concern with "the number of apartments within three miles of the area." Additional commenters made appeals for another traffic study and worried about the fate of an existing tavern. Some of the public comments were more mundane suggestions; one resident, for example, worried about pedestrian safety and said "there should be a 'no turn on red' sign." Opposition was not monolithic. Some residents highlighted the project's ability to improve the village area and the local housing supply.

Importantly, these comments were not confined to lot dimensions and setbacks – the two regulatory issues at stake in the special permit waivers. While density comments could theoretically be tied to these regulatory concerns, some Westwood residents appeared far more focused on higher-level issues related to neighborhood character and proximity to other apartments.

In January, about six weeks after the initial presentation, the developers reduced the number of apartments from sixteen to twelve and increased the number of parking spaces from sixty-two to eighty-five.[6] The revised proposal also increased the buffers, ensuring greater privacy screens between the development and surrounding neighbors. Final approval for the twelve-apartment version came in late April, about five months after the project was first introduced.

### Too Tall for the Neighborhood: Two Townhouses in Newburyport

A request for a variance in Newburyport – a wealthy coastal town north of Boston – generated similarly active public participation. In 2014, a corner lot near a highway ramp and a bike trail became available. Previously home to an Indian restaurant (Mr. India), a small coin-operated laundry, and a one-bedroom apartment, the building had first been abandoned and then later demolished (Rogers 2017). In 2014, developers proposed a pair of three-story, attached townhouses. By April 2015, the proposal had been discussed at six Zoning Board meetings and had already been significantly redesigned.

At the April meeting, the developer applied for variances for building height and setbacks. Both the proposed building's height and its distance from neighbors did not comply with Newburyport zoning code.[7] The attorney representing the builder explained that the setbacks were required because the corner lot was oddly shaped and small as a consequence of prior eminent domain use. Moreover, she contended that the soil prevented a basement, requiring both parking and utilities to be at ground level, instead of below grade. She argued that these factors, along

---

[6] The first floor commercial property added to the complexities around parking.
[7] The proposal would eventually also require a special permit for the two-family use. This use is allowed by permit in the given location. The most active meetings were the ones centering on the variances described here.

with other taller buildings nearby, constituted a hardship justifying the variance from Newburyport's building height requirements.

The public meetings reviewing this variance request were notably active. Most participants spoke against the project. Some of the comments were directly responsive to the specific variance(s) requested. Indeed, 23 percent of comments featured concerns about the building height, making it the second most frequently raised issue. These comments focused on how the building height would affect the views from the nearby bike trail. One resident "believed the aesthetics have improved, but height impacting the 'public abutters' of the rail trail is still impacted." Another "liked [the] improved direction of design, but [was] concerned with what it does to the rail trail and view of the river."

Many other comments, however, were considerably more distant from the regulatory issues ostensibly central to the meeting. Indeed, other frequently mentioned concerns included safety (23 percent), traffic (10 percent), other compliance problems (9 percent), aesthetics (7 percent), and parking (7 percent). At least some of the safety comments highlighted the challenge of having a corner lot near a dangerous intersection. Meeting participants worried about cars pulling out of the driveway, especially given the tight tandem parking design on-site. These parking and safety issues are tenuously connected to building height and setbacks – the two regulatory issues at hand at this variance request meeting.

Complications kept the proposal in front of the zoning board for months. Eventually, the board rejected the plan in summer 2016, leading the developer to abandon the project altogether. In summer 2017, the board approved a different developer for a separate – and, most importantly, smaller – proposal on the site.

While there is no doubt that the site presented the type of challenges that the planning and zoning appeals process is designed to adjudicate, it is unlikely that all, or even most, of the spirited opposition across many meetings was because of the added difficulty that four cars coming and going would present. Worries about increased density, aesthetics, and neighborhood change were pivotal. Local news coverage at the time of the final approval for the second owner's proposal focused on the building's height – and whether, given its height, it fit in with the surrounding neighborhood. City councilor Ed Cameron, one of two city councilors who participated in the opposition, said: "I did offer public comment last year in opposition to a proposal at the Mr. India site which I thought was way too high and blocked a public vista from the rail trail. It's my understanding that what the ZBA recently approved is lower in height, so

I'm hopeful that it will be more in scale with the surroundings" (Rogers 2017).

A long letter to the editor about a different, and much larger proposal may be more revealing. This letter – headlined "Urbanization has gone too far" – is a strong statement against a proposal to replace a parking lot near the library with a hotel, tavern, condos, and more parking. The letter begins, "Just when you think our city is as jammed as it can be, another idea is conjured up to create more overcrowding, congestion and traffic." Later in the letter, the resident draws an analogy between this large proposal and the two-unit one described above: "This is another Mr. India scheme – an attempt to construct a building that is too large for the size of the lot – if not actually, certainly aesthetically" (Isabella 2016). In the politics of neighborhood defense, public debates about seemingly narrow regulatory issues can quickly become bigger conversations about neighborhood change.

## Turning Ten Acres into Seven Homes in North Reading

The Westwood and Newburyport projects both featured well-above-average commenting activity. Two others, one in North Reading and one in Lawrence, offer examples of projects that received more modest amounts of public attention and participation. Even in these cases, neighborhood defenders take advantage of the regulatory opportunities offered to them to expound on a wide range of concerns.

In March 2017, a developer introduced a proposal for a seven-unit subdivision on two adjoining plots totaling ten acres in North Reading, a suburb north of Boston. The proposal kept the existing historic house and barn that sat on the land, and added a cul-de-sac to provide access to the new single-family houses. The plan required a special permit and one waiver from requirements regarding curves in the new street.[8] The public comments at this meeting featured concerns about flooding, aesthetics, density, neighborhood character, noise, and septic systems. For example, one commenter said she wanted to see one less home to "preserve the nature of the property," and another worried about water running onto his property. One expressed concerns about headlights shining in his windows. At a subsequent meeting that only drew a few additional comments, one resident expressed concerns about the impact on traffic saying "currently the (existing) road is poorly maintained and adding more

---

[8] Specifically, this proposal asked for a waiver from the requirement for "a tangent of 150 feet in length to separate all reverse curves on primary and secondary streets."

traffic is only going to make it worse." As with the previous projects, many of these comments stretched beyond the narrow regulatory issues related to street shape.

After some modest modifications – including a new row of rhododendrons to shield the concerned neighbor's windows from headlights – the board approved the project in mid-July, four months after the initial March meeting.

### Rebuilding with Modest Opposition in Lawrence

Our final project was proposed not in a suburb, but in Lawrence, Massachusetts – a socioeconomically disadvantaged, majority Latino old industrial city north of Boston. In June, 2015, a developer proposed rebuilding on a lot after the prior six-unit building (with three parking spaces) burned down. His plans featured a single-family home on one side of the lot and a duplex on the other. The developer needed a variance because the two-building proposal was too big for the lot size per Lawrence land use regulations. Notably, he was allowed to rebuild the original six-unit structure without obtaining any variances or special permits.

Commenters expressed concerns about parking, safety, and aesthetics. Two neighbors worried about whether the site design – especially the parking area – might cause damage or reduce safety on their properties. One noted that "there had always been cars in front of the garage at this house which is problematic to him. He has had to replace his fence and garage door due to driving calamities." Another also complained of "of problems with cars and trucks hitting her fence. She said that she cannot call the Police because they will not come over." Again, the variance request was about lot size – not parking. While obviously the two are tangentially related, the emphasis on parking shows that the meeting did not just narrowly focus on the regulatory issue in question.

The board ultimately concluded at the initial meeting that they could not approve the project. Two months later, the developer offered a slightly modified version of the proposal that passed the zoning board of appeals without public comment.

### CONCLUSION

This chapter offered an initial foray into the world of public meetings. It showed how the regulations introduced in the last chapter lead to opportunities for members of the public to express support or, more frequently, opposition to new housing developments – a point we evaluate more rigorously in the next chapter. Specific regulatory conditions are necessary for these public meetings to take place. Once they are triggered, however, members of the public have the opportunity to raise a wide variety of concerns that are tangentially related to the specific regulation from which a developer is seeking an exemption. We explore the influence that these comments might have in Chapter 6.

We have thus illuminated the first part of our theoretical framework: regulations create opportunities for neighborhood defense. We have also illustrated the range of proposals and regulations that trigger such opportunities and provided an initial glance into how they unfold. The next two chapters turn to the second key part of our puzzle: who participates in these forums and how they use these opportunities to stop or delay the construction of housing.

# 5

# Who Are the Neighborhood Defenders?

The opening of this book described a meeting in Cambridge, Massachusetts, in which a small group of neighbors unanimously opposed the construction of new housing. Citizen opposition to market rate housing is striking. A wealth of previous research has documented strong opposition to subsidized housing, and has linked NIMBY reactions to anti-poor sentiment and prejudice (Pendall 1999; Tighe 2010; Trounstine 2016, 2018). Subsidized housing inherently connotes offering neighborhood resources to a group with characteristics different from those of current residents. These Cambridge residents, however, were not faced with subsidized housing that would have provided neighborhood access to some unknown "other." They opposed the development of market-rate condominiums whose occupants likely would have been fairly similar to, or more affluent than, the current residents.

Moreover, the proposed development was neither on the site of a beloved park, nor would it have transformed a small single-family home into a large apartment complex. The proposal was to convert an abandoned warehouse into four condominium units. On its face, such a development seems like a boon to neighbors' property values and overall neighborhood quality.

Who are these individuals who so enthusiastically oppose projects and play such a pivotal role in the construction of new housing? What motivates them to fight, and what tactics (and land use regulations) do they employ in their battle? This chapter and the following one take up these questions.

The individuals attending the Cambridge meeting offer some suggestive patterns. First, they are neighbors for whom the costs of new housing – from construction noise to disruptions in parking – are most severe. Many of the community voices featured in this book, at the Cambridge meeting and elsewhere, highlight their status as immediate neighbors and longtime residents. They describe in detail the noise, parking, and structural integrity challenges potential developments pose. Here is how these Cambridge residents described their connections to the neighborhood:

- "I lived on the street for going on 80 years now. We bought the house in 1947 and we've been there. We have four generations of family living there right now."
- "I'm a resident of Regent Street ... and I've been there about 30 years."
- "I live at [XX] Regent which is directly next to this property and I have a written statement."[1]
- "I live on Creighton Street. My backyard is next to the abutter on Creighton Street's backyard."

These ties are based on longevity, proximity, and homeownership. Participants use these connections to highlight the costs of new housing.

- "When the condos across the street from my house went in. ... I did not suspect that it would cause my house and others on the street to sink."
- "I ... now have to possibly put up with a lot of noise and light on roof decks. ... [N]ot only will they block out any view I have in the back of my house, but they could cause a lot of problems. I mean, anybody that gets drunk and falls off the roof, they're falling in my yard. ... It's right on the property line."

What's more, many are highly knowledgeable. Some are experts in local zoning codes and come prepared with handouts and careful reviews of complex developer plans:

- "I've done a little research and this is all information from the property database in Cambridge. So we witnessed – this is showing the .... recent trends and the developments over the past year where

---

[1] We have redacted the exact address to preserve the privacy of individuals participating at these meetings.

we've seen industrial buildings become multi-family units, and given that we're in Zone B, my understanding is that there's a 2500 square foot requirement."

- "I think it's zoned for two [family], not four, and that it should be two."
- "This building's built up to the property lines."

In many respects, then, these active participants may differ from the city's residents as a whole. Indeed, renters – who compose 61 percent of Cambridge's population (City of Cambridge 2016) – were entirely absent from this meeting. Moreover, no one who was *seeking a home* in Cambridge attended. In Cambridge, like many of the communities featured in this book, demand for housing far outpaces the supply. More than half of all single-family homes in Cambridge sold for above the asking price in 2016 (Lamacchia 2016). The rental market is similarly pricey (McMullen 2016). Despite this housing crunch, no one suffering its ill effects came to the meeting to highlight the desperate need for additional housing in the city. Instead, the voices amplified at this public hearing were those of homeowners bent on defending their neighborhood.

This chapter more systematically explores these neighborhood defenders. Combining new data on zoning and planning board meetings with the Massachusetts voter file and a commercial property database, we find that the individuals who participate in community meetings on new housing developments differ starkly from the broader population. They are older, whiter, longtime residents, and more likely to be homeowners. They overwhelmingly oppose the development of new housing, with only 15 percent of meeting attendees showing up to support proposed housing projects. In concert, the meeting minutes reveal that these forums are dominated by an unrepresentative and privileged group of neighborhood defenders.

## UNEQUAL PARTICIPATION AND LOCAL DEMOCRACY

In Chapter 2, we outlined two forms of bias among neighborhood defenders. First, demographically, they will be socioeconomically advantaged: they are more likely to be homeowners, white, longtime residents, men, older, and frequent voters. Second, the concentrated costs of development weighed against its diffuse benefits should disproportionately incentivize a small group of neighborhood defenders to show up in opposition to proposed new housing in far greater numbers than housing proponents.

These predictions present a bleak portrait of local democracy. Rather than serving as an opportunity for effective civic engagement of under-represented groups (Stone and Stoker 2015), the mediation of competing interests (Dahl 1961; Berry, Portney, and Thomson 1993), and deliberative democracy (Gutmann and Thompson 2012), neighborhood meetings instead, in our account, amplify a small, unrepresentative group with strong views (Mansbridge 1980; Fiorina 1998; Cain 2015). Neighborhood-oriented policies only work if the interests of those participating represent those of the broader community. We find that, in housing policy, neighborhood meetings are forums for neighborhood defense.

## PUBLIC MEETING MINUTES

To measure who participates in local housing politics and their views on proposed developments, we use the Massachusetts meeting minutes described in depth in the previous chapter. Using these minutes to evaluate participation and views is quite distinct from previous efforts to understand opinions and behaviors surrounding housing policy. These approaches have analyzed mass public views on housing developments (Marble and Nall 2017; Hankinson 2018). Studying the mass public has many virtues. It allows us to understand the challenges associated, with, say, passing housing legislation at the city and state levels. It does not, however, cleanly illuminate the crucial political dynamics unfolding at neighborhood meetings. Meeting attendees are not necessarily representative samples of the general population; in fact, they almost assuredly are not.

Alternatively, other researchers have used case studies to trace meeting dynamics (Mansbridge 1980). These approaches, too, provide valuable insights into how the policy institutions work in practice. Indeed, we use these types of case studies at multiple points in this book to illuminate how individuals use land use regulations to stop developments. By studying just one or several meetings, however, case studies are more limited in their ability to draw broader conclusions about how processes operate for different projects, policy questions, or locations.

Perhaps the best analogue to our work is political scientist Mirya Holman's (2014) analysis of city council meeting minutes. She analyzes the content of city council meeting minutes to understand whether the gender of a mayor leads to the emphasis of different policies. While her work centers on a different question and uses different methodological techniques, her approach (like ours) systematically explores what gets said when local government officials meet in public.

Using these minutes, we coded all public comments on projects comprising more than one housing unit. Each observation – at the comment level – includes the name and address of the meeting participant.[2] We also code whether the individual supports, opposes, or is neutral about a proposed housing development. Finally, as noted in the previous chapter, when available, we also coded the reason(s) the participant expressed.

Even without merging these data with any other information, we can make valuable observations. We can learn the proportion of individuals who support or oppose the development of additional housing and the reasons they typically cite. We can also learn how often individuals attend these meetings. However, combining the data we collected with other information enables us to describe and understand meeting participants in much greater detail.

## Demographics of Meeting Attendees

Because we have the names and addresses of these individuals, we can merge them with several databases to learn more about their demographic characteristics. First, the Massachusetts voter file contains a remarkable amount of information about registered voters, including individuals' age, gender, partisanship, history of voter turnout in elections at all levels, and registration date at current address (which we use as a rough proxy for duration of residence).

Using a fuzzy matching algorithm, we link meeting commenters with registered Massachusetts voters.[3] We were able to match 2,784 of the 3,327 people in the set of participants (83.7 percent). As many people

---

[2] If an individual speaks multiple times at a meeting about different housing developments, she receives one observation per housing project. If participant makes multiple comments about the same project at the same meeting, her comments are concatenated into one observation. Finally, if the same individual attends multiple meetings to comment about the same project, she is coded as one observation per meeting.

[3] We matched on name and address, the only data on participants available. Due to a large number of typos and misspellings, we used a fuzzy string matching algorithm and manual review of the matches. A majority of the people who we were unable to match are likely in the voter file, but could not be matched due to name duplication and missing addresses.

commented more than once, we were able to match 85.4 percent of speakers to the voter file.

While the voter file contains a variety of helpful demographic information, it does not include three variables that are plausibly important predictors of meetings attendance: homeownership, income, and race. Fortunately, we are able to use CoreLogic property records to learn about individuals' homeownership status and home values. Like the voter file and our meetings minutes, these data contain names and addresses, allowing us to merge individuals' property records with information about their demographics and meeting attendance.[4]

### Name Matching

The Massachusetts voter file does not record the race of each registered voter. An individual's name, gender, age, and location, however, can provide valuable clues about his or her race. Using a Bayesian prediction algorithm developed by political scientists Kosuke Imai and Kabir Khanna (2016), we can estimate the probability that a voter is in one of five groups: White, Black, Hispanic, Asian, or Other. We include more technical details on this procedure, including validation of the results, in the appendix.

To bolster these estimates, we also use Latino surnames in a separate analysis to evaluate whether Latinos are over- or underrepresented in planning and zoning board meetings. Surname alone is highly predictive of Hispanic ethnicity (Word et al. 2000), and is widely used in social science research to identify individual ethnicity (Barreto, Segura, and Woods 2004; Wei et al. 2006; Henderson, Sekhon, and Titiunik 2016). We evaluate commenter ethnicity in all towns in our sample with a Latino

---

[4] We matched voters to the property tax database using fuzzy string matching on names and address. For properties owned by multiple individuals, we matched each owner separately. We restricted the tax properties to single family and multifamily homes (including condominium buildings of any size), and excluded apartment buildings and anything owned by a corporation. In order to simplify matching and since we are interested in homeowners representing their own neighborhoods, we required that the voter's town and the property's town be the same. In some cases, voters matched to more than one property. When this happened, we first sought to use the property whose actual address matched the registered voting address of the voter (rather than where the mailing address of the property matched the voter's address). When this did not uniquely identify a property, we use the property with the highest assessed value of those that matched. Overall, we matched 46 percent of voters and 73 percent of commenters to a home in the tax property database.

population greater than 10 percent. We focus on this subset of towns to ensure there is a sufficiently large number of Latino residents to draw reliable conclusions about the representativeness of meeting attendees.

## WHO PARTICIPATES

All of our analyses feature comparisons between two groups of people: meeting commenters and all voters. This is different than comparing individuals to the entire population of their city or town. We know that voters are, on average, older and more socioeconomically advantaged than the general population (Verba, Schlozman, and Brady 1995; Schlozman, Verba, and Brady 2012). Thus, if anything, differences that we describe below would be larger if the comparison group were instead the general population.

Table 5.1 shows striking differences between commenters and voters.[5] Perhaps most starkly, 73 percent of commenters own homes, compared to 46 percent of noncommenters – a twenty-seven percentage point gap. Commenters are older by a similar margin; 75 percent of commenters are over the age of fifty, compared to 53 percent of voters – a difference of twenty-two percentage points. Commenters are also more likely to be white by a margin of eight percentage points; 95 percent of commenters are white, relative to 87 percent of voters in our sample cities. There also are sizable gender gaps: women constitute 51 percent of the voter file, but only 43 percent of the commenters at development meetings.

TABLE 5.1 *Demographic differences between commenters and all voters*

| Demographic | % of Commenters | % of Voters | Difference |
|---|---|---|---|
| Women | 43.3 | 51.3 | −8.0 |
| Democrats | 32.0 | 31.7 | 0.2 |
| Whites | 95.0 | 86.7 | 8.2 |
| Age>50 | 75.0 | 52.6 | 22.4 |
| Homeowners | 73.4 | 45.6 | 27.8 |

*Differences on gender, race, and homeownership are statistically significant; there is no difference for Democrats (or any other party).*

[5] Appendix Table C.1 provides results from t-tests of the difference in means between commenters and voters. All differences are strongly significant with the exception of political party, where we find no differences between meeting commenters and registered voters.

Meeting participants have also lived at their residence for longer (prox-
ied by the length of their voter registration at that location) and are more
active voters. The individuals who participated in development meetings
voted at roughly twice the frequency of those who did not.[6] We find minimal differences in partisanship; Democrats and Republicans participate
at similar rates.

We find similar disparities in meeting participation when we estimate
more sophisticated regression models (Appendix Table C.2). When we
consider all of these individual characteristics jointly, race, age, gender,
homeownership status, length of residence, and frequency of voting all
strongly predict a person's likelihood of commenting at a planning and
zoning board meeting. Partisanship again appears to have no relationship
with one's propensity to comment. A homeowner is twice as likely as a
non-homeowner to comment at a meeting. A thirty-year-old is 20 percent
as likely to comment as a seventy-year-old, and a man is 40 percent more
likely than a woman to comment.

Without individual data on income and net worth, we not able to
directly include wealth in our analyses. However, we can use homeownership and home value as a proxy for household wealth. While
homeownership and value are rough measures, we should expect them
to be particularly relevant in housing politics (Fischel 2001). We have
found that homeownership strongly predicts participation. Homeowners
are more than three times as likely to comment in public meetings as non-
homeowners. Interestingly, though, among homeowners, property value
does not predict whether an individual comments at a planning or zoning
board meeting (Appendix Table C.3). In other words, while homeownership is strongly linked with participation in land use politics, the value of
that home – conditional on owning one in the first place – is not.

Finally, the vast majority of commenters live in the immediate vicinity
of the housing projects under review. Eighty-two percent of commenters
live in the same census tract – a rough measure of neighborhood – as the
housing development.[7] Additionally, 41 percent of commenters live in the
same census block as the development. This is remarkable; census blocks

---

[6] We measure voting frequency as the share of elections between 2010 and 2016 in which
in individual voted. The total number of possible elections varies by town.

[7] Census tracts roughly approximate neighborhoods. We use census tracts as our measure of distance because we do not have consistence definitions of neighborhoods in
each town. Additionally, we would expect neighborhood sizes to vary across places:
larger towns with higher population density, such as Cambridge, will have geographically smaller neighborhoods, while less dense places may have neighborhoods that are

are the smallest unit of census geography, and generally correspond to areas enclosed by single street blocks. Nearly half of all commenters live on the same block as proposed developments.[8] These data reveal that – as anticipated – community meetings are dominated by *neighborhood* defenders – that is, individuals from the immediate surroundings. The wider community, in contrast, is barely represented.

Participants are not representative of their communities, and they are generally more socioeconomically privileged than those who do not attend. This is pattern is true both across towns – we see higher levels of participation in wealthier towns than poorer towns – but also within towns. In poorer, economically struggling towns, more privileged residents, especially homeowners, are most likely to participate in planning and zoning board meetings. Similarly, in the wealthiest towns, where the residents are relatively privileged compared to those in less wealthy towns, we see that more advantaged people, compared to their neighbors, are more likely to participate.[9]

Only a small minority of meeting attendees are high-intensity participators. Eighty-three percent of the commenters spoke at only one meeting. The average person made 1.3 comments, and 45 people made 5 or more comments. Among the participants that we matched to the voter file, the only significant predictors of the number of comments made are political party and voting frequency. Democrats were less likely to make multiple comments, and Republicans were more likely to do so.

## Participation by Race

Across our sample of meeting participants, commenters are overwhelmingly white. Ninety-five percent of meeting participants are white, compared with 80 percent of the adult population in our sample cities. Latinos compose 8 percent of the sample adult population but a mere 1 percent of commenters. Black representation is somewhat better, but still reflects white advantage. While the sample city adult population is 4 percent black, only 2 percent of meeting commenters are black. Table 5.2

geographically larger, such that measuring actual distance between the commenter's home and the housing development may mean different things in different places.
[8] There are generally multiple census blocks in a single identifiable community or neighborhood.
[9] Appendix Table C.4 splits the sample of towns by income tercile. We see generally consistent results across income groups, especially on gender, homeownership, and voting activity.

TABLE 5.2 *Number of commenters and comments by race*

|  | Commenters | Comments |
|---|---|---|
| White | 2,460 | 3,487 |
| Black | 50 | 60 |
| Hispanic | 22 | 29 |
| Asian | 43 | 61 |
| Other | 5 | 7 |

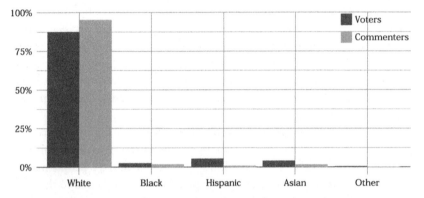

FIGURE 5.1: Commenters and voters by estimated race

ranks each racial and ethnic group by the number of commenters and comments provided.

Figure 5.1 graphs voters and commenters by race. Whites are substantially more likely to participate in planning and zoning board meetings. This pattern is consistent across the most and least diverse towns. For example, in Worcester, a town where the adult population is 64 percent white, we estimate that 88 percent of commenters are white. Despite a black population of 10 percent, only two of the sixty commenters in Worcester were black. Figure 5.2 plots the share of white and nonwhite commenters and voters for four of the more diverse towns in our sample. These differences hold even when we control for a variety of other demographic characteristics, including homeownership.

The underrepresentation of people of color remains stark when we manually code the ethnicity of the 318 commenters who spoke at planning and zoning board meetings in towns that were at least 10 percent Latino. Only three had identifiably Latino surnames. In Lawrence – which is 79 percent Latino – only one of 42 commenters had a Latino

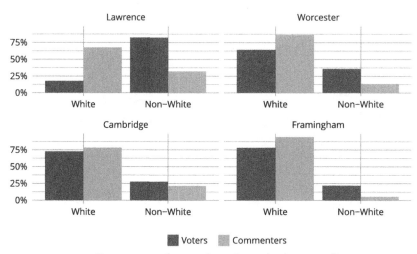

FIGURE 5.2: Comments and voters by estimated race, most diverse towns

surname. Less than one percent of commenters in these high-diversity communities had Latino surnames.

The underrepresentation of Latinos among commenters is remarkable. It is far more stark than in other political arenas. For example, 9.2 percent of voters in 2016 were Latino (Krogstad and Lopez 2016). This means that the 12 percent of eligible voters and 17 percent of the general population who are Latino are certainly underrepresented among actual voters. However, the political inequalities among voters pale in contrast with those among meeting participants (Krogstad 2016). Indeed, even representation among political elites is better than among meeting participants. Ten percent of the 115th Congress is Latino (Bernal 2017). In Lawrence, Massachusetts – where only two percent of meeting participants (and 79 percent of the city's population) were Latino – Latinos make up 40 percent of the town's planning board (Town of Lawrence 2018). The representation of Latinos at community meetings ostensibly designed to enable participation is shockingly low.

The underrepresentation of Latinos in Lawrence Planning Board meetings also suggests that descriptive representation – having political representatives who share one's own demographic traits alone may not help redress racial participation gaps. While descriptive representation has been helpful in mitigating other racially disparate local policy outcomes (Sances and You 2017), it appears not to have significantly boosted Latino participation in Lawrence's land use institutions.

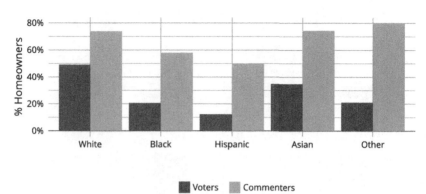

FIGURE 5.3: Homeownership rates for voters and commenters by race

While we see large differences in participation by race, the gap in participation between homeowners and non-homeowners persists across different racial and ethnic groups. Figure 5.3 compares homeownership and participation by race. Consistent with national racial disparities in homeownership rates, there are marked differences between racial groups; whites are substantially more likely to own homes. Homeownership, however, does not have a differential impact on political behavior across racial groups. It increases the likelihood of commenting at a zoning or planning meeting by roughly equivalent amounts – between twenty and thirty percentage points across all racial and ethnic groups.

## BIAS TOWARD OPPOSITION

In addition to being demographically unrepresentative, meeting attendees overwhelmingly oppose the construction of new housing. A mere 15 percent of comments expressed support for new housing. A total of 62 percent were in opposition to proposed housing projects, and the remaining 23 percent of comments were neutral. Figure 5.4 plots the share of comments in opposition to proposed developments by town. The incentives to show up and oppose new housing appear far stronger than those to participate in support. In no town does the share of supportive comments exceed 50 percent.

What's more, ballot referendum results allow us to compare mass public opinion on housing with the views of meeting attendees. In 2010, Massachusetts held a referendum to repeal Chapter 40B, a law promoting affordable housing that permits developers to bypass local zoning regulations if (1) the town's housing stock is less than 10 percent

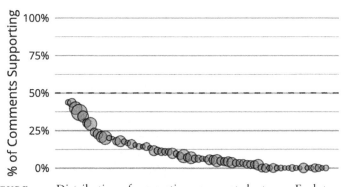

FIGURE 5.4: Distribution of supporting comments by town. Each town is represented by a circle, sized proportionally to the number of comments in the town. Towns with less than ten comments each are omitted.

affordable, and (2) at least 20 to 25 percent of the proposed units have long-term affordability restrictions. Across the state, a majority of voters favored keeping the law, and the referendum to repeal Chapter 40B failed, with only 42 percent of the vote.

In many respects, using Chapter 40B vote returns as our measure of public opinion is a tough test. Chapter 40B deals exclusively with affordable housing. We would expect opposition to affordable housing to be greater than opposition to market-rate housing based on prior scholarship (Tighe 2010).[10] If anything, then, our measure of general public opinion is biased toward opposition and should be more similar to the opinions evinced in our meeting minutes.

The upper panel of Figure 5.5 shows the distribution of the vote supporting 40B by town. Across the cities in our sample, 56 percent of voters in the referendum adopted the pro–affordable housing position and opposed repeal of Chapter 40B. There was majority opposition to the repeal in sixty-one of the ninety-six towns in our sample for which referendum vote returns are available.[11] This comports with state-level figures, where 58 percent of voters opposed the repeal. This a significantly greater level of support for housing construction than evinced by the mere 15 percent of meeting commenters who spoke in support of specific new housing proposals. The relative toughness of this particular test

[10] Only 3 percent of negative comments cited affordability. Thus, there is little evidence that our commenter data would be biased toward opposition because it featured market-rate, rather than affordable, housing developments.
[11] We do not have 40B repeal results for Boylston, Massachusetts.

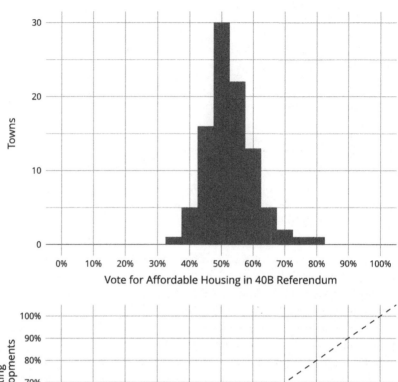

FIGURE 5.5: Support for 40B referendum

makes the forty percentage point difference between 40B support and support for housing proposals at public meetings all the more striking.

The lower panel of Figure 5.5 shows the relationship between town-level vote against repealing Chapter 40B and the percentage of comments in each town that were supportive of multifamily housing developments, for the seventy towns where there were at least ten comments. While there is a positive correlation between opposition to the 40B repeal and positive comments, in every town, fewer than half of the meeting comments were supportive. For example, in Cambridge, 80 percent of voters opposed the repeal of Chapter 40B – the highest level of support for affordable housing across the cities and towns in our sample. In contrast, only 40 percent of comments at development meetings supported the construction of new housing. Indeed, almost every town in Massachusetts exhibited significantly higher support for Chapter 40B than for the development of specific multifamily housing projects. While voters in these towns supported affordable housing construction in the abstract, a substantial majority of those who attended development meetings did so to oppose specific projects.

## PREDICTING OPPOSITION TO NEW HOUSING

While meeting commenters are overwhelmingly opposed to the construction of new housing, opposition is not uniform. As Table 5.3 shows, women, Republicans, and homeowners are significantly more likely to oppose the construction of new housing, all else equal.[12] Frequent voters are more likely to support new developments.

Interestingly, while partisanship did not predict participation in planning and zoning board meetings, it is associated with attitudes toward new housing. Democrats are more likely to support projects and less likely to be neutral or oppose them than independent or Republican

TABLE 5.3 *Demographic differences between commenters speaking in favor and in opposition to developments*

| Demographic | % of Supporters | % of Opponents | Difference |
|---|---|---|---|
| Homeowners | 65.9 | 74.4 | −8.5 |
| Women | 38.5 | 43.2 | −4.7 |
| Whites | 93.1 | 95.7 | −2.5 |
| Age>50 | 78.4 | 75.9 | 2.6 |
| Democrats | 41.5 | 29.1 | 12.4 |

*Differences on gender, party, and homeownership are statistically significant.*

[12] Appendix Table C.5 provides logistic regression results predicting commenter positions.

participants. This finding is consistent with Democrats having more progressive views on housing (Marble and Nall 2017), but contrasts with much of the media coverage on the NIMBY movement, which suggests that NIMBYism is particularly prevalent among progressives (Capps 2015; Paul 2015). Within the progressive places facing housing crises likely to engender NIMBYism, Republicans are more likely show up to meetings in opposition to new housing.

Race similarly is a powerful predictor of opposition to new housing. Figure 5.6 compares the proportion of comments that support development by estimated race. Black support for new housing is significantly higher than other racial and ethnic groups, by a margin of more than thirty percentage points. Still, majorities of all racial and ethnic groups – including black people – oppose the construction of new housing.

This is true for both homeowners and renters across all groups. Figure 5.7 illustrates support for new construction by both race and homeownership status. While white and Asian renters are slightly more supportive of new housing than their home-owning counterparts, their endorsement of new housing falls far short of black levels of support. Among black commenters, homeowners are slightly more supportive of new housing, but there are too few individuals in each category to be confident that these differences are meaningful. On balance, black homeowners and non-homeowners alike are more supportive of development than members of any other group.

Finally, we also find some suggestive evidence that white meeting participants in diverse communities are less supportive of new housing.

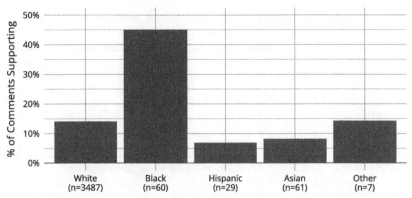

FIGURE 5.6: Comments supporting development by estimated race of commenter

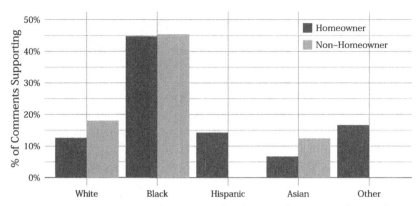

FIGURE 5.7: Comments supporting development by estimated race of commenter

Among communities that were greater than 10 percent Latino, 73 percent of white meeting attendees opposed the construction of new housing – ten percentage points higher than opposition among all meeting participants. This comports with evidence from Trounstine (2018) and Rothstein (2017) that land use regulations were created and used as tools of racial exclusion. It also is consistent with a wide body of research on racial threat, which argues that dominant whites see growing racial diversity as a threat to their influence (Key 1949; Giles and Buckner 1993).

## NEIGHBORHOOD DEFENDERS NATIONALLY

The analyses presented herein use data from one state. Massachusetts's town meeting tradition and strong local zoning control might make housing opponents particularly potent. Or, they may incentivize participation from a particularly unrepresentative set of citizens. While we are unable to rigorously quantify the extent to which these neighborhood defenders dominate political discussions in other states, suggestive evidence indicates that these trends hold, at least to some extent, elsewhere.

City leaders nationally recognize the potential of a small but motivated group to shape local politics generally, and housing policy in particular. While mayors largely see policy arenas like schools and policing as dominated by majority public opinion, almost two-thirds of city leaders believe that housing development is dominated by a small group with strong views (see Figure 5.8). To put that figure in perspective, the only

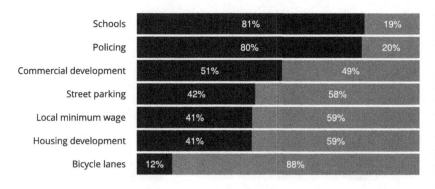

Majority public opinion ■ Small group with strong views

FIGURE 5.8: Survey of mayors: Majority public opinion or small group politics

policy arena that mayors in our survey believed was more dominated by a vocal minority was bicycle lanes.

Just as importantly, the motivation to participate in such meetings exists in a variety of different urban contexts. The desire to defend one's neighborhood is not limited to high-demand housing markets. Even within cooler housing markets, particular neighborhoods are highly desirable. This likely means there is a group of existing residents with a powerful motivation to limit additional development.

To see this principle in operation, consider the Lower East Side of Milwaukee, Wisconsin. While the city of Milwaukee as a whole is not experiencing the same exploding housing prices and development pressures as its coastal counterparts, the role of neighborhood defenders in stymieing development in the city's Lower East Side is remarkably similar to the accounts we analyzed in Massachusetts. The Lower East Side is currently experiencing remarkable change, with an influx of newcomers moving into a community that historically featured large commercial and industrial properties. This renewed interest has been accompanied by a significant uptick in proposed housing development to provide residential accommodations for these newcomers.

One such example was a proposed forty-unit apartment building at 1400 E. Boylston Street in 2013. Because the proposed apartment building required a zoning change, it had to go through, as one reporter described it, "a lengthy process of neighborhood and committee meetings" (Jannene 2014). Neighbors vociferously objected to the plan. One neighbor worried: "There is a palpable level of discomfort with this plan.

While parking is of primary concern, there are also many, many questions about why the existing zoning in the neighborhood even allows for the current [level of 22 units]." Another neighbor argued: "As longtime members of the East Village we feel ... such a development is grossly oversized for this mainly residential area. I have checked with other neighbors to see how they feel about such a development. ... Such a development would be inappropriate for our neighborhood and we strongly request that you vote against this."

One neighbor circulated a petition to stop the development:

This development is out of sync with our neighborhood in size, density, aesthetic, and intention. For over 100 years we have proudly been one of Milwaukee's only downtown adjacent neighborhoods that features single-family, duplex, and low-density apartment buildings. This has allowed us to enjoy a wonderful quality of life and property values that have withstood more than one economic downturn.

These neighbors were backed by their neighborhood association, which had formal powers to negotiate with the developer. The East Bank Neighborhood Association voted to "oppose the project as presented to us as presented by the developer in November" (Horne 2013). As a consequence of these neighborhood objections, the developer moved on to a different project where he was able to construct housing that complied with the existing zoning code, thereby bypassing neighborhood involvement (Jannene 2014).

While we are unable to systematically document the demographics of these neighbors as we can in Massachusetts, the city's leaders strongly believe that these individuals are unrepresentative of their broader communities. Milwaukee Mayor Tom Barrett has remarked, "I didn't realize everyone on the East Side was an architect" (Jannene 2014). An interview with a Milwaukee alderman confirmed that the mayor used this comment repeatedly. The alderman was struck by "well-informed design critiques from professors" at local community meetings. He noted at his community meetings that there were "a lot of regulars" and that he "know[s] who I'm going to run into ... architects and lawyers. Lawyers show up in lawyerly manner." He also believed that a disproportionate share of meeting attendees were homeowners.

The presence of neighborhood defenders in Milwaukee suggests that these dynamics are prevalent even in low-income communities. We further discuss in the next chapter how these dynamics play out in less advantaged cities and towns.

CONCLUSION

This chapter has uncovered two related forms of bias. The first is that a demographically unrepresentative (and privileged) group disproportionately participates in public meetings on housing development. The second is that the concentrated costs and diffuse benefits of housing development spur a group of highly affected individuals to both participate and oppose new housing. Historical analyses of land use regulations argue that they were created by wealthy white homeowners as a tool for protecting their home values and exclusive access to public goods (Rothstein 2017; Trounstine 2018). Our research shows that the same group of people is using these regulations today to stop the development of new housing.

What's more, many of the developments these individuals are showing up in force to oppose are small subdivisions or townhouse developments – a point underscored in the previous chapter's analysis of the projects that trigger public hearings. If anything, we might have expected opposition to new housing to be more muted in our analysis, reflecting the more modest character of the proposals that make up the bulk of our database.

Left unanswered by this analysis are the tactics these neighbors use to persuade zoning and planning board officials. In the next chapter, we turn to how these neighborhood defenders shape housing policy.

# 6

# Neighborhood Defense Tactics

The previous chapter illustrated that the neighborhood defenders who speak at zoning and planning board meetings are demographically unrepresentative of their broader communities. Moreover, they are overwhelmingly opposed to the construction of new housing – opinions that are at odds with the broader community's views on housing. Left unexplored, however, are the types of arguments they use, the reasons they give, and the tactics they use while opposing housing developments.

Chapter 4 showed that meeting participants use these forums to raise far-ranging concerns – not just those related to the narrow regulatory issues that triggered the meetings. This does not mean, however, that participants eschewed mention of regulations altogether. Residents cited a variety of issues that sometimes aligned with the various preexisting laws and regulations. Some of them presented themselves as experts in these regulations. One even brought handouts describing the city's zoning code. Indeed, by linking their claims with existing laws, these residents also implicitly raise the specter of litigation.

By showing up and commenting, neighborhood defenders can delay, modify, or outright block an unwanted housing proposal. Perhaps most straightforwardly, the expression of wide-ranging concerns and expertise by neighbors could change board members' minds. For example, hearing participants express concerns about crumbling foundations could convince a board member who initially supported a project to change her position. Even if the board member still thinks a project has merit, these neighborhood concerns may lead her to ask the developer to provide new water and structural engineering studies, both of which make building more challenging.

Moreover, neighborhood defenders might threaten or file legal action. Lawsuits are extraordinarily costly to everyone involved. Even if they do not outright succeed in blocking a development, they can impose years of delay and extra costs on actual proposals and deter other potentially beneficial ones from even getting started.

Finally, neighborhood defenders can organize and magnify their already unrepresentative voices to further influence housing decisions. Through neighborhood associations or social networks, they might connect with one another to sign petitions, push for ballot initiatives or budget overrides, nominate themselves to become members of a zoning or planning board, or threaten electoral consequences to politicians who defy them.

In this chapter, we outline many potential avenues that neighborhood defenders might employ to impact housing in their community. We also consider the potent role that race might play in driving neighborhood defense, and the extent to which neighborhood defenders predominate in disadvantaged communities. Using a combination of quantitative data on legal filings and qualitative insights from the meeting minutes data, we find that neighborhood defenders employ all political and legal options at their disposal, using their expertise, motivation, and organization to stymie the construction of new housing in their communities.

## PARTICIPANTS EXPRESS A WIDE RANGE OF CONCERNS

Roughly half of the meeting minutes we studied provided details about the reasons individuals supported or opposed new housing proposals. We introduced these coded reasons in the previous chapters and summarized them for a subset of projects in Chapter 4. Figure 6.1 displays these reasons across all projects, grouped by position taken.[1] Perhaps the most striking result is the variety of reasons offered, including flood susceptibility, septic systems, environmental concerns, neighborhood character, and parking, among other things. Moreover, there are notable differences in the reasons provided by supporters and opponents. Supporters of new

---

[1] Two coders used a codebook available in the appendix to classify meeting minutes; coders agreed 100 percent of time about whether a comment should be labeled support/oppose/neutral. They selected the same set of nineteen total topic categories 85 percent of the time.

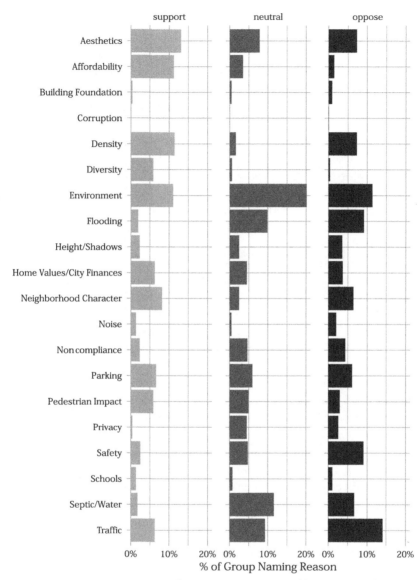

FIGURE 6.1: Reasons given by commenters, grouped by position taken

housing were significantly more likely to mention affordability concerns. Opponents, in contrast, were more likely to raise traffic, environmental, flooding, and safety concerns.

Commenters raise issues that reflect the contexts in which their communities are situated. Almost one quarter of opposing comments cited traffic, and most of these highlighted specific instances of congestion. A Manchester-by-the-Sea woman observed that "traffic has increased at a fast rate even without the new building" in her community. One Foxborough man remarkably "commissioned his own traffic study as he feels the impact of cars and children on the area have not been adequately addressed. He has lived in the area for a few years and compares the peak traffic periods to a demolition derby."[2] Similarly, almost 15 percent of comments opposing new housing mention flooding concerns, and many of these cited specific instances of water in basements, yards, or nearby streets. A Newburyport woman noted that "Boyd Drive already experienced flooding. The impact on existing homes was not assessed." A Reading man explained that "a couple of homes on Dustin Road have a lot of water and flooding problems, and opined that rain gardens will not work."

Many commenters framed concerns related to density, the environment, flooding, shadows, neighborhood character, parking, schools, pedestrian impact, and traffic as community concerns – consistent with their status as neighborhood defenders. Traffic concerns were about fast or heavy traffic in the neighborhood. Flooding worries sometimes invoked stories of a neighbor's basement or a local road. Parking fears highlighted the dearth of street parking in the neighborhood. Septic and water complaints flagged neighborhood-level problems. In contrast, a relatively small share of meeting participants raised explicitly self-interested concerns about depreciating home values. Less than 10 percent of project opponents flagged diminished home values or city finances. This is not to say that home values were not in the back of neighborhood defenders' minds when they worried about, say, neighborhood flooding; frequent floods could certainly have a deleterious impact on home values. But, for the most part, neighborhood defenders did not directly raise economic self-interest when rallying other residents and city officials to their cause at public hearings.

## LAND USE REGULATIONS

These wide-ranging, community-oriented concerns often effectively tie into existing land use regulations. As we outlined in Chapter 3,

---

[2] This commenter's ability to commission his own traffic study also illustrates the unrepresentative resources that many of these participants have available to them. Traffic studies typically cost thousands of dollars.

Massachusetts cities and towns have accumulated a wide variety of laws that limit the construction of new housing. Some explicitly limit the development of multifamily housing by outright prohibiting it, or by setting such onerous requirements for its construction that it is essentially banned. Others do not explicitly restrict the construction of multifamily or multiple units of housing, but in effect limit its construction by imposing significant environmental, septic, lot configuration, or parking requirements. Many commenters explicitly or implicitly tied their concerns to these land use regulations. As we noted in Chapter 4, these cited regulations were not always the same as the ones that triggered the public meeting in the first place. They nonetheless prove to be potent tools of neighborhood defense.

Just under 10 percent of meeting comments explicitly reference existing land use regulations. One commenter in Arlington "inquired about setbacks, the parking reduction bylaw, and whether the project would go before the Commission." An Acton meeting participant "ha[d] no issues with the proposal but noted that peer review may have to be done for the Stormwater piece of the project." At the same Acton Zoning Board meeting, another participant "asked that the north boundary houses have a privacy screen [and] asked for the applicant to confirm that the setbacks complied." A Concord man similarly questioned compliance with existing laws. He "expressed concerns about the encroachment on the meadow and opined that the development does not align with the spirit of the Planned Residential Development Bylaw."

Many other comments at least implicitly connect with community regulations. One commenter in Seekonk was "very concerned with water problems and the wildlife in the area." Seekonk's zoning code features six regulations on developments near water that extend beyond the state's rules. Among them are limitations on buffer zones around "isolated vegetated wetlands" and regulation of vernal pools that "are not certified by the state" (Pioneer Institute for Public Policy Research and Rappaport Institute for Greater Boston 2005). A Northbridge man also had a number of concerns related to water and wetlands "not[ing] that there is a moving body of water (wetland area) to the rear of his property; the proposed subdivision roadway ... will require a wetland crossing." He further "explained to the Board that his 1.6 acre house lot is situated at the bottom of a steep bank, noting concerns with drainage and the potential impacts the development will have on the aquifer area of his existing well." Like Seekonk, Northbridge's zoning code includes multiple stringent environmental regulations, including four wetland regulations and five septic regulations above and beyond state requirements. Indeed, comments related to the environment, flooding, parking, and septic systems in particular were often closely connected with existing land use regulations.

## EXPERTS IN THE FIELD

Participants' comments also indicate a high level of familiarity with complex land use regulations. A sizable minority of participants in planning and zoning board meetings were experts – often professionally – in local zoning codes. Many commenters showcased their professional backgrounds in law, design, engineering, architecture, and real estate in making assessments of housing projects that affected their communities. An engineer in the town of Andover critiqued a developer's traffic study and stormwater analysis: "He stated that as an engineer he knows what kinds of games can be played with numbers. He gives no credibility to these counts. He added that Merrimack College traffic is not de minimus. . . . He asked for a written report from the DPW on the impacts of proceeding with the facility."

One Brookline engineer came prepared to discuss concerns about parking and environmental contamination at a July 2016 Zoning Board meeting:

As an engineer, I agree there is a concern around the liability. . . . I personally am in favor of below ground parking, but that brings another set of concerns. This particular site was a funeral home. . . . I don't know if there's been an environmental study done, what kind of chemicals are on the site.

At the same Brookline Zoning Board meeting, an architect expressed her concerns:

I'm an architect. . . . I think we're all in agreement that there is a genuine need for affordable housing. There is a need that has to be met and met with a good quality building that works in all aspects of its design, not as we see here, an ill-conceived project that doesn't work. . . . I'll start with massing. This building is a monster.

She went on to describe problems with the scale, setbacks, height, and overall aesthetics. A physician at the meeting used his professional expertise to highlight what he perceived to be health and safety concerns:

I'm a physician, so if it makes sense, I'll talk about health and safety concerns around this project. . . . One concern we have is around fire safety. The building, because it occupies so much of the site, means it can only be accessed by fire-fighters on two sides now, which for such a huge unit potentially raises a safety concern. . . . We [also] share the concern that there will be inadequate guidelines for exiting cars.

He then returns to the problem of emergency vehicle access, again highlighting his professional background:

Now, as a physician, I can tell you that access for emergency vehicles is critical to preventing increased mortality and decreasing good outcome for patients when they have emergencies. . . . There are national standards about this. National standards say . . . a first responder with a defibrillator should arrive in four minutes to 90 percent of emergency incidents. . . . We're already at a breaking point.

Imagine being an advocate of increased housing supply and deciding to attend this meeting in Brookline. The dominance of these high-knowledge attendees could make participation intimidating for anyone who shows up for a planning and zoning board meeting and is not equivalently expert in land use matters. Political scientists Arthur Lupia and Anne Norton (2017) suggest that the use of sophisticated language in meetings such as these could act as a form of political power that drowns out other policy discussion, threatening the ability of deliberative democratic institutions to work as intended.

Indeed, one would need to have a high level of knowledge about local land use to effectively make arguments in such a context. Moreover, at a more mundane level, conversations about the parking reduction bylaw are probably fairly boring to a prospective meeting attendee who is not an expert in zoning or very motivated by a particular proposal. The highly expert or intense views of a disproportionately oppositional group of meeting attendees mean that housing supporters would likely have to show up with similar expertise in order to be interested and effective in planning or zoning discussions. Indeed, opponents' intensity may be especially salient. As one housing investor we interviewed put it, "My hard-earned experience is that the NIMBYs . . . bring an extremely high level of passion, time and anger to this issue. Proponents of housing tend to be busier . . . and less angry and passionate, more likely to blow off a 4-hour slugfest at city hall on a Tuesday evening. The resulting impact on the political process is profound. One NIMBY equals 2 or 3 housing advocates."

These wide-ranging resident comments can change board members' minds. Neighborhood concerns at the Brookline Zoning Board meeting led board members to demand a number of additional studies, including reports from a traffic analyst and from the Brookline Fire Department. In response to multiple neighbors complaining about massing and building height, one zoning board member asked for a specific type of shadow study featuring "sophisticated 3D animation." In making their demands, these zoning board members explicitly referenced neighborhood concerns:

Some of the comments [from neighbors] we heard tonight and some of your responses have left me with the impression that some of the things that were submitted to the Board were sort of half-baked, that there weren't sufficient studies yet of the impact of cueing on the street, that the parking system is still under investigation as to what is going to be selected or how it's going to work

Another board member similarly highlighted commenters' worries:

Several people have referred to power failures that go on in the neighborhood. God knows I'm familiar with those. How difficult would it be get information about power failures that go on, just to factor those in?

These board responses are remarkably similar to the meeting in Cambridge that opened the book. The sophistication of many of these commenters makes them particularly persuasive and potent opponents to the development of new housing. They marshal their influence to persuade board members to outright reject proposals or to continue review to subsequent meetings.

## LITIGATION

Frequent attendance at meetings in some instances indicates citizens' willingness to pursue legal challenges against developers or the local government. Multiple individuals in our data set attended meetings with lawyers or identified themselves as lawyers opposing projects in a personal capacity. According to February 2017 Duxbury Planning Board meeting minutes, one man attended a meeting and stated "that he is an attorney and asked who is present from Battelle [the developer], noting that he is concerned that Battelle is getting a windfall without paying taxes." In Medway, a husband and wife brought an attorney to a zoning board meeting to contest the developers' plans to use what they believed to be a private road. The meeting minutes outline the attorney's concerns:

The way that the deeds were written ... grants ownership of the road to the owner of each lot. [T]herefore, their permission would be required in order for the developer to gain access to Fern Path. As a representative for, Mr. and Mrs.

[X], he informed the developer and the Board, that the [X's] do not give permission for access to the private road. Additionally based on conversations with other neighbors, it is [the lawyer's] understanding that they also do not intend to give permission for access.

One lawyer came to a Zoning Board meeting to suggest that the developer and the town were not following appropriate legal procedures. The meeting minutes noted that he "understands counsel's approach at requesting a pro forma but stated that it has to be requested after looking at the development comprehensively."

This type of legalistic talk could be dissuasive in the same way that high levels of expertise were above. Indeed, the presence or threat of lawyers is likely intimidating and limits the type of back-and-forth discourse that is integral in a deliberative democracy. Moreover, as with the highly expert language, legalistic talk is likely highly persuasive – again creating hurdles for less informed and legally connected individuals to speak up.

What's more, lawsuits themselves are enormously powerful tools of delay. Just the threat of a lawsuit can have an impact; even an unsuccessful lawsuit can stretch on for years. Our interviews with housing lawyers, developers, and town officials emphasized lawsuits' importance as tools of obstruction. One housing lawyer worked on a project that had obtained wide neighborhood support. "One cantankerous neighbor," however, posed "a credible threat to litigate" and successfully slowed down the project. The neighbor's threats lead the developer to fully redesign the project such that the project no longer required a zoning variance. Another housing lawyer similarly recalled an affordable housing development in which one individual "sued 3–4 times, nuisance lawsuit after nuisance lawsuit, to delay a project even though it was very clear he would lose." While the project was eventually permitted, the process took longer and was far more costly than it would have been without the neighbor's litigious involvement. Local town officials had remarkably similar experiences. One planning director observed that developments in her town featured "lots of lawsuits" and that "neighbors cost developers money." She exclaimed, "If I were a developer, I wouldn't touch [TOWN NAME]!"

Lawsuits are costly to developers, neighbors, and the town alike. As one developer we interviewed put it, "When neighbors appeal me, they also appeal the town. The town had to spend $40–50,000 on outside counsel, and I had to spend $40,000 on the appeal, and the neighbors paid $30,000 in legal." These direct costs are further compounded by the carrying costs developers must pay as a consequence of the delay in development. Lawsuits are powerful tools that can limit the quantity of housing provided and shift proposals to jurisdictions where residents are less able or likely to litigate.

### Infill in Ipswich and a Lawsuit

A proposal to build a two-family home in Ipswich, a coastal town of about fourteen thousand people north of Boston, illustrates how neighborhood defenders use lawsuits to impose delays. The owner of a sizable lot in the in-town zoning district sought to add a second two-family home to the parcel on which one already existed. Such infill development – in which underused parcels of land are developed to their full potential – was encouraged by the zoning rules. But the lot, while large, was relatively narrow and deep, necessitating a variance to a parcel shape regulation. The owners first went to the Zoning Board of Appeals in April of 2010. The next five monthly board meetings featured extensive discussions about the proposal before board members voted it down in September. The following year, the owners changed their plans and then applied to the planning board for a special permit instead of a variance. The proposal was on the agenda of six planning board meetings across four months – a delay of well over one year at this point – before the board ultimately voted unanimously to approve the special permit.

In August of 2011, a few weeks after the planning board granted the special permit, one of the neighboring families – a couple who spoke against the project at every zoning and planning meeting with recorded public comments – filed a lawsuit in Massachusetts Land Court.[3] The lawsuit challenged whether the permit was properly granted under in-town residential zoning requirements. After four months of motions and procedure, the Court sided with the planning board and ruled against the neighbors who brought the lawsuit. While the neighbors were ultimately unsuccessful in their attempts to stop the development, they were able to delay the project by an additional four months. In 2016, the same couple who brought the lawsuit was part of another (this time successful) zoning lawsuit on a different project. These types of repeated delays – imposed

---

[3] *Sammon, Joseph* v. *Hone, Brian*, Docket No. 11-MISC-452291 (Mass. Land Ct. Aug. 18, 2011).

by a small group of neighborhood defenders – signal to developers that the community will be an expensive one in which to do business.

## Environmental Lawsuits in California: CEQA

The use of lawsuits as a neighborhood defense tactic is hardly unique to Massachusetts. In California, lawsuits under the California Environmental Qualify Act (CEQA) seeking to block or delay development are commonplace and potentially significant contributors to the state's housing crisis.[4] Housing lawyer Jennifer Hernandez analyzed all CEQA lawsuits. As we noted in Chapter 2, she found that – consistent with Chapter 5's findings on the demographics of neighborhood defenders – these lawsuits disproportionately occur in wealthier and whiter communities (Hernandez 2018). These lawsuits heavily center on housing development, with 25 percent of all CEQA lawsuits focused on the development of new housing.[5] These housing-related lawsuits mostly challenge multiunit infill development in which underused parcels are developed into multifamily housing (Hernandez 2018).

Habitat for Humanity's experience attempting to build affordable condominiums in Redwood City highlights the power of CEQA as a tool for neighborhood defenders. Habitat sought to build affordable condominiums in downtown Redwood City. The city of 75,000 is located halfway between San Jose and San Francisco in a region facing, by many measures, the steepest housing cost pressures in the United States. In 2017, after a myriad of reviews and planning and zoning board meetings, the city approved a six-story, twenty-unit building with condominiums targeting residents earning between $63,000 and $85,000 per year (Clark 2018). This proposal already represented a substantial downsizing, by about half, from Habitat's original plans three years earlier (Bradford 2018).

As part of the city approval in the spring in 2017, the council determined that the proposal did not present CEQA concerns. This ruling

---

4 There is some debate of the extent to which CEQA is a substantial driver of the California housing crisis. One prominent critique of some of the focus on the CEQA, a report from scholars at the University of California at Berkeley, argues that the effect of CEQA lawsuits is overstated in discussions of the housing crisis because CEQA lawsuits are just one tactic – subsequent to local regulations and other public forums – that obstructs housing construction (O'Neil, Gualco-Nelson, and Biber 2018).
5 Other targets of CEQA lawsuits include infrastructure projects and local regulations.

exempted the project from additional impact studies. After the city's approval, a group of neighbors – led by a local criminal defense attorney whose office is next door to the proposed development – first appealed the decision and then filed a CEQA lawsuit. The lawyer and his allies clearly saw themselves as neighborhood defenders, framing themselves as "the conscience of the community" (Bradford 2018). The lawyer emphasized that the barriers to filing such a lawsuit were quite low, consistent with our account of land use regulations facilitating the aims of neighborhood defenders: "The thing that works is you have to find some way where they're violating their own plan, and its not that hard to do." The lawsuit stalled the project for well over a year. According to Habitat for Humanity, the delay has added $4 million to the cost of the project (Bradford 2018).

## Lawsuits and Housing Permitting

To build on these illustrative case studies, we more systematically analyze the use of lawsuits as a neighborhood defense tactic. We anticipate that places with more regulations – and therefore more opportunities for neighborhood defenders to plausibly fight unwanted developments – should experience more lawsuits challenging project approvals. Since lawsuits are costly and add delay, we should expect places with more lawsuits to see fewer new multifamily dwellings constructed.

Figure 6.2 illustrates the posited relationship between regulations, lawsuits, and permitting. More restrictive land use institutions should, separately from lawsuits, have a negative relationship with permitting – as we find in Chapter 3. The source of this negative relationship includes the shadow studies, parking studies, environmental reviews, and additional meetings – among other things – that neighbors are able to force using existing regulations. In addition, we anticipate that regulations will also be positively associated with lawsuits, as neighbors take advantage of existing rules as a justification for legal action (or threatened legal action).

We focus our analysis on Massachusetts lawsuits because – as we outlined in Chapter 3 – Massachusetts cities and towns feature unusually detailed land use regulations that are unavailable elsewhere, allowing us to empirically connect regulations with lawsuits. While we cannot observe threatened lawsuits, a search of the Massachusetts court dockets provides a count of the number of lawsuits filed in each city or town. To identify lawsuits per town between 2005 and 2017, we collected

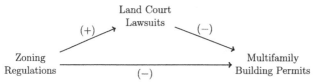

FIGURE 6.2: Hypothesized relationships between regulations, lawsuits, and building permits

information on all court cases featuring the terms "zoning," or "planning," where the municipal zoning or planning board was included in the name of one of the parties.[6]

During this time period, 1,679 lawsuits related to residential land use were filed. There was a remarkable range in our data: Weston – an affluent suburb of Boston with a population of only 11,000 people – had a whopping 25 lawsuits, while 4 municipalities had 0. Overall, however, the number of lawsuits per town is small, with the mean town experiencing 8.9 lawsuits and 80 of the 187 cities and towns featuring 5 or fewer. The primary mechanisms by which neighbors restrict multifamily housing development is thus not actual lawsuits; rather, many of the other strategies described in this chapter – including credible threat of legal action, use of expertise to demand additional studies, organization, and persuasion – likely play a bigger role.

That said, filed lawsuits may play some role in restricting development. It is perhaps unsurprising that Weston – featuring the highest number of lawsuits in our data set – has permitted no multifamily housing developments in the last sixteen years. To investigate the link between regulations and lawsuits, we use two different analyses. First, we examine the connection between regulations and lawsuits, which we normalize by dividing total community lawsuits by the total number of housing units.[7] Second, we investigate the link between the number of lawsuits per housing unit and the share of permits allocated to multifamily housing.

---

[6] We identified lawsuits featuring zoning using the Bloomberg Law database. This procedure is similar to Glaeser and Ward (2009), which searched Massachusetts Land Court records only for a state-level analysis. In conversations with developers and our own analysis of court dockets, we found that many zoning cases were filed in other Massachusetts courts as well. Land Court cases made up 46 percent of the cases in our dataset. Thirty-nine percent were filed in Superior Court, 13 percent in the Appeals Court, and 3 percent in the Supreme Judicial Court.

[7] We use 2000 US Census figures for total number of housing units and adjust lawsuits to use a per-housing-unit basis, because the raw number of lawsuits in part might proxy for total population or total housing units in an area.

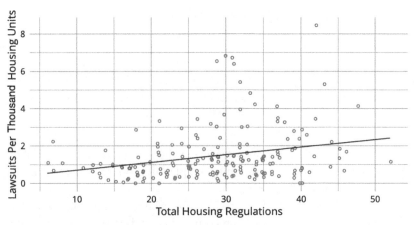

FIGURE 6.3: Scatter plot of number of housing regulations and lawsuits filed per ten thousand residents. Lawsuits increase with additional regulations.

Figure 6.3 shows a strong positive relationship between the total number of housing regulations in a town and the number of lawsuits (per thousand housing units). Towns with more regulations get sued over zoning and building permits more often. Figure 6.4 shows a strong negative relationship between lawsuits and the share of multifamily housing permits in each town. The more lawsuits in the town, the lower the share of permitted units in multifamily buildings. Thus, lawsuits appear to be one mechanism by which land use institutions restrict development. As posited, more restrictive places have more lawsuits, and these lawsuits, in turn, are negatively linked with multifamily permitting.[8]

This relationship between lawsuits and housing development illustrates the power of small groups (or even individuals) to engage in the politics of delay. Lawsuits do not require large groups and can, in fact, be driven by just one person. One housing lawyer we interviewed lamented that the current standard of litigation essentially provides "individuals [with] a veto." The meeting minute data include numerous instances of lawsuits or litigious threats typically involving one individual, a couple, or a small group of neighbors.

[8] Appendix Tables D.1 and D.2 present OLS results these relationships. Table D.1 shows positive, statistically significant relationships between the total number of regulations in a town and the number of lawsuits. We also find positive relationships between lawsuits and the number of cluster, multifamily, parcel shape, senior housing, and septic system regulations. Table D.2 shows a negative statistically significant relationship between lawsuits and multifamily housing permits (defined several different ways).

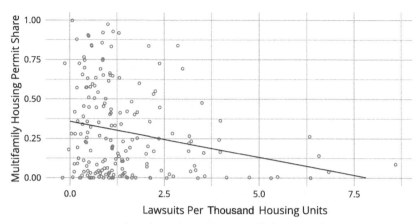

FIGURE 6.4: Scatter plot of number of lawsuits filed per ten thousand residents and share of multifamily housing permits. The share of multifamily housing permits decreases with lawsuits.

The import of lawsuits as a form of opposition exacerbates the political inequalities we documented in Chapter 5. Individuals and groups of neighbors must have sufficient financial resources to sue, limiting its use as a neighborhood defense tactic to the most advantaged residents and communities.

## Lawsuits and Affordable Housing Regulations

Lawsuits also may offer an avenue to subvert state regulations promoting affordable housing. In the previous chapters, we outlined a fairly unique piece of affordable housing legislation in Massachusetts: Chapter 40B. Under Chapter 40B, development proposals in which at least 25 percent of units are affordable may bypass many local zoning laws in communities where less than 10 percent of the housing stock is affordable. In many respects, it is similar to the failed SB 827 in California, which would have allowed housing developers proposing projects near mass transit to circumvent local zoning codes.

While Chapter 40B still requires public hearings and allows local governments some say over the process, town officials are required to review projects under much more flexible rules, and these decisions are subject to state appeal. While on its face this procedure would seemingly limit the influence of neighborhood defenders, in practice, it may incentivize citizen lawsuits. As one housing lawyer we interviewed put it, "Neighbors have no other way to raise legitimate concerns." She found that the Chapter 40B framework "really amps up litigation." With typical avenues – such as persuading planning or zoning board officials at meetings – cut off for some types of projects, individuals feel they are left with no option other than to file suit. Massachusetts Land Court lawsuits related to zoning have increased markedly since Chapter 40B's inception in 1969 (Glaeser and Ward 2009). While there are many possible sources of this increase, this growth in lawsuits is consistent with Chapter 40B inducing litigious behavior.

The ability and willingness of neighborhood defenders to pursue all legal avenues to stop or delay development makes housing reform challenging. Indeed, even if housing is largely taken out of the hands of the local governments most predisposed to respond to neighborhood defenders, these individuals can still use lawsuits to stop or slow down state-supported efforts to construct new housing.

## ORGANIZED INTERESTS: THE POWER OF NEIGHBORHOOD ASSOCIATIONS

The minutes reveal that, in some cases, neighbors appear to be coordinating with one another and organizing in advance of public meetings. This cohesion enhances their political influence. Organization may render neighborhood defenders' arguments more persuasive on their faces. What's more, power in numbers might allow neighborhood defenders to marshal influential local elected officials to their cause.

Many commenters note that they have spoken to other members of their community. Others indicate that presentations at public hearings have been coordinated, with one neighbor speaking about building foundations, with another reflecting on parking concerns. Some came prepared with written documentation of neighborhood opposition.

In 2015, a developer in Taunton, Massachusetts, proposed building two three-unit buildings and one single-family home. Neighbors strongly opposed. One noted: "There are 64 homes in Winthrop Heights across Winthrop Street and there are all single family homes. He stated there is no need for more multifamily dwellings. He is OK with it being single family dwellings. *He submitted [a] petition signed by approximately 83 abutters opposed to triplexes*" (emphasis added). In Salem, Massachusetts, a neighbor attended a December 2015 meeting to oppose a proposed eighteen-unit development and supplied a neighborhood petition bolstering his viewpoint. According to the minutes, he "strongly opposes the project and presents additional signatures of a previous received petition of opposition that was read into the record at the previous public meeting."

This coordination need not solely be in the service of neighborhood defense. A 2015 Amesbury, Massachusetts, Planning Board meeting offers an example of neighbors coordinating in *support* of a proposed development. One neighbor noted she was "one of 64 abutters who heartily endorse" the proposed Hatter's Point development. Another highlighted how she and other neighbors had organized to clean up the site, underscoring close neighborhood ties: "I've lived there for nearly 11 years. During this time, I lived through the broken promises of the previous developer. I was forced to spend my limited personal resources *along with my neighbors* to demolish much of the dangerous structure at Hatter's Point" (emphasis added).

This coordination can occur by both informal and formal mechanisms. Informally, neighbors have many day-to-day interactions with one another. The racial and economic homogeneity of many American neighborhoods helps facilitate these conversations; these kinds of communities have higher levels of social capital, with more trust, friendship, and cooperation among neighbors (Putnam 2007). Moreover, these neighbors share a common interest in preserving their home values and the quality of their public goods. It naturally makes sense that they might talk about those common interests. And, when a proposed housing development poses a putative threat to those common interests, it is reasonable that those same neighbors might inform one another about planning and zoning board meetings, encourage one another to attend, and coordinate a plan of attack.

Moreover, some communities feature more formal institutions that encourage and, in some cases, enforce neighborhood cohesion. Neighborhood and homeowners' associations proliferated in the middle of the twentieth century to enforce restrictive covenants, defend neighborhoods (Sugrue 1996; Kruse 2005; Trounstine 2018), and serve as a check on developers during urban renewal (Berry, Portney, and Thomson 1993). Much like the neighborhood meetings studied in the previous chapter, white homeowners dominated both types of associations. These institutions received support and legitimacy from both municipal officials and powerful real estate interests (Sugrue 1996; Kruse 2005; Trounstine 2018). They were able to use this advantaged position to pressure municipal elected officials, reshape the implementation of zoning and land use regulation, and impact a variety of housing construction decisions (Frug 2006; Trounstine 2018).[9]

Berry, Portney, and Thomson (1993) note that neighborhoods "often reign supreme ... in development issues. They do so, in part, because neighborhood associations are often seen as the legitimate bearer of neighborhood interests on questions that affect the direct physical status of the neighborhood" (169). Indeed, city governments often have institutional mechanisms in place to directly incorporate neighborhood association views into city policy making. While the procedure varies from city to city, Berry, Portney, and Thomson (1993) find that, in the places they studied, most cities had one or more offices devoted to soliciting and incorporating neighborhood associations' preferences.

The meetings feature multiple appearances from neighborhood associations. In Lawrence, Massachusetts, they were especially active. At a 2017 zoning board meeting, the president of the  Mt. Vernon Neighborhood Association spoke in opposition to three different projects in her neighborhood. The first – 401 South Broadway – featured an infill single-family home. The president of the association stated:

[S]he, being the President of the Mt. Vernon Neighborhood Association, was representing many that could not be at the meeting. She said that many of her Mt. Vernon neighbors were opposed. She said that the open space is decreasing at a rate that is harmful to the neighborhood. She felt that the additional home would cause an increase in traffic flow on Gorham St.

Consistent with historical accounts underscoring the political power of neighborhood associations, the neighborhood's city council representative echoed her concerns in opposing the project: "Councilor David Abdoo, Councilor of District E, stated that [his] position remained unchanged and he was still opposed to the development citing the same reasons as [the Mt. Vernon Neighborhood Association president] had expressed." The zoning board unanimously denied the proposal.

The neighborhood association president expressed similarly vociferous opposition to a second infill housing development proposed at that same meeting. She once again worried about the traffic issues imposed by a new single-family house. She "stated that the neighbors

---

[9] Homeowners' associations exert considerably more legal power than neighborhood associations. Neighborhood associations can pressure political actors, but they lack direct control over local land use and relied on voluntary contributions. In contrast, homeowners' associations have direct control over local property and can raise money using assessments (Frug 2006).

responded to this matter. She agreed that Weare St. is very narrow and she felt that there was not enough land to construct another home. She said it would also generate more cars." Once again, she succeeded in blocking the proposal, with the zoning board voting to deny the request 4-1.

Finally, the neighborhood association president highlighted her political connections at this meeting in opposing an infill duplex. She "stated that she was speaking on behalf of many neighbors. She said that there is not enough land and a cul-de-sac would not help. She noted that the Mayor and Councilor Laplante opposed the project." Once again, the zoning board unanimously denied the request.

Lawrence's neighborhood associations also coordinated with one another. In response to a fifty-five-unit proposal, the president of the South Lawrence West Neighborhood Association: "stated that both she and ... the President of the Sacred Heart Neighborhood Association met with these gentleman. She said that neither she nor [the Sacred Heart Neighborhood Association president] are in favor and stated that this is a highly congested area that they both had concerns on the public safety issues." The zoning board unanimously denied the proposal.

In the previous chapter, we outlined the stark underrepresentation of Latinos in land use politics in Lawrence, a city that is 79 percent Latino. These qualitative insights from Lawrence zoning board meetings suggest that neighborhood associations may play a critical role in empowering the city's white minority to dominate decisions on housing policy and defend their neighborhoods. While the language is different, the outcomes share a great deal with those pursued by mid-nineteenth century neighborhood associations that expressly formed to protect white neighborhoods (Sugrue 1996; Kruse 2005).

What's more, these associations are empowered by their local government. The Lawrence city government's website includes information about all of the neighborhood associations, including meeting times and contact information. It describes these organizations as "grassroots residents groups that work towards bettering their particular neighborhoods. They are neither City agencies nor City Departments. The City recognizes their efforts and collaborates to maintain and beautify all neighborhoods in Lawrence" (City of Lawrence 2019). The city supports neighborhood associations by helping them foster partnerships with local colleges universities, event coordination, training, incorporation, grant writing, and group development (City of Lawrence 2019).

Lawrence is hardly alone in the prominence of its neighborhood associations. Worcester, Massachusetts, features active and oppositional neighborhood associations. At one meeting we outline later in this chapter, the zoning board required the developer to negotiate with the neighborhood association to no avail. In our discussion of Milwaukee, Wisconsin, land use politics in the previous chapter, the city required the developer to bargain with the neighborhood association.

In Los Angeles, the city government empowers local Neighborhood Councils under the auspices of the city's Department of Neighborhood Empowerment. The Neighborhood Councils are "advisory bodies, who advocate for their communities with City Hall on important issues like development, homeless and emergency preparedness" (Department of Neighborhood Empowerment 2019). When development projects necessitate public hearings, the Neighborhood Council is officially notified and invited to participate in proceedings. The City of Minneapolis is so concerned about the lack of diversity in its city-funded neighborhood organizations that it has threatened to cut municipal funds for groups that fail to meet diversity goals. Many neighborhood groups balked at the city's deadline and process for designing the policy, leading the city had to loosen deadlines for neighborhood groups to meet diversity goals (Otárola 2019).

In short, neighborhood associations are potent players who enhance the power of homeowners in land use politics.

## POLITICAL ACTIVISM

Participation in public meetings may also signal a strong willingness to get involved in other parts of the political process – potentially empowered or mobilized by new information or formal neighborhood associations. Individuals unhappy about planning processes may organize a recall petition. They could bring together election campaigns in favor of candidates who support their vision for community office.

They could even run for political office or nominate themselves as candidates for boards. While the process varies between communities, generally, when a planning board or zoning board has an opening, community residents can submit their names for consideration. One developer we spoke with believes that many of the individuals who join these boards are neighborhood defenders seeking to reform local land use institutions. It is certainly not a stretch to imagine that at least some of the highly sophisticated real estate professionals attending public meetings would also be willing to volunteer as members of local planning and zoning boards.

## Valentine Estate

Finally, meeting participants might mobilize broader, town-level opposition to stop or delay a development. In one town we studied, meeting participants organized a town referendum vote to spend millions in government resources to stop an unwanted housing development. Ashland, Massachusetts, is a small town of fifteen thousand residents west of Boston. In 2014, a developer applied for a Chapter 40B permit on a 7.67 acre plot of land known as the Valentine Estate. Only 3.7 percent of the town's housing stock is affordable, well below the state's 10 percent threshold for 40B projects. The developer proposed four buildings: two three-story structures with twenty-nine units and two four-story structures with forty units. They set aside thirty-five units as affordable (Hilliard 2017).

While Chapter 40B allows developers to ultimately bypass many local zoning rules, it still mandates multiple Zoning Board of Appeals public hearings and board approval. Neighbors showed up to these hearings apoplectic. One neighbor (who had a background in permitting) described the development as "an insult to the citizens of Ashland. I have never seen such an atrocity" (Roy 2014). At a 2015 zoning board hearing, multiple neighbors highlighted traffic problems. One neighbor came prepared with "aerial photos of the development sites." He raised "questions concerning the site distance and the development bedroom statistics included in the study."

In response to neighborhood opposition, the town imposed multiple delays, requiring studies and legal fights. As public hearings stretched into 2016, neighborhood opposition remained firm, and appeared to become more organized. One neighbor asked whether "it would be acceptable for a group of concerned citizens to provide the Board with written comments." He noted that "more than 500 signatures had been obtained opposing the project."

In an interview, the developer described years of hearings and $500,000 in permitting fees. The hearings featured individuals lamenting "the turtles, the snails, the wetlands, the traffic." The town ultimately agreed to allow 99 units of housing – far lower than the proposed 140. The developer agreed to 120, but the town would not budge.

While neighborhood defenders mounted multiple lawsuits and appeals, neighbors and town officials worried that the developer would ultimately prevail in court (Hilliard 2017). They consequently took extraordinary action: They organized a Town Meeting vote on whether the municipality should purchase the Valentine Estate for $3.5 million. The Town Manager endorsed the decision to purchase the property, arguing that "[o]ne of the things we really value as a town is our open space and the woods. Things that give our suburban town a little more of that rural character" (Bosma 2018b). In spring 2018, the town brought this purchase to a full town vote in a ballot referendum. This budget override passed resoundingly, with 83 percent of the vote in support of taking on extra town debt to purchase the property (Bosma 2018a). As of this writing, the town has built nothing on the property.

While what happened in Ashland is clearly unusual, the political proceedings there illustrate the political clout neighborhood defenders can exert delaying and stopping the construction of new housing. Neighborhood defenders can persuade town officials and mobilize broader segments of the town to stop unwanted development. What started as a more typical neighborhood defender story – with an unrepresentative group of neighbors fighting a development at planning and zoning meetings – became a broader political movement, as neighborhood defenders pushed the town and their fellow citizens to become involved.

While publicly purchasing property to stop a development might seem extreme, such efforts are not unique to Ashland. In Weston, Massachusetts, ten neighbors of a proposed Chapter 40B development at Dickson Meadow pushed the town to buy the parcel of land so that the town could oversee the construction of a smaller development. Although the neighbors were ultimately unsuccessful on that front, they did manage to change the layout of the development and delay the project substantially (Robitaille and Bratt 2012). Arlington, Massachusetts, neighbors furious over a proposed Chapter 40B development at the Mugar Wetlands have pushed the town to buy the property. As of this writing, the town has discussed the possibility of using a mix of funds from the Community Preservation Act tax surcharge and bigger grants from conservation groups to purchase the land and prevent the development (Buell 2015). The broader political organization of neighborhood defenders is a potent force against housing development in many local communities.

## THE ROLE OF RACE

The previous chapter highlighted racial disparities in who participates in housing politics. Consistent with the historically exclusionary aims of many zoning and land use regulations (Rothstein 2017; Trounstine 2018), people of color are starkly underrepresented in land use forums. Our detailed data on comments made at public meetings may also provide a window into whether race and racial bias drive opposition to the construction of new housing.

Determining whether a comment is rooted in racism can be challenging to parse in some instances. A Supreme Court ruling on land use ordinances underscores this point. Arlington Heights, Illinois, prohibited the construction of multifamily dwellings virtually everywhere in the community. While the regulation did not include any explicitly racial language, it effectively precluded blacks from residing there. Moreover, at least from the perspective of the community, this was by design. At the city council meeting where this ordinance passed, community members supported it on racist grounds. Letters to the newspaper similarly endorsed the ordinance because of its capacity for racial exclusion. Despite this racist community sentiment, the Supreme Court upheld the ordinance in 1977 because there was no clearcut evidence that the city council members intended to exclude people from their community on the basis of race (Rothstein 2017, 54).

Even among the mass public, it is difficult to parse whether the objections of housing development opponents are rooted in race. Social norms likely deter the use of explicitly racist language at public meetings. Moreover, planning and zoning board officials have a strong incentive to keep that sort of language out of public meetings (or, at least, public meeting minutes) at the risk of future litigation due to racial bias. Nonetheless, many of the nearly 11 percent of commenters who cited "neighborhood character" in opposition to a housing project may be using racially coded language.[10] Indeed, many activists and media observers view such concerns in this light. Urban planner Rick Jacobus (2017) notes: "If you are like me, when someone says they want to 'preserve the character' of a community, what you hear is that they want to exclude poor people and people of color." A few of the comments that fell under the neighborhood

---

[10] Public safety may, on its face, also seem like it includes concerns evincing underlying racial biases. In most cases, however, these comments concerned emergency vehicle access and pedestrian safety in heavy traffic.

character umbrella appear to be racialized. One man in Beverly – a town that is 83 percent white – critiqued the design of a building as "ridiculous" and said "Beverly is going to look like Chelsea." Sixty-two percent of Chelsea's population is Hispanic. Chelsea is six towns away from Beverly. It is unlikely the commenter invoked it randomly. He went on to ask if "there is a restriction put on the building that there is to be no Section 8 housing in the building." Several other comments in the database similarly argued that their homogenous communities would resemble much more diverse ones if a project were approved.

It is difficult to disentangle, however, whether most of the "neighborhood character" comments are about race, class, or both. A Dighton woman, for example, opposed a project because she felt it was "not consistent with the neighborhood. A multi-family home built on a slab is going to negatively impact the values of homes in the neighborhood. The other homes in the neighborhood are single family homes that are owner occupied." There may very well be racial undertones to this woman's opposition – and there are almost certainly some class concerns. However, there is nothing in her comments that clearly ties her opposition to racial bias. Many of the comments that referenced neighborhood character across a variety of towns were remarkably similar to hers. A Concord man "spoke in opposition to the project and the change in the neighborhood character." A woman in Hudson "was worried about the character of the neighborhood and how this doesn't fit in."

While we cannot find many explicit attempts to exclude people of color in the meeting minutes, this does not mean that the sentiment is absent. Rothstein (2017) eloquently describes this challenge in his discussion of the Arlington Heights, Illinois, Supreme Court decision:

We can't prove what was in council members' hearts in Arlington Heights or anywhere else, but in too many zoning decisions the circumstantial evidence of racial motivation is persuasive. I think it can fairly be said that there would be many fewer segregated suburbs than there are today were it not for an unconstitutional desire, shared by local officials and by the national leaders who urged them on, to keep African Americans from being white families' neighbors. (54)

We cannot know what is in the hearts of individuals who speak at these public meetings. Given the racial homogeneity of many of these Massachusetts towns and their virulent opposition to the construction of any new housing, it is hard to imagine that racial animus is not a part of these planning and zoning board meetings. Moreover, many of the comments highlighting neighborhood character are almost certainly rooted in anti-poor bias, suggesting that some neighborhood defenders use zoning codes as a means of maintaining community class status.

## NEIGHBORHOOD DEFENDERS IN LOW-INCOME CITIES

The story presented thus far in this chapter features legalistic experts bent on racial and socioeconomic exclusion and likely conjures images of affluent and advantaged neighborhood defenders protecting the boundaries of their affluent and advantaged communities. Readers might be left wondering whether these dynamics unfold similarly in lower-income communities. Some evidence presented thus far suggests yes. The quantitative analysis in Chapter 5 showed that advantaged and oppositional neighborhood defenders dominated planning and zoning board proceedings regardless of town demographics. Interviews and case study evidence revealed that "lawyerly" and expert neighborhood defenders obstructed developments in Milwaukee. Moreover, this chapter's exploration of neighborhood defenders in Lawrence – an overwhelmingly Latino city whose median household income falls well below the state average – features institutionally and politically powerful neighborhood defenders. We turn to meeting minutes in Massachusetts towns – Worcester and Lowell – to better understand the dynamics of neighborhood defense in less advantaged communities. Both are former industrial cities located more than twenty-five miles from Boston; they have considerably lagged the Greater Boston area's explosive economic growth.

Table 6.1 juxtaposes Worcester and Lowell's demographic characteristics with the other cities and towns in our meeting minutes sample. Worcester and Lowell are significantly larger, more dense, and more diverse than our sample as a whole. They are also significantly poorer, as measured by both median household income and median housing value.

In Worcester, we see examples of expert language remarkably similar to those in more advantaged communities like Concord and Andover. For example, Worcester Zoning Board meeting minutes in 2015 describe how one man sharply opposed the construction of thirty-six low-rise condominiums in his neighborhood:

[NAME] stated that he represents the Brown Square Neighborhood Group and that he served as a Zoning Board member for eight years. He stated that he does not believe the proposal meets the statute regulations to be considered hardship. He believes that the petition should be denied and that the developer is only looking to maximize for profitability. This does not fit in with the character of the neighborhood.

TABLE 6.1 *Demographics of Worcester and Lowell compared with our entire meeting minute city/town sample*

|  | Sample mean | Worcester | Lowell |
| --- | --- | --- | --- |
| Population | 25,772 | 184,508 | 110,558 |
| Population density | 1,976 | 4,845 | 7,842 |
| Population growth 2010–2015 | 5 | 2 | 4 |
| Median age | 42 | 34 | 33 |
| Percent over 65 | 15 | 12 | 10 |
| Percent white | 86 | 58 | 50 |
| Percent black | 2 | 11 | 7 |
| Percent hispanic | 5 | 21 | 18 |
| Median household income | 97,650 | 45,599 | 46,972 |
| Median house price | 431,844 | 206,500 | 234,100 |
| Distance from Boston (miles) | 24 | 40 | 25 |
| Observations | 97 | | |

These comments also highlight the prevalence of neighborhood associations as tools of neighborhood defense. Moreover, this speaker's biographical details confirm our supposition earlier this chapter that many neighborhood defenders are past and future zoning board members.

Another man at the same meeting highlighted multiple problems with a proposed development that were closely tied with city regulations regarding parking, emergency vehicle access, and wildlife. The meeting minutes describe his comments:

[NAME] stated that the ball field has tournaments all summer long and parking is horrendous. During the winter, the right-of-way is narrowed down to allow one car to go down the street at a time. Emergency vehicles had issues accessing a house this winter. There are several cul-de-sacs in that area where Franklin Street is the only way in and out. [NAME] stated that the neighborhood character and social structure would be negatively affected and property values will be affected too. He is also concerned with what clear cutting will do to the wildlife in the area.

These comments are virtually indistinguishable from concerns raised in Acton and Brookline – affluent communities facing much starker housing cost pressures – earlier in this chapter.

As in Acton and Brookline, Worcester Zoning Board members were deeply concerned about neighborhood opposition. Meeting minutes described one board member's response to neighborhood opposition in a 2015 meeting reviewing the development of low-rise condominiums:

[Worcester Zoning Board Chair] stated that he believes that the design looks like this is an institution. The project needs to have a lot of landscaping to be more appealing. He is concerned the density is very high and also about the amount of impervious area. He would like to see the applicant meet with the neighborhood again because right now there is a big gap from what is proposed to what the neighbors want.

Other board members concurred in a unanimous vote. This meant that discussion of the proposal would be continued through the next meeting six weeks later, and that construction approval was delayed by a further two months. At the subsequent meeting, neighborhood opposition to the proposed low-rise condominium development remained intense, despite the developer having reduced the number of housing units from thirty-six to twenty-four. This neighbor's comments perhaps most succinctly described his community's concerns: "[NAME] stated that there was no compromise or agreement at the neighborhood meeting. They do not want this type of project in the neighborhood." The board agreed: "[Worcester Zoning Board member] stated that the applicant addressed some of his concerns, but that he is concerned with this development not quite fitting in to the neighborhood and the traffic that will be due to the density. [Worcester Zoning Board member] concurred." The developer opted to withdraw his proposal at this point; neighborhood opposition successfully killed the project.

These dynamics were not limited to a unique set of commenters at one particular meeting. We found multiple examples of them at Worcester Planning and Zoning Board. In 2016, for example, one man highlighted regulatory requirements in response to a proposal to build an infill single-family dwelling that did not conform with frontage requirements:

[NAME] stated that parcel is not within an RS-7. ... [NAME] stated that the lot is too small to sustain a home relative to the character of the neighborhood and that when he purchased his home he was told the lot was unbuildable. There is no housing shortage in Worcester and commented on average time houses are listed before sale. He stated that much of the lot is unusable and maintains a steep incline. [NAME] stated that his home exists within 2 feet to the property line and the proposed home is 14.5 feet from his home. [NAME] also has concerns about stormwater and erosion issues as a result of the construction.

Other neighbors expressed similar sentiments: "[NAME] stated concerns about environmental impact and requested a study. She also stated concerns about aesthetics, parking and safety." A third neighbor "stated that the neighborhood character does not match the proposal relative to yard size and the lot is too small. Stated concerns about parking on the street." The Worcester Zoning Board largely agreed with these concerns, leading the developer's attorney to request a continuance extending the public hearing by an additional two months. While the project scale was much more modest than the previous condominium example – a single-family house compared with twenty-four condominium units – the meeting process was remarkably similar. Ultimately, the Worcester Zoning Board approved the single-family house with significant modifications, but not without an additional month of studies and public meetings.

More systematically, a striking 77 percent of the ninety-four comments in Worcester between 2015 and 2017 opposed the construction of new housing. Only four of the ninety-four comments expressed support for a proposed housing development. This opposition is actually ten percentage points higher than in Massachusetts cities and towns as a whole.

This is remarkable given Worcester's financial woes. The city is facing a significant fiscal crisis, with some estimates suggesting that the city will need to put one-third of its revenues toward retirement benefits by 2020. More than 35 percent of the city's land is tax exempt, making it hard for the city generate enough property tax revenue to cover its expenses (Petrishen 2014). From a city finance perspective, additional housing development would bring much-needed property tax revenue.

In Lowell, however, the scene at public meetings was considerably different. We were only able to locate two zoning board meetings between 2015 and 2017 in which members of the public spoke. Two of the comments were in favor of proposed developments, while two were opposed. Supporters of a redeveloped Hebrew school highlighted problems with vacant properties: "[NAME] stated that the former Hebrew school has been vacant for 14 years. There is currently vandalism and drug problems as a result of the vacant building, so she is excited about the development of the property." A second commenter echoed the woman's concerns and thought "the proposed project would be positive." An opponent to the project brought up concerns related to parking that are now likely quite familiar to our readers:

[NAME] stated that he believes that the proposed rear parking lot for the residential units is inadequate. He noted that the city also does not plow Academy Drive. If the spaces on the proposed parking lot are used by residents of the proposed units, then the people who go to the synagogue will park on the street, which is a problem because there is not enough room.

The fourth commenter spoke in opposition to the construction of a single-family dwelling on a vacant lot:

[NAME] stated that the houses in the neighborhood are already crammed together. The neighborhood is congested and loud and this proposed development would add to that. He also mentioned that many homes on the street are being operated as multifamily dwellings when they are not supposed to be. He feared that the proposed single family home would also be operated as more than a single family. [NAME] also noted that there are too many cars on the street as it is now and neighbors do not take care of their properties.

In some respects, these two oppositional comments share a great deal with analogous statements in Worcester and more affluent communities in Massachusetts. On the other hand, opposition to housing projects – at least as reflected in meeting attendance – is clearly more limited in Lowell than in other communities we studied.

Moreover, perhaps in part because there were fewer opponents, Lowell Zoning Board members were considerably less responsive to neighborhood opposition. In response to the abutter who worried about the construction of a single family lot, several zoning board members highlighted the potential value of the development relative to its current use as a vacant lot:

Member [NAME A] stated that something should be done with the unsightly lot. He felt that proposing a single-family home would be more beneficial than leaving it vacant. Member [NAME B] agreed, stating that he was in favor of the application. He commented that bad neighbors should not have an impact on the development of the property.

The Lowell Zoning Board unanimously approved the proposal. Perhaps reflecting the slightly more widespread neighborhood concern, the Hebrew School project elicited a bit more pushback from the board. Board members asked a few more pointed questions about parking and how the parking lot would be maintained after snowstorms. Satisfied with the developer's answers, the board unanimously approved the conversion of the former religious school, so long as the developer met certain conditions regarding parking and snow removal.

Worcester and Lowell suggest that there may be more variance in the politics of neighborhood defense in low-income cities. While Worcester's meeting minutes were virtually indistinguishable from those of more affluent communities, Lowell's meetings featured little neighborhood activism. While neighborhood defense may not be uniform in less advantaged communities, it nonetheless appears to be more endemic than media accounts centered on San Francisco and Boston would indicate – especially in desirable neighborhoods within these lower-income localities.

## POLITICAL INEQUALITY AND LAND USE

After reading about the tactics residents use to oppose new housing, many may find some of their concerns familiar or, indeed, sympathetic. Most individuals who have lived in a community for any length of time can cite examples of unscrupulous developers cutting corners and proposing projects with deleterious consequences to their surrounding community. While some of the commenters expressed deeply troubling preferences clearly aimed at racial and economic exclusion, the views of many meeting participants are not in and of themselves problematic. Moreover, the long-standing political dominance of developers and the growth machine in urban politics (Logan and Molotch 1987) may make strong neighborhood defense more appealing.

What is troubling, however, is that many other voices are not heard at these meetings. This is in part a consequence of costly barriers to participation. Lacking the time, sense of efficacy, and knowledge to participate, renters and other unrepresented voices stay home. Moreover, even those that do show up may find themselves intimidated by neighborhood defenders' high levels of expertise. Most importantly, potential supporters have little incentive to show up at neighborhood meetings. The marginal benefits of an additional unit of housing pale in comparison to the concentrated costs faced by neighbors.

While these trends are generalizable, they are not monolithic, especially in low-income cities. Evidence from Milwaukee and Worcester illustrates that there are politically powerful neighborhood defenders in disadvantaged cities. They may, however, be more unevenly distributed and primarily concentrated in advantaged and gentrified neighborhoods within these less affluent cities.

We have illustrated important demographic and attitudinal disparities in who participates. Moreover, we have highlighted the strategies that sophisticated neighborhood defenders employ, which render them highly effective and introduce even greater participatory barriers.

We have not, thus far, delved in great detail into communities that lack neighborhood defenders. The brief case study of Lowell presented in this chapter provides some suggestive evidence that these communities may be more likely to quickly approve developments. In communities with rapidly escalating housing costs, this could contribute to the gentrification of low-income neighborhoods. We turn to these communities in our concluding chapter, and explore how gentrification has fractured the coalition for land use reform.

# 7

## Gentrification, Affordable Housing, and Housing Reform

Faced with a system in which developers, urban planners, and advantaged homeowners controlled the construction of housing, local policy makers gave power to neighbors to shape what could be built in their communities. Cities and towns recruited neighborhood voices to participate in forums that evaluated whether proposed developments complied with an ever-growing list of regulations. At these venues, community members could offer their neighborly insights on whether or not a project comported with local requirements over wetlands, flood mitigation, traffic management, or parking spaces.

What at first glance seemed an effective way of preventing developers from running roughshod over local communities, however, appears to be yet another case of an institution captured by advantaged and powerful interests. Instead of providing voice to underrepresented residents, planning and zoning board meetings amplify the voices of older, white homeowners. Moreover, because land use regulations govern everything from wetlands to parking, these advantaged neighbors have many opportunities to influence local planning and zoning officials, and to shape the development of new housing. Sometimes these neighbors are able to stop new developments. At a minimum, they are able to delay or extract significant concessions. This process reduces the production of all types of housing units – both market-rate and affordable.

In Chapter 2, we outlined a theory arguing that the intersection of participatory disparities and land use regulations hampers the construction of new housing. One implication of our argument is that, in places with high housing costs, neighborhoods or municipalities with lower levels of participation and more relaxed regulatory environments will see gentrification. We turn now to exploring how land use regulations and participatory institutions may contribute to gentrification, and how gentrification pressures pose a significant obstacle to broad-based housing policy reform.

There is a wide consensus that many cities and towns across the country need more housing. Whether the housing shortage is due to population growth, migration, low rates of new construction, or other causes, the solution is more housing. Civic leaders, YIMBY (Yes in My Backyard) activists, and affordable housing advocates all agree on the need to increase the supply of housing. Here, however, the agreement ends. Some groups, especially those in the YIMBY movement, argue that building more market-rate housing will address both the general housing crisis and the affordable housing shortage, by increasing supply and reducing prices. Neighborhood groups, concerned about affordable housing, argue that building more market-rate housing will not actually address the affordable housing shortages in their communities. They also worry that it might be making the housing crunch worse for many through gentrification, which displaces current residents in some neighborhoods.

## GENTRIFICATION

In Washington, DC, gentrification is so intense – and so disproportionately felt in communities of color – that the city is being sued for policies that a civil rights lawyer claims intentionally displaced low-income, black residents. Lawyer Aristotle Theresa argues that the administrations of former mayors Adrian Fenty and Vincent Gray intentionally sought to attract white Millennials at the expense of current city residents: "These policy documents say outright, we are planning to alter land use in order to attract people who are of a certain age range, in order to attract people who are a certain profession" (Wang 2018). The out-migration of blacks from Washington, DC, has been extraordinary: the city was 71 percent black in 1970, but less than 50 percent in 2018 (Starr 2018).

While gentrification is not universal, it is a widespread challenge in many cities, as working-class neighborhoods and communities of color become prohibitively expensive for longtime residents. Indeed, while more housing is at the core of any solution to the housing crisis, one divisive problem, as obvious as it may seem, is that new housing is, by definition, *new*. Given the lack of undeveloped land in most cities, the housing shortage cannot be solved by replicating the current housing stock. Instead, new housing must replace older, less-dense buildings, and it is an imperfect substitute. While in some cases the increased supply will reduce prices and rents, in many other cases the new housing is part of a different market serving a different population. When dense housing is built in a wealthy suburb where the housing stock is mostly large single-family homes, the new housing might allow less wealthy residents to move in. In contrast, new housing in cities, especially luxury condominiums, creates opportunities for wealthier residents to move into poorer areas, potentially leading to gentrification. Indeed, developers looking to maximize rents or sale prices in high-cost cities will build expensive housing. When affordable housing is built, it is often mixed with new luxury housing to make the full development profitable. New middle-class housing is squeezed out by legal mandates for low-income housing on one end and developers' desire to maximize profits on the other. Moreover, limited mandates hardly provide sufficient affordable, low-income housing to meet exploding demand.

Thus, neighborhood defenders in the suburbs and neighborhood defenders in urban neighborhoods might be taking similar actions for very different purposes. Neighborhood defenders in wealthy communities fight against developments that allow more people – potentially more low- and middle-income people, depending on the nature of the development – access to the high-quality public goods in their communities. Neighborhood defenders in low-income communities facing gentrification contest projects that threaten their displacement from their homes.

Gentrifying communities face a number of structural disadvantages in mounting a successful neighborhood defense. First, they are often more laxly regulated and zoned for higher density housing. Wealthy neighborhoods typically are zoned for lower-density construction. Some are historic areas protected by a multitude of preservation requirements. Many city officials and members of the public prefer to keep them in their current form. *Gawker*'s Hamilton Nolan is emblematic of this viewpoint: "Do you have to bulldoze all of the real pretty San Francisco neighborhoods and build awful glass cubes where beautiful Victorian homes once stood? No. You can build new things in other places" (Capps 2016).

Indeed, research on Los Angeles zoning changes finds that upzoning occurred more frequently where political resistance was most muted; neighborhoods with large numbers of homeowners – especially homeowners with access to valuable amenities – saw little change in land use regulations (Gabbe 2018). This means that, even in low-income communities with a large and highly motivated group of neighborhood defenders, there will be few institutional mechanisms available for them to use in the politics of delay.

| Item delivered | Refund sent |
|---|---|

ce you won't get a refund. The seller's responsible for return shipping charges, so

k the item as sent.

# ong Road

Ensure
NANA
Mandarin
Chiken

Cereal
MILK
Hot cheese

Second, these communities are less likely to have large numbers of high-intensity neighborhood defenders. As we outlined in Chapter 2, disparities in participation based on socioeconomic status are well-documented in political science research (Verba, Schlozman, and Brady 1995; Schlozman, Verba, and Brady 2012). Moreover, the results in Chapter 5 show that participation is higher among white homeowners. While even one motivated neighborhood defender can certainly make a difference – just one person filing a lawsuit can delay a project – larger groups attending meetings are likely to be more persuasive to planning and zoning board officials. On average, we anticipate fewer of these sorts of groups in less advantaged neighborhoods. Indeed, in Chapter 5 we found that participation in planning and zoning board meetings was higher in wealthier communities.

Third, even when neighborhood defenders in gentrifying communities do mobilize, their voices may carry less weight with local officials. Sociologist Jeremy Levine (2017) shows that city leaders in Boston largely ignored residents of color when they invoked community concerns. In previous chapters, we found that advantaged residents were more likely to participate in land use forums, highlighting community concerns in the process – and, seemingly, their views were incorporated into important land use decisions. Even in less advantaged communities – places like Milwaukee, Wisconsin and Worcester, Massachusetts – the voices represented at these meetings were those of the most privileged. In contrast, Levine's in-depth analysis of seventy-six community meetings in Boston shows that not all voices are amplified in planning and zoning board meetings. Even when less advantaged individuals are present at these meetings, their viewpoints are marginalized. This unequal responsiveness is consistent with national-level evidence that political elites are more attentive to the preferences of wealthy constituents (Gilens 2014).

These factors mean that many low-income communities of color in high-demand housing markets receive a disproportionate share of housing development. Economists who favor increasing the supply of market-rate housing largely ignore this spatial inequity. While virtually everyone involved in housing policy agrees that we need to build more housing, those focused on building more *regionally* ignore the fact that this region-wide construction may in fact come with deleterious *neighborhood-level* consequences. Kriston Capps, writing for CityLab, describes this problem:

From a regional perspective, any and every city in a metro area could be building more. Any and every new housing unit adds to the supply and lets out some pressure. But, from a neighborhood perspective, the view is different. Neighborhoods that build less than others are sometimes given a pass because they are beautiful or historic or wealthy or powerful (and often all of those things). The lack of new construction in wealthier neighborhoods puts pressure on less wealthy neighborhoods. ... This pressure builds up until it explodes in distressed neighborhoods. (Capps 2016)

Legal scholar John Mangin explicitly links this spatial inequity with gentrification: "[G]entrification and exclusion are intimately related at the neighborhood level. If a high-demand, high-cost neighborhood won't build, developers and people looking for housing will be diverted to the nearest low-cost neighborhoods. That increases demand and development and leads to gentrification" (Mangin 2014).

By pushing for more housing regionally without considering these disproportionate *neighborhood-level* impacts, much of the housing legislation targeting more relaxed zoning has exposed significant political fissures among housing advocates.

## MARKET RATE VERSUS AFFORDABLE HOUSING

Communities experiencing significant gentrification thus have good reason to feel marginalized in the politics of land use. What's more, many of them are unconvinced that solutions centered on the increased production of market-rate housing *alone* will ease the suffering of low-income residents crowded out by gentrification. One Boston-area affordable housing advocate referred to these supply-side housing policy solutions as "trickle-down" initiatives, and was deeply skeptical that they would work: "That's not the case in our city."

Even if the production of more market-rate housing does improve affordability – a premise that some housing advocates deeply contest – it is easy to see why these perceptions would exist among both residents of gentrifying communities and housing advocates. Imagine living in a community primarily comprised of middle- and low-income residents and people of color – places like the neighborhoods in Washington, DC, that have experienced rapid displacement. Suppose a developer proposes building a ten-unit condominium building with market-rate units. Because of changes in the housing costs in your city (and gentrification pressures in your neighborhood), the cost of those market-rate units places them out of reach for existing neighborhood residents. Instead, they will provide homes to newcomers largely from different income and racial backgrounds than existing residents.

Now imagine that a group of advocates insists that these units will actually improve affordability in your neighborhood. If these units are not approved, they insist, housing prices will go up even more than they already are. From your perspective as a current neighborhood resident, this line of argument may be difficult to swallow. Even a (potential) slight reduction in regional sale and rental prices from what they would have been in the absence of this development will do little to help you and many of your neighbors in the face of exploding citywide and neighborhood housing prices.

As we outlined in Chapter 2, some affordable housing advocates believe that in high-cost cities like San Francisco and Washington, DC, there are two related but separate housing crises. One is a shortage of market-rate housing, creating cost pressures even on fairly affluent renters and home buyers. The second is a dearth of subsidized or affordable housing – reachable for low-income home seekers. While building more market-rate housing could help ease the former crisis, there is less evidence on whether the benefits of redressing market-rate shortages will trickle down to low-income home seekers.

This has created significant fissures between YIMBYs – who fight for the production of *all* new housing – and many affordable housing advocates, who push for strategies involving the production of more publicly subsidized housing via paths like inclusionary zoning and city and state-level affordability requirements and rental protections. One affordable housing advocate we interviewed described the YIMBY movement as a "hornet's nest," noting: "Progressive groups, especially in communities of color, are lining up against it. A lot of people are involved without realizing the negative stuff." These cleavages may create significant obstacles to building coalitions to support legislation targeting the production of more housing generally (or the production of more affordable housing).

## SB 827: CONFLICT BETWEEN YIMBYS AND AFFORDABLE HOUSING ADVOCATES

This sharp divide between YIMBYs, affordable housing advocates, and communities of color is brought into sharp relief by the debate over (and ultimate failure of) proposed housing legislation in California. In 2018, California State Senators Scott Wiener and Nancy Skinner proposed tackling restrictive zoning with Senate Bill 827, which would have required California cities to permit mid-rise apartment construction (buildings up to forty-five to fifty-five feet tall) near train stations and bus stops (Grabar 2018). Since a huge swath of California's cities fell within a "1/2 mile radius of a major transit stop" or a "1/4 mile radius of a stop on a high-quality bus corridor," the bill would have allowed higher-density housing construction in a number of neighborhoods presently composed of single-family housing (Wiener 2018). An analysis from the *Los Angeles Times* found that "190,000 parcels in L.A. neighborhoods zoned for single-family homes are located in the 'transit-rich' areas identified in SB 827." Yeghig L. Keshishian, the spokesman for the LA Department of City Planning, said, "While we are still evaluating the full effects of the bill, close to 50 percent of the city's single-family homes would be impacted under SB 827"(Zahniser, Dillon, and Schleuss 2018). The effects were even starker in San Francisco, where the *Los Angeles Times* found that "almost all" single-family housing would be similarly affected by the bill (Dillon 2018*a*).

### Early Support from YIMBYs

Many academics, urban planners, and YIMBYs expressed early support for SB 827. Marlon Boarnet, the chair of the Department of Urban Planning and Spatial Analysis at USC's Price School of Public Policy, said, "This is a bold vision" (Zahniser, Dillon, and Schleuss 2018). The California Tech Network – a group of one hundred CEOs, co-founders, and technology investors supporting the construction of more housing in California – wrote a letter to Senator Wiener strongly endorsing the bill. They cited the crushing burden California's astronomical housing prices placed on their workers:

We the undersigned California technology leaders wish to voice our support for SB 827. ... The lack of homebuilding in California imperils our ability to hire employees and grow our companies. We recognize that the housing shortage leads to displacement, crushing rent burdens, long commutes, and environmental harm, and we want to be part of the solution. We hope to grow our businesses in California, but it's difficult to recruit and retain employees when they could accept jobs in other states and pay a fraction of California's housing costs. (Calfornia YIMBY Tech Network 2018)

They were joined by several leading environmental groups, including the National Resources Defense Council (NRDC), Climate Resolve, and Environment California. The groups wrote a joint letter of support to Senator Wiener:

The shortage of affordable housing in California is decades in the making. A failure to maximize transit opportunities, and to allow adequate housing – including affordable housing – near those transportation centers, has contributed to displacement, longer commutes, more vehicle miles traveled, increased greenhouse gas emissions, loss of open space, and worsening urban sprawl. In this context, housing development near public transportation can be a key element in achieving California's climate goals, by offering more people the opportunity to use transit for their daily trips. (Climate Resolve, NRDC and Environment California 2018)

At first glance, it appeared as though SB 827 had attracted a powerful group of allies who could usher the bill to success.

### Strange Bedfellows and the Death of SB 827

At the same time, a powerful coalition of seemingly disparate interests lined up in opposition to SB 827. Perhaps most unsurprisingly, homeowners and neighborhood associations in single-family districts – the sorts of neighborhood defenders featured throughout this book – prominently opposed the legislation. The Sherman Oaks Homeowners Association in Los Angeles, for example, met with its state senator and assembly member, and sent formal letters to state senators sitting on the committee analyzing the bill (Sherman Oaks HA 2018).

The Sierra Club – a powerful environmental interest group – joined homeowners' associations in favoring a less aggressive approach to development. In a press release, Lindi von Mutius, the Sierra Club chief of staff, argued:

This bill has the right aim, but the wrong method. We know that some members of the legislature are working to refine the bill to make it less damaging in approach. We hope they are successful because we need more transit-oriented development that is appropriately sited to ensure smart, walkable communities that improve quality of life, reduce pollution, and fight climate change. (Kash 2018)

The Sierra Club expressed concerns about the loss of local control, linking state preemption of zoning laws with a host of other state-level preemption efforts:

At the heart of this bill is what a coalition of labor, good government groups, and a host of others call state-level preemption. These bills strip local governments from the decision-making process. Last year we saw this used in Louisiana and Tennessee in an effort to stop local housing mandates for developers, using the same very blunt instrument – removal of local zoning authority. They have also been applied across blocking local fracking bans, deregulating factory farms, suppressing the minimum wage, and … restricting local elected officials' ability to advocate for public lands protection. (Kash 2018)

In linking state-level preemption of zoning laws in liberal California with conservative-led preemption of progressive causes like raising the minimum wage, the Sierra Club attempted to paint SB 827 as fundamentally contrary to progressive interests.

Moreover, because the bill failed to tackle *affordable* housing explicitly, it also attracted the ire of a diverse coalition of affordable housing advocates. In February 2018, thirty-seven housing and tenant advocacy organizations and transit equity groups from Los Angeles wrote Senator Wiener to oppose the bill. They worried that SB 827 would undermine existing affordability requirements in Los Angeles neighborhoods and generate new housing that is out-of-reach for many existing residents:

[D]ozens of housing, community, labor, transportation, and environmental organizations have collaborated to create policies and plans that create more density around transit while *intentionally* producing deeply affordable units and ensuring local, quality jobs are created as we create a more sustainable city. ... If SB 827 passes, we will lose these incentives for developers to include low-income, very-low income or extremely low-income units in their new buildings near transit. ... If SB 827 passes, we stand to lose out on tens of thousands of affordable homes near transit and we are putting families who depend on rent stabilization at great risk of displacement at a time of severe housing and homelessness crises. (Alliance for Community Transit – Los Angeles 2018)

The Democratic Socialists of America Los Angeles Housing and Homelessness Committee, San Diego Housing and Homelessness Working Group, San Francisco Housing Committee and Climate and Environmental Justice Committee, Long Beach Housing Committee, and Sacramento Housing Committee similarly opposed SB 827 on the grounds that it would intensify gentrification:

We agree that apartment construction in affluent single-family-home neighborhoods would be a step in the right direction, especially if such development were truly affordable to low-income people. But this is not what this bill will accomplish. Instead, SB 827 will result in luxury housing exclusively for the wealthy while displacing and dispossessing the poor and working class. (Democratic Socialists of America Los Angeles 2018)

Some members of this group labeled themselves PHIMBYs: "Public Housing in My Backyard." CityLab described this coalition as "a loose alliance of socialist activists and tenants' rights and affordable housing boosters" who opposed SB 827, "convinced that unleashing market-rate development will not significantly improve the housing situation for low-income people"(Schneider 2018). Coined by Los Angeles

Democratic Socialists of America member Jed Parriott, the PHIMBYs presented their opposition as part of political movement on behalf of low-income and historically marginalized people (Schneider 2018). The PHIMBYs argued that SB 827, as written, would not affect the wealthy cities and towns in California – places where we expect neighborhood defenders to predominate. Rather, its impact, according to many activists, would be most deeply felt in low-income communities of color. Shanti Singh, a member of the Democratic Socialists of America–San Francisco's steering committee said, "If you put race- and class-forward, affirmative zoning and planning into SB-827, you would not see the Marin Counties and the Beverly Hills of the world on the same side as the Boyle Heights [a low-income, gentrifying East Los Angeles neighborhood] (Schneider 2018)." The places least able to mount a neighborhood defense would find themselves receiving the brunt of SB 827's downsides in this account.

Affordable housing advocates did not just express concern over the effects of SB 827; they also felt that the process had excluded their interests – much as the local planning and zoning process has marginalized non-white, non-homeowning community members. Singh complained that YIMBY supporters of SB 827 "do not consult with communities of color. They haven't really tried to work with any tenants rights organizations" (Schneider 2018). According to a *San Francisco Examiner* account, this political exclusion became quite heated: "At a Tuesday rally, YIMBY protestors shouted down people of color at a rally on City Hall steps against Senate Bill 827. .... The voices of black, brown and Asian community members at the rally were drowned out by the young, mostly white pro-housing at any cost group" (Rodriguez 2018). Wing Hoo Leung, the president of the Chinatown-based Community Tenants Association said: "Our members were intimidated by YIMBY. They felt threatened." Shanti Singh, a Democratic Socialists of America member, said of her experience at the rally: "What does it say about you when you're drowning out communities of color talking about their struggles? It was depressing" (Rodriguez 2018).

A combination of steep constituent opposition and a rational interest in preserving legislative power spurred strong opposition among local political elites. Unsurprisingly, wealthy suburbs were vociferously opposed. Palo Alto's mayor Liz Kniss wrote a letter to Senator Wiener on behalf of the city: "The City of Palo Alto is writing to inform you of our 'oppose' position on Senate Bill 827." She argued that the bill would undermine in-progress local efforts to re-zone and encourage development: "SB 827 in its current form could diminish local acceptance of residential development and undermine our local efforts"(City of Palo Alto 2018). The Beverly Hills City Council similarly voted unanimously against SB 827 (Talbot 2018).

In Los Angeles, the city council also voted unanimously to oppose the bill (Islas 2018). Opponents included many councilmembers with progressive and pro-housing leanings. Councilmember Mike Bonin argued: "This is a bad bill. ... This bill was inevitable because our current system is, in some ways, as bad as this bill. Our current system does not protect against gentrification and displacement. Our current system is also not providing the affordable housing that we need for our next generation, for our children and for the people who are moving here." He went on to note: "We can't freeze our city in amber and pretend we don't need more housing. But we also can't blow up our neighborhoods and bury it beneath the Sacramento overreach that is at the heart of this bill"(Islas 2018). Councilmember Joe Buscaino used the now familiar critique of the bill as "too blunt a tool" to solve California's housing crisis. He argued that it was the equivalent of surgeon using a "chainsaw" rather than a scalpel (Islas 2018). San Francisco's Board of Supervisors followed suit, voting 8-3 to oppose SB 827 one week after the Los Angeles City Council's unanimous vote (Sabatini 2018).

Opposition from Los Angeles politicians, in particular, may have proved pivotal in killing SB 827. Randy Shaw, the editor of Beyond Chron and Director of San Francisco's Tenderloin Housing Clinic, wrote:

The California Legislature is not going to pass a land use bill unanimously opposed by the Los Angeles City Council and the city's mayor. Period. I told backers of the bill over two months ago that SB 827 was dead unless they could get Mayor Garcetti [the mayor of Los Angeles] or Los Angeles state legislators on board; that never happened. Wiener needed a Los-Angeles-based co-sponsor from the start. He need a strong ally who Los Angeles unions, community organizations, and tenant groups could trust. This also never happened. (Shaw 2018)

More generally, Wiener's failure to acknowledge gentrification pressures and obtain backing from a broad-based group of affordable housing interests – in addition to his firm base of YIMBY supporters – doomed the bill from the start. Shaw argues that his failure to build a broad coalition reinforced already existing distrust of Scott Wiener. Shaw notes: "Scott Wiener was elected to the Board of Supervisors in 2010 with strong realtor and landlord support. He used that support in 2016 to win a close race against Jane Kim for State Senate. Wiener has been consistently opposed by San Francisco tenant groups, and his record on the Board strongly served real estate interests"(Shaw 2018).

## BUILDING COALITIONS AND A NEW PARTICIPATORY POLITICS

As policy makers consider potential solutions to the participatory inequalities – and the consequent undersupply of housing – outlined in this book, SB 827 offers a number of lessons about how to construct a coalition to support the construction of more housing. Perhaps most importantly, political actors should acknowledge that the production of market rate and affordable housing are distinct policy goals. Building more market-rate housing will not necessarily help those at the bottom of the income distribution – who are often those most affected by sky-rocketing housing prices. Los Angeles City Councilmember José Huizar objected to SB 827 because it offered too much to developers without incentivizing affordable housing: "The affordable housing component should have been the driving force for this." According to StreetsBlogLA:

> Huizar reiterated that the status quo was not desirable . . . and he worried that the process by which the city is updating its community plans would simply continue to be a mechanism by which wealthy communities would protect themselves from future growth and force housing, especially affordable housing, *into communities that have historically taken on most of the burden.* (Islas 2018, emphasis added)

Low-income individuals not only find themselves increasingly unable to afford increasingly expensive housing; they also disproportionately assume the burden of out-of-reach market-rate housing construction in their neighborhoods.

YIMBYs and their allies cannot pretend that building more housing of all types – without affordability requirements – will help everyone. At its most extreme, the construction of multimillion dollar luxury condominiums in the city of Boston may not appreciably relieve low-income residents in the city's poorest neighborhoods of rising costs (Anenberg and Kung 2018). Even if the construction of these new units marginally reduces demand – and therefore prices – in the high-end segments of the market, it is politically quite difficult to make the case that the construction of these ultra-expensive housing units will help the most downtrodden parts of the city.

What's more, policy makers must acknowledge that the participatory process has marginalized communities of color and low-income neighborhoods that may already feel as if they are bearing the brunt of new housing construction. Individuals who already feel marginalized by the process – and believe that developer interests, not community interests, are most important to city governments – are unlikely to trust a policy like SB 827 to help their community. Rather, they might fear a policy like SB 827 is essentially another giveaway to developers.

Instead, programs that deliberately target expensive communities may be more politically palatable. Chapter 40B in Massachusetts – which has been featured in previous portions of this book – is one such example. Unlike SB 827, Chapter 40B uses city and town affordability – not proximity to transit – as the criteria for whether or not to exempt developments from local zoning rules. One affordable housing advocate believed this distinction was critical: "Most of us feel that it's been a good thing for the state. ... It doesn't affect Boston [which is above the qualifying affordable housing threshold]. It gives developers a lot of power, but that's a different dynamic in Weston [one of the wealthiest towns in Greater Boston] than it is in Roxbury [one of the poorest neighborhoods in Boston]." Applied to California, such a policy would likely put affluent communities like Beverly Hills in the bull's-eye, while still allowing local land use regulations to protect low-income neighborhoods of Los Angeles.

Indeed, Chapter 40B has been somewhat effective at encouraging the permitting of additional multifamily housing in Massachusetts (Schuetz 2009). That said, it is not enough. As we showed in Chapter 6, affordable housing proposed under Chapter 40B has still been stopped, delayed, or reduced by neighborhood defenders, and the threat of opposition prevents developers from proposing Chapter 40B housing in some towns. Furthermore, the amount of affordable housing in Massachusetts remains far too low. That said, Chapter 40B has several advantages over other policies designed to bypass local control; it explicitly focuses on affordability and targets the communities with the least existing affordable housing.

Moreover, a process that deliberately includes and considers the views of groups with a stake in the housing crisis will likely prove more politically durable and impactful. One of the chief obstacles to SB 827's passage was its failure to appeal to natural anti-NIMBY constituencies supportive of housing production. Of course, this is easier said than done; tenant groups and YIMBYs, for example, do not necessarily share the same goals. As Randy Shaw notes: "Tenant groups prioritize keeping existing tenants in place. YIMBYs prioritize expanding the housing supply to meet rising population and jobs growth" (Shaw 2018).

## Encouraging Representative Participation

Policies that themselves promote inclusion in the housing participation process may be particularly appealing to the diverse set of groups interested in housing policy. Many groups might be interested in improving attendance at local government meetings. Meetings might, for example, be held at more convenient times to attract a broader subset of the population. Or, city outreach might target *all* neighbors, not just property-owners. In many locations, cities and states require developers to notify "abutters," "adjacent landowners," "adjoining landowners," or "contiguous property owners" located within a certain geographic radius of a proposed development.

All of these legal definitions privilege the status of property ownership; these are not requirements to notify all people living nearby, but all landowners proximal to a proposed project. California, for example, defines "landowner" as "a private person or entity that lawfully holds any possessory interest in real property, and does not include a city, county, city and county, district, corporation, or other political subdivision, public body, or public agency" (State of California 1872). Massachusetts similarly defines abutters in terms of property ownership and instructs developers to use property tax lists from local assessors to locate mailing addresses for property owners:

Any person filing a notice of intention with a conservation commission shall at the same time give written notification thereof, by delivery in hand or certified mail, return receipt requested, to all abutters within one-hundred feet of the property line of the land where the activity is proposed, at the mailing addresses shown on the most recent applicable tax list of the assessors, including, but not limited to, owners of land directly opposite said proposed activity on any public or private street or way, and in another municipality or across a body of water. (State of Massachusetts 1872)

Renters are *not* a part of the abutter or landowner notification process.

As we noted in Chapter 2, recruitment increases political participation. Through recruitment, community members learn about political proceedings of which they may not have been aware. Moreover, they may be more likely to believe that their participation is efficacious if they are expressly asked to participate. Changing notification requirements might help to attract a more representative neighborhood slice.

Such an initiative has the benefit of being both politically attractive and likely inducing a modest increase in the representativeness of public hearing processes. That said, the evidence we presented in Chapters 5 and 6 suggests that, regardless of recruitment procedures, public meetings will likely remain disproportionately comprised of opponents to new development. Changing notification requirements is unlikely to increase the proportion of housing supporters from 15 percent – its current level – to a majority pro-housing coalition. The concentrated costs and diffuse benefits of housing development will probably still incentivize participation from opponents far more than supporters. Moreover, it is not reasonable to expect individuals for whom the benefits of new housing will be diffuse (or indeed, even committed activists) to attend multiple two-plus hour meetings every time a new housing development is proposed in their jurisdiction.

Even the most ambitious efforts at boosting political participation have failed to produce the kinds of results that would meaningfully alter the oppositional tilt of planning and zoning board meetings. Numerous studies have used field experiments to measure the effects of Get Out the Vote (GOTV) techniques (Gerber, Green, and Larimer 2008; Enos, Fowler, and Vavreck 2014). While some of these interventions have produced impressive increases in voter turnout – one boosted turnout by eight percentage points (Gerber, Green, and Larimer 2008) – it is not clear that this higher turnout reduces participatory inequalities. Political scientists Ryan Enos, Anthony Fowler, and Lynn Vavreck (2014) find that GOTV operations generally increase turnout, but two-thirds of the ones they studied *increased* participatory inequalities by turning out individuals already over-represented in politics. GOTV operations yield the worst participatory disparities in low-salience elections. Local elections are low turnout affairs (Hajnal 2010; Oliver, Ha, and Callen 2012; Trounstine 2013; Anzia 2014) that hinge on a relatively limited set of local government responsibilities (Oliver, Ha, and Callen 2012) and are vulnerable to interest group capture (Anzia 2014). Interventions designed to boost turnout at planning and zoning board meetings, then, could just as easily prove motivating to neighborhood defenders, worsening the already sizable representational disparities at these land use forums. Opponents currently dominate supporters of new housing by a margin of fifty percentage points at planning and zoning board meetings. It is unlikely that interventions solely targeting turnout will make a meaningful dent in such a potent oppositional tilt.

## Encouraging Participation from Pro-Housing Interest Groups

The concentrated costs and diffuse benefits of housing developments create powerful obstacles to the creation of a mass pro-housing coalition. But, there are still interest groups on the pro-housing side that might be activated to attend meetings and lobby their local zoning and planning boards. Indeed, a variety of groups profit from a more pro-growth local government (Logan and Molotch 1987). Developers and realtors, for example, stand to reap enormous profits from the construction of more housing. Construction workers (and the unions that represent them) similarly might benefit from the jobs these projects create.

These individuals have the incentive to show up, unlike the members of the mass public who more diffusely benefit from the construction of new housing. Moreover, at least some subsets of these real estate interests may be publicly sympathetic and persuasive. Take the example of this Cambridge union representative:

I'm a business representative for Carpenter's Local 40 in Cambridge at 10 Holworthy Street, and I have the privilege of speaking for over 40 men and women who are lifelong residents of Cambridge, who are in support of this project because of the work opportunities it will provide, but also because the nature of Cambridge, the commitment to affordability will allow them to stay here and live in the same communities with their families.

While he and his workers clearly benefit financially from this project, their motivations are likely seen as more sympathetic and deserving of concern than the developer's profits. In the union representative's words, they are simply community members seeking to earn reasonable livelihoods and maintain local affordability for families.

Despite their incentives and potential influence, these real estate interests are only sporadically represented at these land use forums. While the developer whose proposal is being reviewed always speaks, we seldom found examples of *other* developers showing up in support of a proposal. Realtors and union representatives are also infrequently featured at these forums. These interests, of course, likely have other avenues for exerting power over local political outcomes. They may, for example, have more direct access to zoning and planning board representatives or elected local officials. Still, the fact remains that one group that might be most plausibly motivated to attend a lengthy public meeting on land use is largely absent from these highly influential forums. One remedy, then, to the oppositional bias of public meetings might be to actively recruit real estate interests – especially construction workers – to these land use meetings.

Of course, this possibility, too, comes with a number of potential obstacles. Perhaps most importantly, there are serious normative trade-offs that must be weighed when encouraging greater real estate interest group involvement. As we have noted at various points throughout this book, a local politics in which real estate interests predominate will not necessarily – or even likely – yield more just outcomes. The wholesale destruction of low-income and middle-income communities – especially communities of color – during urban renewal and the gentrification of urban neighborhoods today illustrates what happens when market forces run rampant without any government-imposed commitment to housing affordability. The capture of institutions of direct democracy by interest groups is not on its face a better version of democracy (Gerber 1999).[1]

What's more, an unchecked pro-growth orientation comes with serious environmental concerns (Lubbell, Feiock, and Ramirez 2005, 2009; Mullin 2009). There are many locations in the United States where insufficient water or vulnerability to floods may make managed, highly regulated growth the most environmentally sensible and sustainable option. Allowing short-term real estate interests to drive land use decisions at the expense of the long-term environmental viability of a community is also obviously problematic.

Finally, the incentives for real estate interests to attend these meetings may not be as substantial as they seem at first glance. Zoning and planning boards review proposals on a project-by-project basis. While we should expect the real estate community to come out in droves for a city-wide rezoning discussion, there is no particular financial incentive for one developer to attend another developer's zoning board meeting in support of his development. Similarly, unless a particular construction union has been guaranteed jobs as part of an ongoing housing proposal, workers do not know whether a particular project will directly benefit them – in

---

[1] Gerber (1999) shows that advantaged economic groups primarily exercise their outsized influence in direct democracy by blocking – rather than proposing – ballot initiatives. In this way, they are analogous to the neighborhood defenders in our account who similarly exercise power via obstruction.

the same way that prospective home seekers cannot know whether they might acquire housing at a specific proposed housing development.

Developers and realtors are also not monolithic interests. Large developers, for example, may actually benefit from a more complicated regulatory structure that prices out smaller operations. Some realtors may favor a higher volume of sales, while others may actually prefer a tight real estate stock featuring many bidding wars and fast sales. Thus, even among more specialized interests, there may not be a pro-housing coalition that can be reliably mobilized to attend frequent planning and zoning board meetings.

A nonprofit coalition might be normatively more appealing than one centered on a profit-oriented, pro-growth orientation. Nonprofits and Community Development Corporations are critical players in the production of affordable housing, and have, in many communities, stepped in to produce subsidized housing in the face of federal government retrenchment in this arena (Berry, Portney, and Thomson 1993; Goetz 1993). The presence and efficacy of these interests, however, varies enormously from community to community (Berry, Portney, and Thomson 1993). What's more, these organizations operate under enormous fiscal constraints; with tight budgets and staffing, their capacity to organize may be limited. Asking these already overburdened organizations to take on the task of assembling a pro-housing coalition at every two to three hour planning and zoning board hearing is a tall order. This may be feasible for some larger, high-salience developments, but it is hard to imagine mobilizing such a group for meetings on the more modest projects that comprise so much of the housing production in many communities.

## MEETING REFORMS

What, then, given the current structure of neighborhood meetings might be more effective avenues of reform? The next two sections explore two sets of policies: The first centers on reforming meetings, while preserving neighborhood-based decision-making. The second more radically considers making land use proceedings city-level affairs.

Our research suggests that ameliorating the oppositional bias of meeting attendees will be difficult, at best. But, just because community members are engaged in the politics of neighborhood defense does not mean that zoning and planning board officials need to disproportionately incorporate these critiques in their final decisions. In the meetings we studied, zoning and planning board officials often handed down decisions immediately after deliberating over public comment. What if, instead, like judges, they waited some set period of time – perhaps one day or one week so as not impose massive delays – before issuing a decision on a proposed housing development? A waiting period would allow board officials to more fully incorporate the full body of evidence – including city staff review of proposed developments – rather than overly weigh the critiques from neighborhood defenders that are more recent in their minds. Social psychological research on the availability heuristic shows that we overvalue and overuse information that we can immediately recall. This leads recently acquired information – which is easier to remember – to play more prominently in decision-making (Tversky and Kahneman 1973). With neighborhood defenders' critiques most immediately available, it is unsurprising that many of the land use officials we studied asked for more studies or outright denied projects after hearing from concerned neighbors – and frequently cited those neighborhood defenders in issuing their decision.

Moreover, zoning and planning officials could set clear requirements on what will be required of developers in advance of public meetings, and then stick with those requirements in the face of vociferous neighborhood opposition. For example, local officials might clearly lay out in advance which studies developers are required to complete and the standards by which the studies will be evaluated. Neighborhood defenders then cannot – as in the current system – demand more studies once these requirements have been satisfied.

This procedure has analogues in the movement towards preregistration in research science. This push stemmed from the failure of prominent studies in many fields to replicate in followup studies. The culprit – at least in many cases – was not malicious researcher intent or fraud. Rather, it appears as though researchers' quest to find (and publish) statistically significant results is to blame (Ioannidis 2005; Simmons, Nelson, and Simonsohn 2011). Psychology researchers Joseph Simmons, Leif Nelson, and Uri Simonsohn describe the problem: "After much discussion, our best guess was that so many published findings were false because researchers were conducting many analyses on the same data set and just reporting those that were statistically significant"(Kupferschmidt 2018). Researchers were *p-hacking* – conducting exploratory analyses until they found statistically significant (and therefore publishable) results. Such analyses violated key statistical assumptions, and led to the reporting of false positives, in which authors unveiled statistically significant relationships that do not exist in actuality.

By asking for repeat studies when the initial ones do not support their beliefs, neighborhood defenders are essentially engaging in p-hacking. They are demanding additional exploratory analyses until they find one that backs their desire to delay or block a development. This not only adds costs and delays to housing construction; it also means that cities and towns may base important decisions off of invalid studies. Statistically, if a developer is forced to run a traffic study often enough, one will yield the results that bolster neighborhood defenders' claims – even if the neighborhood does not have noteworthy traffic problems. The same applies in the other direction.

Instead, we advocate for a system in which cities and towns clearly define what evidence is required to evaluate a proposed housing development. The Center for Open Science outlines the benefits of predefining analytic procedures:

When you preregister your research, you're simply specifying to your plan in advance, before you gather data. Preregistration separates hypothesis-generating (exploratory) from hypothesis-testing (confirmatory) research. Both are important. But the same data cannot be used to generate and test a hypothesis, which can happen unintentionally and reduce the credibility of your results. Addressing this problem through planning improves the quality and transparency of your research, helping others who may wish to build on it. (Center for Open Science 2018)

As in the research world, cities and towns should show developers and neighborhood defenders alike what studies will be required *in advance of any meeting*. In this approach, the board would spell out in advance the standards and criteria for a legitimate study that it would accept as definitive. Such a procedure would not only stop neighborhood defenders from demanding studies until they obtained the results they desired; it would also prevent the developer from cherry-picking evidence in support of his project. Moreover, it would prevent local officials from falling prey to the temptation to call for additional studies as a sort of sensible compromise between developers and obstructionist neighbors.

## City- and Town-Level Reforms

The neighborhood-level, project-by-project basis on which housing developments are reviewed makes marshaling a pro-housing coalition challenging. There are few individuals and groups that have the resources and incentives to attend these meetings at a scale that will meaningfully reshape the supply of housing. One more radical proposal, then, might be to change the level of government at which key housing decisions are made. Rather than recruiting and empowering neighborhoods, local governments could instead focus their efforts on city-level proposals to modify their zoning – and then allow developers to build up to the limits of existing zoning with more limited public review.

Minneapolis's 2040 comprehensive plan illustrates the possibilities of city-level reform. In December 2018, the City Council voted resoundingly (12-1) in support of the city's 2040 comprehensive plan. Perhaps most strikingly, the plan abolishes single-family zoning, allowing duplexes and triplexes in all residential areas, including those presently zoned exclusively for single-family homes. The scope of the policy is vast, with more than half of Minneapolis zoned for single-family housing at the time of the land use reform. Housing advocates across the country have eagerly sought advice on how to promulgate Minneapolis's reforms. Tina Kotek, Oregon's Speaker of the House, said, "When Minneapolis took the bold step to address their crisis, it created a sense of momentum. Minneapolis made it clear that the conversation was about addressing historical exclusion and took a big step toward building inclusive communities. That conversation resonates across the United States and it resonates in Oregon" (Mannix 2019).

Importantly, the city-level plan succeeded despite ardent opposition from single-family neighborhoods. As one *Minneapolis Star Tribune* account put it, "Defenders of single-family neighborhoods dominated the thousands of online comments submitted to other city." In response, the plan evolved, allowing triplexes instead of fourplexes on single-family lots. Moreover, pro-density advocates helped bolster the plan as part of the Neighbors for More Neighbors Campaign. Janne K. Filsrand, a volunteer for campaign, said after the successful city council vote, "We as a city recognize that we have challenges that we have failed to address for decades. We ... are committed to doing the work that we need to do, even when it's hard, even if we can't always agree on how we need to do that work" (Otárola 2018). While it remains to be seen how replicable the Minneapolis organizing strategy is elsewhere, the city shows that city-level organizing *can* yield sweeping land use reform.

Shifting the locus of policy-making authority to the city level comes with important tradeoffs. A number of urban politics studies have assessed this question through the lens of at-large and neighborhood-level city council elections. The general consensus has been that institutions channeling neighborhood-level influence enhance minority interests, while at-large, city-level elections respond more to majority preferences

(Meier et al. 2005; Mullin 2009).[2] Political scientists Jessica Trounstine and Melody Valdini (2008) suggest that the extent to which these institutions enhance minority interests is dependent on context. Minority interests must be both substantial and spatially concentrated in order to be amplified by neighborhood-level representation.[3]

The desirability of ensuring minority influence over the policy-making process is context dependent. If the minority in question is a historically disadvantaged group, we might feel considerable enthusiasm about using political institutions to enhance minority interests (Guinier 1994). In contrast, if such institutions allow a historically advantaged minority to hoard resources, support for institutional protections of minority interests likely wanes. Our analysis of neighborhood-level participatory institutions suggests that, in the case of land use politics, the balance of power is tilted in favor of entrenched, advantaged interests. It may therefore make sense to at least consider city-level political processes as potentially more representative of broader community interests.

Our analysis of meeting minutes data suggests that, at a minimum, city- and town-level conversations about zoning are considerably more likely to attract supporters of multifamily housing. In Chapters 5 and 6, we featured data on participants in planning and zoning board meeting minutes about specific housing development proposals. We also collected analogous data for the same cities and towns about participants in meetings surrounding city- and town-level *zoning proposals* centered on the construction of multifamily housing. These meetings encompassed a wide array of topics, including changes to the Master Plan, the introduction of mixed-use zoning (allowing commercial and residential development to occur in the same neighborhoods and buildings), and changes to parking bylaws, among other things. Because there were many fewer zoning proposals than specific housing developments over the three-year period we studied, these data only feature 374 meeting participants.

[2] The extent of this relationship varies by context and racial and ethnic group (Welch 1990). Moreover, while the bulk of research suggests that neighborhood-level elections favor concentrated interests, Welch and Bledsoe (1988) find that at-large elections provide more voice to middle-class and wealthy interests relative to neighborhood-level participation.
[3] Trounstine and Valdini (2008) also show that these effects differ by gender and race of the candidate: at-large districts boost the representation of white women, while neighborhood-level districts increase the proportion of black men in city councils. Candidates of other races and genders do not appear to be affected by city-level institutions.

As with our analyses in Chapters 5 and 6, we coded whether participants supported or opposed proposed zoning changes that would allow for higher density. We find *much* higher levels of support for town-level proposals that would increase density in the community than for specific projects. While a mere 15 percent of planning and zoning board meeting attendees showed up in support of specific housing developments, a striking 39 percent of meeting participants endorsed zoning changes that would permit greater density – a gap of more than twenty-five percentage points. Perhaps unsurprisingly, when people are asked to consider density in the abstract, they appear considerably more supportive than when contemplating specific housing developments in their own neighborhoods.

Importantly, though, even town-level mobilization has its limitations. While 39 percent is certainly higher than 15 percent, it still represents a minority of meeting participants. In other words, even city- and town-level zoning proposals that would permit more multifamily housing fail to attract majority support in public meetings.

Moreover, framing public conversations around city-level zoning may work well in communities where mass public opinion supports the construction of new housing. But, in places where the public as a whole is concerned about development – even projects far from their own backyards – town-level zoning changes may provoke considerable consternation. In a town like Ashland, Massachusetts – where community members were willing to support a multi-million-dollar ballot referendum to stop one development – such proposals would likely fall flat.

In addition, city-level politics are potentially more vulnerable to developer capture. Classic urban politics abounds with accounts of business domination of political regimes, with the interests of marginalized neighborhoods largely overlooked (Logan and Molotch 1987; Stone 1989). While the dominance and role of business-led coalitions has historically evolved (Altshuler and Luberoff 2003), private real estate interests remain highly influential, especially when neighborhood voices are more institutionally muted.

What's more, similar to project-by-project proposals, city-level land use reform may also be stymied by institutional veto points. As of this writing, zoning changes in the Massachusetts communities central to this book require a super majority of two-thirds of the city or town's legislative body. At present, a bipartisan coalition of Massachusetts lawmakers is seeking to reform this and other aspects of state zoning law. In December 2017, Republican Governor Charlie Baker submitted Bill H.4075,

"An Act to Promote Housing Choices," to the Massachusetts House of Representatives, noting, "When a majority of a city or town legislative body wants to adopt zoning that will encourage housing production, state law should not stand in the way. I urge your prompt enactment of this legislation" (Governor Charlie Baker 2017). While Massachusetts is somewhat unusual in imposing this supermajority requirement, it is not alone. In Texas, for example, cities are permitted by state law to require a supermajority of the city council to "overrule a recommendation of the zoning commission that a proposed change to a regulation or boundary be denied"(American Planning Association Texas Chapter 2013). Other states similarly allow local governments to impose supermajority requirements at their discretion.

Finally, moving conversations about housing to the city-level misses the fact that housing shortages are usually *regional* problems. In the Boston region that has comprised much of the empirical basis of this book, the city of Boston has joined with 14 other surrounding inner core suburbs to commit to building 185,000 new housing units by 2030 (Logan 2018). These communities contend that one or two regional cities cannot shoulder the burdens of the housing crisis alone. Somerville, Massachusetts, Mayor Joseph Curtatone summarizes the challenge:

Our region is in the midst of housing emergency. It is a crisis of housing affordability and availability that has deep and disastrous impacts on individuals and families. And it is not contained by municipal boundaries it is a problem of such scale and scope that it demands cities, towns, and the state come together to develop bold regional solutions. That is our charge, and I'm encouraged to be announcing a regional goal as the result of our first phase of work. But this first phase is only a beginning. It is incumbent on us all to continue our work and implement actionable plans to achieve this goal. (Harmon 2018)

This kind of regional commitment – across advantaged and disadvantaged communities – is critical; when we concentrate a disproportionate share of the housing development in disadvantaged urban neighborhoods, we contribute to gentrification and displacement. What's more, we deny families access to the high quality public goods that are disproportionately located in America's highly zoned suburbs (Trounstine 2018).

### Federal Government Retrenchment

The limitations of these local solutions suggest that higher levels of government may be better suited to addressing the needs of low-income home seekers. Indeed, in his seminal work, political scientist Paul Peterson (1981) argues that, because they are highly constrained by competition from surrounding local governments and the regulatory powers of higher levels of government, local governments are ill-suited to promulgating redistributive programs like affordable housing. Instead, he makes the case that the federal government is better equipped to implement these sorts of policies. Political scientist Edward Goetz (1993; 2013) forcefully argues that local governments cannot make up for federal retrenchment in housing spending.

Indeed, publicly subsidized housing has been the subject of decades of cutbacks at the federal level (Goetz 1993; Dreier, Mollenkopf, and Swanstrom 2004; Goetz 2013). During the Reagan administration, the federal government withheld capital funds responsible for the rehabilitation, modernization, and day-to-day maintenance of public housing from many public housing authorities. A report from the Urban Institute described the horrifying consequences: "By the end of the 1980s, many housing agencies were coping with aging properties that had dangerous problems like broken elevators, malfunctioning incinerators, mold, and leaking pipes that spewed raw sewage"(Popkin 2017). The federal government could scarcely maintain its existing subsidized housing stock, let alone expand the supply to meet need.

The challenges facing public housing have not lessened in the intervening decades. The Department of Housing and Urban Development has experienced sharp declines in funding; between 2001 and 2013, public housing capital funding fell from $3 billion to $1.78 billion (Cohen 2014). HUD's most recent Capital Needs Assessment (in 2010) estimated that the backlog of public housing capital need stood at $26 billion. The most recent Trump administration budget – which proposed eliminating this fund altogether (Booker 2018) – would dramatically worsen this shortfall.

Local government leaders are deeply concerned about these cutbacks. In the 2017 Menino Survey of Mayors, we asked a nationally representative sample of cities with more than seventy-five thousand inhabitants what they believed the chief obstacles were to improving access to housing across several groups. Fifty percent of mayors cited the lack of state or federal funds as one of the two biggest obstacles to improving access to housing for low-income families. Thirty-eight percent said that these cutbacks would similarly hamper efforts to improve access for elderly and disabled residents. Without dramatic infusions of state and federal aid, local leaders feel ill-equipped to reach housing policy goals that might help to alleviate the housing crisis, including increasing the availability of multi-bedroom units, increasing homeownership rates, and modernizing and replacing older housing stock (Einstein, Glick, and Palmer 2018). In short, fully addressing community housing needs – especially for low-income residents – is impossible without substantial policy interventions from higher levels of government.

Federal reinvestment in housing must be accompanied by land use reform. Indeed, without such reform, neighborhood defenders will continue to be able to stymie the construction of affordable and market-rate housing alike. Substantial government interventions in the housing market – such as public housing and Low Income Housing Tax Credits – are hindered by these privileged neighbors (Harrison and Kraemer 2019). Land use reform *alone* cannot solve the nation's housing crisis. Rather, it should serve as the first step in a multipronged progressive housing agenda.

## Facing the Housing Crisis

Facing staunch local opposition at planning and zoning board meetings and little support from the federal government, even the most affordability-minded local leaders face formidable obstacles in enacting progressive housing policies. Addressing this housing crisis requires a multi-pronged approach. Local governments must reform how they regulate the construction of housing and how they incorporate public input. Importantly, they should accompany these changes with careful consideration of how to ensure the production of *affordable* housing; producing more market-rate housing alone will not help all of those suffering the ill consequences of the housing crisis. While these changes would likely yield substantial improvements in the production of market-rate housing, local governments are probably more limited in their capacity to make significant headway on affordability challenges on their own. State and federal governments must step in as partners alongside local governments to address the inability of a wide swath of the American population to access safe and affordable housing.

We need housing. However, the conversation over what gets built, where it gets built, and how it addresses not just the housing crisis, but the severe shortage of affordable housing, is far from complete. In some communities, neighborhood defenders have stopped the conversation by preventing new housing, but in doing so they are pushing the costs of development to other communities. In other places, underprivileged voices are not heard in this conversation. In these localities, new housing is being built, but it does not serve the needs of many in the community who need help. New housing will necessarily cause communities to change. The ability of some communities to resist such change, keeping out density, traffic, or less wealthy residents, and maintaining "neighborhood character," represents tremendous privilege, and pushes the necessary housing to less privileged places, creating gentrification and displacement. Addressing the housing crisis requires more than changes to zoning regulations; successful policy solutions must recognize the participatory politics of housing and the ways that citizens and bureaucrats shape the development process.

# A

# Appendix to Chapter 3

TABLE A.I *Regressions of zoning regulations on permitted buildings*

| Regulation type | MF units share | MF bldgs share | MF units number | MF bldgs number | MF units logged | MF bldgs logged |
|---|---|---|---|---|---|---|
| All regulations | -0.009** (0.002) | -0.005** (0.001) | -16.061** (4.656) | -0.979** (0.376) | -0.029 (0.018) | -0.026* (0.012) |
| Cluster regulations | -0.024 (0.015) | -0.02** (0.007) | -47.788 (31.281) | -3.208 (2.497) | 0.042 (0.121) | -0.006 (0.081) |
| Growth regulations | -0.052** (0.013) | -0.016* (0.007) | -74.005* (28.54) | -3.667 (2.3) | -0.334** (0.109) | -0.166* (0.074) |
| Inclusionary regulations | -0.001 (0.021) | -0.005 (0.01) | -23.065 (43.352) | -1.889 (3.455) | 0.185 (0.166) | 0.078 (0.111) |
| Multifamily regulations | -0.066** (0.013) | -0.032** (0.006) | -124.124** (27.097) | -9.211** (2.176) | -0.465** (0.104) | -0.345** (0.069) |
| Parcel shape regulations | -0.06** (0.011) | -0.032** (0.005) | -109.205** (23.741) | -8.084** (1.907) | -0.328** (0.093) | -0.241** (0.062) |
| Senior housing regulations | -0.052* (0.026) | -0.036** (0.012) | -70.733 (54.504) | -6.841 (4.334) | -0.072 (0.21) | -0.058 (0.141) |
| Septic regulations | -0.031** (0.009) | -0.017** (0.004) | -54.401** (18.053) | -4.313** (1.439) | -0.129 (0.07) | -0.127** (0.047) |
| Subdivision regulations | 0.012 (0.014) | -0.002 (0.007) | -2.589 (29.06) | 1.729 (2.313) | 0.162 (0.111) | 0.118 (0.074) |
| Wetlands regulations | -0.002 (0.004) | -0.002 (0.002) | -2.571 (8.376) | 0.219 (0.667) | 0.019 (0.032) | 0.005 (0.022) |

Each row and column corresponds to a separate OLS regression. For all regressions, N = 187 Massachusetts cities and towns. Dependent variables are based on the units permitted by building type in each town from 2000 to 2015. The first two models use the share of multifamily units and multifamily housing buildings, respectively. The third and fourth models use the actual number of multifamily units and buildings, and the fifth and sixth models use the logged number of multifamily units and buildings. Independent variables are defined as the number of regulations of each type in the LHRD.

## CHURCH REDEVELOPMENT APPENDIX

### Where Church Properties Were Sold

In Table A.2, we estimate the number of churches sold in a town as a function of the following town level traits, all standardized to be centered at zero: (1) number of parishes (church presence), (2) distance from Boston, (3) median household income, (4) support for the 40B affordable housing referendum in 2010,[1] (5) the existing number of housing units, and (6) measures of land use regulation. Only the underlying church presence affects the number of churches sold in a town. There is no consistent relationship between the other variables – most notably, land use regulations.

TABLE A.2 *Binomial regressions of church property sales by town by regulations, church presence, and other town-level variables (all standardized)*

|  | All regs | Multifamily regs | All other regs |
| --- | --- | --- | --- |
| Church presence | 0.286* | 0.305* | 0.274* |
|  | (0.130) | (0.123) | (0.133) |
| Distance from Boston (miles) | 0.045 | 0.016 | 0.053 |
|  | (0.110) | (0.095) | (0.111) |
| Median HH income 2000 (k) | −0.200 | −0.231* | −0.195 |
|  | (0.126) | (0.116) | (0.124) |
| Support for housing referendum | 0.064 | 0.089 | 0.060 |
|  | (0.108) | (0.102) | (0.107) |
| Housing units 2000 | 0.294 | 0.284 | 0.305 |
|  | (0.153) | (0.153) | (0.156) |
| All regulations | −0.065 |  |  |
|  | (0.145) |  |  |
| Multifamily regulations |  | 0.017 |  |
|  |  | (0.110) |  |
| All other regulations |  |  | −0.080 |
|  |  |  | (0.141) |
| Observations | 135 | 135 | 135 |

Standard errors in parentheses
**p < 0.01, *p < 0.05

[1] We explore Chapter 40B in greater depth in Chapter 5.

## Which Church Properties Were Redeveloped?

We estimate two logistic regression models investigating church property redevelopment in Table A.3. In Model 1 the dependent variable is whether the parcel was redeveloped into anything (housing, office space, retail). In Model 2 the dependent variable is whether the parcel was redeveloped into *housing*.[2] The table shows that there is no substantial or significant relationship between land use regulations and whether a parcel is redeveloped. The biggest effect is that of the lot size. The largest lots were less likely to be redeveloped.[3]

TABLE A.3 *Logistic regression models estimating the effects of regulations on a property being redeveloped and being redeveloped into housing (all variables standardized)*

|  | Church redeveloped? | Becomes residential |
|---|---|---|
| Count: All regulations | 0.088 | −0.085 |
|  | (0.491) | (0.333) |
| Distance from Boston (miles) | 0.052 | −0.164 |
|  | (0.297) | (0.194) |
| Support for housing referendum | −0.175 | −0.192 |
|  | (0.374) | (0.302) |
| Median household income 2000 ($000s) | 0.764 | 0.397 |
|  | (0.419) | (0.257) |
| Housing units 2000 ($000s) | 0.203 | 0.146 |
|  | (0.368) | (0.254) |
| Parcel size (logged) | −0.458** | −0.459** |
|  | (0.161) | (0.151) |
| Observations | 180 | 180 |

Robust standard errors in parentheses
$**p < 0.01$, $*p < 0.05$

[2] We exclude parcels over 500,000 square feet and those under 600,000 square feet. Parcels over 500,000 square feet were extreme outliers on the high end. There were a couple of parcels this size that became housing and then the next largest was approximately 200,000. At the low end, we wanted to only include parcels that could plausibly become any type of housing. We chose a 6,000 foot cutoff because that is the largest median size (by neighborhood) in Boston of a multifamily house plot.

[3] For example, Boston College bought the (now) former archdiocese headquarters, a 43 acre campus in the Brighton neighborhood near the college (for $100MM). The College has repurposed it as conference space, and moved its art museum to a former building on site.

TABLE A.4 *Logistic regression models estimating the effects of regulations on a church becoming multifamily housing (all variables standardized)*

| | All regs | MF regs | Other regs | Both regs |
|---|---|---|---|---|
| Distance from Boston (miles) | −0.403 | −0.458 | −0.392 | −0.447 |
| | (0.255) | (0.246) | (0.266) | (0.241) |
| Support for housing referendum | 0.128 | 0.054 | 0.273 | −0.007 |
| | (0.387) | (0.328) | (0.380) | (0.370) |
| Lot size (SqFt 1000s) | 0.248 | 0.228 | 0.213 | 0.252 |
| | (0.257) | (0.221) | (0.245) | (0.241) |
| Property was only land | −0.193 | −0.395 | −0.190 | −0.348 |
| | (0.539) | (0.513) | (0.531) | (0.548) |
| Count: All regulations | −0.757* | | | |
| | (0.372) | | | |
| Count: Multifamily specific regs | | −0.890** | | −0.820** |
| | | (0.210) | | (0.211) |
| Count: All other regs | | | −0.551 | −0.192 |
| | | | (0.346) | (0.354) |
| Observations | 116 | 116 | 116 | 116 |

Robust standard errors in parentheses
**p < 0.01, *p < 0.05

Table A.4 presents results from logistic regressions estimating the effect of regulations on whether a property was redeveloped into multifamily or single family housing, conditional on the property being redeveloped into housing, using the same controls as provided previously. We find that the number of regulations overall and the number of multifamily housing regulations significantly reduce the likelihood that a property becomes multifamily housing.

### Density of Church Redevelopments

Table A.5 models the density (units per acre) of residential church redevelopments using OLS.[4] We include two specifications. In Model 1, the independent variable is a measure of *all regulations*, while in Model 2, multi-family regulations and all other regulations are disaggregated. We find that the total number of regulations has a negative effect on density. However, when the types of regulations are split by multifamily and all other regulations, the effect of multifamily housing regulations is negative

---

4 The average parcel is about .7 acres.

TABLE A.5 OLS *models estimating the effects of regulations on new housing density (all variables standardized)*

|  | Units per acre | Units per acre |
|---|---|---|
| Distance from Boston (miles) | 1.113 | 1.053 |
|  | (1.365) | (1.409) |
| Support for housing referendum | 3.394 | 3.215 |
|  | (2.130) | (2.138) |
| Property was only land | −1.259 | −1.455 |
|  | (3.321) | (3.231) |
| Count: All regs | −5.106** |  |
|  | (0.894) |  |
| Count: Multifamily specific regs |  | −2.048 |
|  |  | (1.339) |
| Count: All other regs |  | −3.664** |
|  |  | (1.269) |
| Observations | 111 | 111 |
| R-squared | 0.253 | 0.255 |

Robust standard errors in parentheses
**p < 0.01, *p < 0.05

but not significant; only the effect of all other regulations is statistically significant.

## Distance and Parcel Size Subsets

In Chapter 3, we examined the effects of housing regulations on multi-family housing development. Here, as a robustness check on our results, we restrict our samples to two subsets of highly comparable properties. Doing so helps confirm that the differences in housing developments and density that we observe are due to differences in regulations, rather than other factors. We first restrict our results to midsize parcels, excluding the top and bottom quartiles of lot sizes. We may be concerned that very large and small parcels could attract more unusual developments, which would bias our estimates of the relationship between regulations and property development. Second, we restrict the sample only to cites within fifteen miles of Boston. Focusing on parcels close to Boston accounts for the fact that proximity to the city may drive housing demand.

Figure A.1 replicates Figure 3.11 for each of the two smaller subsets of more directly comparable properties. The top row plots each development by the number of each type of regulations for all church plots between the twenty-fifth (.3 acres) and seventy-fifth percentile (1.6

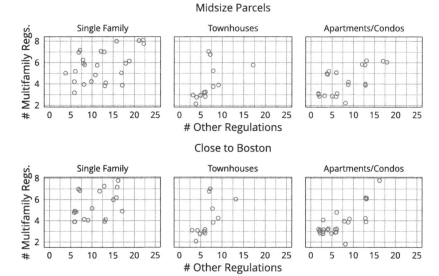

FIGURE A.1: Type of housing developed by the number of multifamily and other housing regulations in the town for subsets of church properties. *Midsize Parcels* are those in the twenty-fifth to seventy-fifth percentiles of lot sizes. *Close to Boston* includes all properties within fifteen miles of Boston.

acres) in size and the bottom row does so for all plots within fifteen miles of Boston.

Analyses of these subsets provides more evidence for the link between regulations (of all types) and building multifamily housing. Some single-family housing gets built in towns with a variety of regulations. However, nearly all multifamily housing is built in communities with fewer regulations, and virtually all development in highly regulated towns is single family housing. This holds for the set of modestly sized parcels, and for all parcels close to Boston. Even in the inner-ring cities and towns – featuring transit access and high housing demand – high regulations restrict multifamily housing.

Figure A.2 documents that density relationships hold when focusing on the modestly sized parcels and those close to Boston. Because density is calculated by dividing the number of units by the total size of the land, places with very large and small parcels might have artificially low or high densities, respectively. Removing very large and small parcels from our analysis ensures that our results are not driven by these artificial densities. Moreover, the fact that our results do not change even when restricting our analyses to cities and towns close to Boston shows that,

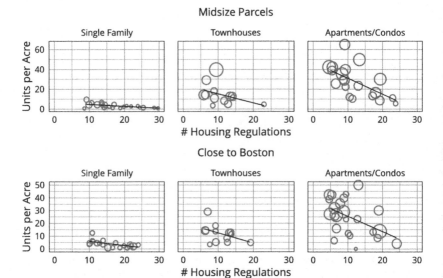

FIGURE A.2: Density of housing redevelopments by housing type and town housing regulations for subsets of church properties. *Midsize Parcels* are those in the twenty-fifth to seventy-fifth percentiles of lot sizes. *Close to Boston* includes all properties within fifteen miles of Boston. Density of all housing types decrease with regulations. Circle size is proportional to the number of housing units in the development.

even in the highly developed areas where the demand for housing is seemingly limitless, regulations reduce density. All of these results hold when we examine statistical models controlling for distance from Boston, town-level vote returns on an affordable housing referendum, whether the parcel was previously developed land, and the density of housing provided. All else equal, places with more regulations produce lower-density housing.

# B

## Appendix to Chapter 4

### COMMENT CODING

Every time a public participant at a zoning or planning meeting was identified by name and address, and spoke about a project that implicated multiple housing units, we coded (a) their demographics, (b) the address of the project they spoke about, and (c) whether they were supportive, neutral, or opposed, and (d) the reasons they offered to justify their position (when available). The two major coding decisions were how to code participants' tones and reasons for support or opposition.

**Tone:** The support/neutral/oppose variable is coded support or oppose if the coder can detect any hint in either direction. Most supportive comments were quite explicit and included phrases such as "I support this project" and "This is good for the town." Oppose comments fell into two categories. Some explicitly expressed opposition in general: "This is bad for the town," "I'm opposed to this project." Other comments coded "oppose" focused on specific reasons (discussed later) with a negative tone or valence: "I'm worried about traffic," "It will make the street more dangerous," or "It doesn't fit the neighborhood." Comments coded neutral were generally sincere, or at least neutrally phrased questions. Asking "How will this affect the wildlife" would be coded neutral. Many of these neutral comments likely came from skeptical or even opposed residents who couched their views in a formally neutral question. We coded these as neutral rather than try to guess or assume why they were asking about things with a negative valence. This should make the coding reasonably conservative.

**Content:** When possible, we coded the substance of each commenter using the scheme depicted in Table B.1. We allowed for multiple content areas per commenter such that a person who raised both traffic and environmental concerns would get both comment codes.

TABLE B.1 *Comment issue coding scheme*

| Category | Description/Examples |
|---|---|
| Density | Arguments that the new development will make the population too dense in the area |
| Height/shadows | The building will be too tall/short and will cast unacceptable shadows. Includes arguments about wind from the building (often a result of the height) |
| Parking | Too much strain on parking, proposal doesn't account for enough parking. |
| Traffic | Vehicular traffic only (not pedestrian) |
| Schools | Arguments that the development will harm/improve/influence the quality of the local public schools |
| Affordability | Arguments about the development increasing housing prices, including affordable housing, etc. includes income diversity |
| Diversity | Arguments about impact on diversity. Includes disabilities (handicap accessible) |
| Flooding | Construction may lead to flooding either during or after. Project may affect drainage. |
| Building foundation | Construction will damage the foundation of neighboring buildings |
| Noise | Construction causing noise or the development making the area noisier |
| Privacy | New housing too close with views into property and other related concerns |
| Trees/Green space/ Environment | Arguments about trees, parks, green space, wildlife, and environmental impact; includes air pollution concerns |
| Aesthetics | "It's ugly." "It doesn't match the other buildings" "building doesn't fit." Includes arguments about visual and historic character of area. |
| Not compliant with zoning | Concerns that the development does not comply with zoning laws (often argue that zoning laws are agreed to after a collective participatory process, therefore should not be ignored) |
| Safety | Raises safety concerns about children, snow removal, intersections etc. |
| Pedestrian | Includes pedestrian/bicycle traffic. Also sidewalk issues. |

| Category | Description/Examples |
|---|---|
| Neighborhood character | To show difference between density and explicit fears of socioeconomic/racial diversity, arguments about preserving history and questions of "fit" that are not about the building itself. Concerns about who will be moving into the neighborhood and using neighborhood resources; arguments that this is a "great addition to the neighborhood." Arguments about "changing" the neighborhood. |
| Home value/city revenues | Includes arguments about a development decreasing property values and reducing city revenues, "hurting my property values," or questions about whether a property will be a "net financial gain for the city." |
| Septic/water system | Only applies to suburbs without sewer systems |

# C

## Appendix to Chapter 5

TABLE C.1 *Difference in means between commenters and all voters*

| Variable | Commenters | | Noncommenters | | |
| | N | Mean | N | Mean | Difference |
|---|---|---|---|---|---|
| Age | 2,566 | 58.711 | 1,535,520 | 50.893 | 7.818** |
| Reg. length | 2,580 | 17.377 | 1,618,375 | 11.828 | 5.549** |
| Female | 2,580 | 0.433 | 1,618,375 | 0.513 | −0.080** |
| Reg. Democrat | 2,580 | 0.320 | 1,618,375 | 0.317 | 0.002 |
| Reg. Republican | 2,580 | 0.112 | 1,618,375 | 0.111 | 0.001 |
| Reg. Independent | 2,580 | 0.566 | 1,618,375 | 0.563 | 0.002 |
| % Elections voted | 2,580 | 0.502 | 1,618,375 | 0.272 | 0.230** |
| Homeowner | 2,580 | 0.734 | 1,618,375 | 0.456 | 0.278** |
| Property value ($k) | 1,895 | 550.223 | 738,309 | 490.967 | 59.256** |

**$p < 0.01$

TABLE C.2 *Logit models of commenters relative to full voter file*

|  | (1) | (2) | (3) |
|---|---|---|---|
| Age | 0.004** | 0.002 | 0.003 |
|  | (0.001) | (0.002) | (0.002) |
| Registration length | 0.008** | 0.014** | 0.013** |
|  | (0.002) | (0.002) | (0.002) |
| Female | −0.342** | −0.351** | −0.346** |
|  | (0.040) | (0.040) | (0.040) |
| Democrat | 0.122 | 0.116 | 0.130 |
|  | (0.069) | (0.070) | (0.070) |
| Independent | 0.130* | 0.153* | 0.164* |
|  | (0.064) | (0.064) | (0.064) |
| % Elections voted | 2.006** | 1.883** | 1.907** |
|  | (0.076) | (0.077) | (0.077) |
| Homeowner | 0.703** | 0.695** | 0.699** |
|  | (0.047) | (0.048) | (0.048) |
| White | 0.463** | 0.291** | 0.323** |
|  | (0.094) | (0.097) | (0.099) |
| Towns | 97 | 97 | 97 |
| Commenters | 2566 | 2566 | 2566 |
| Town controls |  | X |  |
| Town FEs |  |  | X |
| Observations | 1,538,086 | 1,538,086 | 1,538,086 |

*Note:* *p < 0.05; **p < 0.01

TABLE C.3 *Logit models of commenters relative to full voter file – homeowners only*

|  | (1) | (2) | (3) |
|---|---|---|---|
| Age | 0.003 | 0.001 | 0.002 |
|  | (0.002) | (0.002) | (0.002) |
| Registration length | 0.002 | 0.007** | 0.006* |
|  | (0.002) | (0.003) | (0.003) |
| Female | −0.412** | −0.425** | −0.404** |
|  | (0.047) | (0.047) | (0.048) |
| Democrat | 0.176* | 0.174* | 0.194* |
|  | (0.079) | (0.081) | (0.081) |
| Independent | 0.148* | 0.162* | 0.176* |
|  | (0.074) | (0.074) | (0.074) |
| % Elections voted | 1.638** | 1.546** | 1.564** |
|  | (0.087) | (0.088) | (0.089) |
| White | 0.141 | 0.100 | 0.135 |
|  | (0.113) | (0.116) | (0.118) |
| Property value (000s) | 0.000** | 0.000 | 0.000 |
|  | (0.000) | (0.000) | (0.000) |
| Towns | 97 | 97 | 97 |
| Commenters | 1888 | 1888 | 1888 |
| Town Controls |  | X |  |
| Town FEs |  |  | X |
| Observations | 722,509 | 722,509 | 722,509 |

*Note:* *p < 0.05; **p < 0.01

TABLE C.4 *Logit models of commenters relative to full voter file by town median income*

| | Town Median Income Tercile | | |
|---|---|---|---|
| | (1) | Lower (2) | (3) |
| Age | 0.005 | 0.005 | −0.002 |
| | (0.003) | (0.003) | (0.003) |
| Registration length | 0.015** | 0.006 | 0.019** |
| | (0.003) | (0.004) | (0.004) |
| Female | −0.374** | −0.256** | −0.403** |
| | (0.071) | (0.073) | (0.066) |
| Democrat | −0.045 | 0.174 | 0.211 |
| | (0.126) | (0.127) | (0.112) |
| Independent | 0.008 | 0.210 | 0.227* |
| | (0.118) | (0.116) | (0.103) |
| % Elections voted | 1.803** | 1.674** | 2.202** |
| | (0.130) | (0.138) | (0.133) |
| Homeowner | 0.729** | 0.790** | 0.576** |
| | (0.080) | (0.088) | (0.080) |
| White | 0.524** | 0.439* | 0.009 |
| | (0.159) | (0.220) | (0.149) |
| Towns | 32 | 33 | 32 |
| Commenters | 823 | 784 | 959 |
| Town FEs | X | X | X |
| Observations | 749,510 | 374,893 | 413,683 |

*Note:* $^*p < 0.05$; $^{**}p < 0.01$

TABLE C.5 *Logit models predicting supporting comments*

|  | (1) | (2) |
|---|---|---|
| Age | 0.01 | 0.01 |
|  | (0.005) | (0.005) |
| Registration length | 0.004 | 0.004 |
|  | (0.01) | (0.01) |
| Female | −0.31** | −0.31** |
|  | (0.10) | (0.10) |
| Democrat | 0.44** | 0.44** |
|  | (0.16) | (0.16) |
| Independent | −0.04 | −0.05 |
|  | (0.16) | (0.16) |
| Pct elections voted | 0.65** | 0.65** |
|  | (0.16) | (0.16) |
| # of comments | −0.04 | −0.04 |
|  | (0.03) | (0.03) |
| Homeowner | −0.43** | −0.43** |
|  | (0.10) | (0.10) |
| Prob. white | −0.70** |  |
|  | (0.22) |  |
| Prob. max. white |  | −0.47* |
|  |  | (0.20) |
| Constant | −1.60** | −1.74** |
|  | (0.33) | (0.34) |
| Observations | 3,629 | 3,629 |

Note: *p < 0.05; **p < 0.01

## Race Matching

As the algorithm requires the geographic location of each voter, the first step is to geocode the address of each individual in the voter file to identify their census block.[1] Due to disparities between addresses as recorded in the voter file and addresses recorded by the census bureau, we were not able to match every address. Seven percent of voters were not geocoded, and roughly 20 percent were only geocoded at the census tract (rather than block) level. For the voters that we could not geocode, we used county-level census data instead of block-level data for the race estimates. Furthermore, in some cases, voter gender and age were missing, such that, for some race estimates, we could only use some of the variables.

---

[1] We geocoded each address to its 2010 census block using the Geocode from the US Census Bureau. https://geocoding.geo.census.gov/geocoder/.

TABLE C.6 *Summary of race matching variables*

| | Block +<br>Age + Sex | Tract +<br>Age + Sex | Tract +<br>Sex | County +<br>Age + Sex | County +<br>Sex | Total |
|---|---|---|---|---|---|---|
| Voters | 1,149,190<br>71% | 277,105<br>17% | 75,502<br>5% | 109,225<br>7% | 7,353<br>0% | 1,618,375 |
| Commenters | 1,890<br>73% | 480<br>19% | 14<br>1% | 196<br>8% | –<br>– | 2,580 |

TABLE C.7 *Race estimates by group*

| | | Voters | Commenters |
|---|---|---|---|
| Mean probability | White | 0.84 | 0.92 |
| | Hispanic | 0.06 | 0.02 |
| | Asian | 0.05 | 0.03 |
| | Black | 0.04 | 0.03 |
| | Other | 0.01 | 0.01 |
| Maximum probability | White | 0.88 | 0.95 |
| | Hispanic | 0.05 | 0.01 |
| | Asian | 0.04 | 0.02 |
| | Black | 0.03 | 0.02 |
| | Other | 0.01 | 0.00 |
| $Pr(White) \geq .5$ | White | 0.87 | 0.95 |
| | Nonwhite | 0.13 | 0.05 |

Table C.6 summarizes the different types of race estimates and the number of commenters and voters for each. Overall, 71 percent of voters were geocoded to a census block, and their race estimated using their age, gender, and the demographics of the census block. An additional 22 percent used census tract instead of census block for race estimation, using either age and sex (17 percent) or age alone if sex was missing (5 percent).

The Imai and Khanna (2016) algorithm produces probabilities that each voter belongs to each of the five groups. Thus, we can measure race three different ways: using the raw probabilities, assigning each voter to the group with the highest probability, and assigning voters to just two categories, *White* and *Nonwhite*, based on if the probability of being white is 50 percent or higher. Table C.7 summarizes the race estimates for voters and commenters using all three measures, and Figure 5.1 plots the race estimates using the second measure for all five groups. For all three measures of race, commenters are more likely to be white

than voters; there are statistically significant differences between the proportions of commenters that are white (or probabilities that a voter is
white) compared to voters, relative to the other groups. For most of
our analyses (including all regression models), we use the simple binary
*White/Nonwhite*, because the number of minority commenters is relatively small. When we look at individual groups, we use the maximum
probability measure instead.

### Race Estimate Validation

Because the Massachusetts voter file does not include race and there are
no other precise aggregate racial statistics on voters, the true distribution
of voters across racial groups in the towns in our sample is unknown. In
order to validate our race estimates, we use the best comparison group
possible, the distribution of citizen voting age population (CVAP) by
town from the 2016 American Community Survey (ACS). Figure C.1
plots the white CVAP percentage and the estimated proportion of white
voters by town, ordered from the lowest percentage of white CVAP to
highest. The percentage of voters estimated to most likely be white corresponds very closely to the single-race white CVAP population in each
town. On average, the percentage of white voters is only 2.6 percentage
points higher than the white CVAP. This difference may be attributable to
several factors, including that whites may be more likely to be registered
to vote than members of other groups, that mixed-race people may have

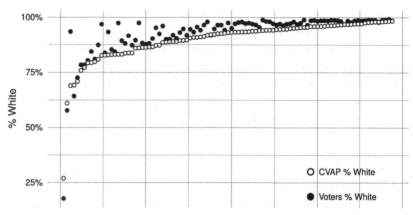

FIGURE C.1: Race estimate validation: Town percentage CVAP and town voters
percentage white

names that the race estimating algorithm determined are white, and that the algorithm is systematically underestimating the minority population by a few percentage points. However, given our primary interest is comparing voters to commenters, this small difference between actual white CVAP and estimated white voters will not affect our results. We should expect any differences between actual and estimated race to be the same among both voters and commenters, such that differences between the two groups are unbiased.

# D

# Appendix to Chapter 6

TABLE D.1 *Regressions of zoning regulations on lawsuits per thousand housing units*

| Regulation type | Lawsuits | |
|---|---|---|
| All regulations | 0.041** | (0.011) |
| Cluster regulations | 0.159* | (0.074) |
| Growth regulations | 0.108 | (0.069) |
| Inclusionary regulations | −0.056 | (0.103) |
| Multifamily regulations | 0.33* | (0.064) |
| Senior housing regulations | 0.323* | (0.128) |
| Septic regulations | 0.139** | (0.043) |
| Parcel shape regulations | 0.137* | (0.059) |
| Subdivision regulations | −0.059 | (0.069) |
| Wetlands regulations | 0.031 | (0.020) |

Note: $*p < 0.05$; $**p < 0.01$. Each row corresponds to a separate OLS regression. For all regressions, N = 187 Massachusetts cities and towns. Dependent variable is defined as the total number of lawsuits, 2006–2017, per 1,000 housing units. Independent variables are defined as the number of regulations of each type in the LHRD.

TABLE D.2 *Regressions of lawsuits on permitted buildings*

| Dependent variable | Lawsuits | |
|---|---|---|
| Multifamily units share | −0.045** | (0.014) |
| Multifamily buildings share | −0.02** | (0.007) |
| Multifamily units | −81.27** | (30.256) |
| Multifamily buildings | −8.346** | (2.38) |
| Log multifamily units | −0.371** | (0.115) |
| Log multifamily buildings | −0.284** | (0.076) |

Note: $*p < 0.05$; $**p < 0.01$. For all regressions, N = 187 Massachusetts cities and towns. Independent variable is defined as the total number of lawsuits, 2006–2017, per 1,000 housing units. Dependent variables are calculated using units and buildings permitted by building type in each town from 2000 to 2015.

# References

Alliance for Community Transit – Los Angeles. 2018. "RE: SB 827 (Wiener) Planning and Zoning – Transit-Rich Housing Bonus – Oppose." Available at allianceforcommunitytransit.org/l-a-community-organizations-oppose-sb-827/. Accessed on September 14, 2018.

Altshuler, Alan, and David Luberoff. 2003. *Mega-Projects: The Changing Politics of Urban Investment*. Washington, DC: Brookings Institution Press.

American Planning Association Texas Chapter. 2013. "Zoning Regulations in Texas: A Guide to Urban Planning in Texas Communities." Available at www.txplanning.org/guide-to-urban-planning-in-texas/. Accessed on April 10, 2019.

Anenberg, Elliot, and Edward Kung. 2018. "Can More Housing Supply Solve the Affordability Crisis? Evidence from a Neighborhood Choice Model." Finance and Economics Discussion Series 2018-035. Washington: Board of Governors of the Federal Reserve System, https://doi.org/10.17016FEDS.2018.035. Available at www.federalreserve.gov/econres/feds/files/2018035pap.pdf. Accessed on September 14, 2018.

Anzia, Sarah F. 2014. *Timing and Turnout: How Off-Cycle Elections Favor Organized Groups*. Chicago: University of Chicago Press.

Archdiocese of Boston. 2018. "Boston Catholic Directory." *BostonCatholic.org*. Available at www.bostoncatholic.org/Parishes-And-People/Default.aspx. Accessed on June 27, 2018.

Arnstein, Sherry R. 1969. "A Ladder of Citizen Participation." *Journal of the American Planning Association* 35: 216–224.

Badger, Emily, and Inyoung Kang. 2017. "California Today: In San Francisco's Housing Lottery It's the Luck of the Draw." *New York Times*. Available at www.nytimes.com/2018/05/14/us/california-today-san-francisco-housing-lottery.html. Accessed on May 14, 2018.

Barreto, Matt A. 2010. *Ethnic Cues: The Role of Shared Ethnicity in Latino Political Participation*. Ann Arbor: University of Michigan Press.

Barreto, Matt A., and Loren Collingwood. 2015. "Group-Based Appeals and the Latino Vote in 2012: How Immigration Became a Mobilizing Issue." *Electoral Studies* 40(4): 490–499.

Barreto, Matthew A., Gary M. Segura, and Nathan D. Woods. 2004. "The Mobilizing Effect of Majority-Minority Districts on Latino Turnout." *American Political Science Review* 98(1): 65–75.

Berinksy, Adam J. 2005. "The Perverse Consequences of Electoral Reform in the United States." *American Politics Research* 33(4): 471–491.

Bernal, Rafael. 2017. "Latino Representation in Congress at Record High, but Far from Parity." *The Hill*. Available at http://thehill.com/latino/350673-latino-representation-in-congress-at-record-high-but-far-from-parity. Accessed on August 22, 2018.

Berry, Christopher. 2001. "Land Use Regulation and Residential Segregation: Does It Matter?" *American Law and Economics Review* 3(2): 251–274.

Berry, Christopher R. 2009. *Imperfect Union: Representation and Taxation in Multilevel Governments*. New York: Cambridge University Press.

Berry, Jeffrey M., Kent E. Portney, and Ken Thomson. 1993. *The Rebirth of Urban Democracy*. Washington, DC: Brookings Institution Press.

Booker, Brakkton. 2018. "White House Budget Calls for Deep Cuts to HUD." *NPR*. Available at www.npr.org/2018/02/13/585255697/white-house-budget-calls-for-deep-cuts-to-hud. Accessed on September 14, 2018.

Bosma, Alison. 2018a. "Ashland Approves Pot Ban, Two Overrides." *Metrowest Daily News*. Available at ashland.wickedlocal.com/news/20180515/ashland-approves-pot-ban-two-overrides. Accessed on August 1, 2018.

Bosma, Alison. 2018b. "Ashland Looks to Buy Valentine Estate." *Metrowest Daily News*. Available at www.metrowestdailynews.com/news/20180215/ashland-looks-to-buy-valentine-estate. Accessed on August 1, 2018.

Boston Globe Editorial Board. 2005. "Welcome in Brookline." *Boston Globe*. Downloaded from Proquest.

Brabham, Daren C. 2009. "Crowdsourcing the Public Participation Process for Planning Projects." *Planning Theory* 8(3): 242–262.

Bradford, Ben. 2018. "Is California's CEQA Environmental Law Protecting Natural Beauty – or Blocking Affordable Housing?" *Capital Public Radio*. Available at www.scpr.org/news/2018/07/11/84603/is-california-s-ceqa-environmental-law-protecting. Accessed on September 17, 2018.

Bridges, Amy. 1997. "Textbook Municipal Reform." *Urban Affairs Review* 33(1): 97–119.

Buell, Spencer. 2015. "A Big 'No' from Arlington on Mugar Site Plans." *Arlington Wicked Local*. Available at arlington.wickedlocal.com/article/20150528/news/150526532. Accessed on August 1, 2018.

Bui, Quoctrung, Matt A.V. Chaban, and Jeremy White. 2016. "40 Percent of Buildings Could Not Be Built in Manhattan Today." *New York Times*. Available at www.nytimes.com/interactive/2016/05/19/upshot/forty-percent-of-manhattans-buildings-could-not-be-built-today.html. Accessed on January 18, 2018.

Burden, Barry C., David T. Canon, Kenneth R. Mayer, and Donald P. Moynihan. 2013. "Election Laws, Mobilization, and Turnout: The Unanticipated Consequences of Election Reform." *American Journal of Political Science* 58(1): 95–109.

Burns, Nancy. 1994. *The Formation of American Local Governments: Private Values in Public Institutions.* New York: Oxford University Press.

Butera, Candace. 2018. "Are We Worried Sick about the Rent?" *CityLab.* Available at www.citylab.com/equity/2018/01/rent-anxiety-is-making-us-sick/551660/. Accessed on April 10, 2019.

Butterfield, Fox. 2003. "Church in Boston to Pay $85 Million in Abuse Lawsuits." *New York Times.* Available at www.nytimes.com/2003/09/10/us/church-in-boston-to-pay-85-million-in-abuse-lawsuits.html. Accessed on June 27, 2018.

Cain, Bruce. 2015. *Democracy More or Less: America's Political Reform Quandary.* New York: Cambridge University Press.

Calfornia YIMBY Tech Network. 2018. "Re: SB 827 (Wiener) Near High-Quality Transit – Support." Available at www.cayimby.org/technetwork/. Accessed on September 14, 2018.

Cameron, Charles M. 2000. *Veto Bargaining: Presidents and the Politics of Negative Power.* New York: Cambridge University Press.

Campanella, Thomas J. 2017. "How Low Did He Go?" *CityLab.* Available at www.citylab.com/transportation/2017/07/how-low-did-he-go/533019/. Accessed on July 23, 2018.

Campbell, Andrea L. 2005. *How Policies Make Citizens: Senior Political Activism and the American Welfare State.* Princeton, NJ: Princeton University Press.

Capps, Kriston. 2015. "How Fair Housing Will Turn Liberal Cities Conservative." *CityLab.* Available at www.citylab.com/equity/2015/07/how-fair-housing-will-turn-liberal-cities-conservative/398642/. Accessed on August 24, 2017.

Capps, Kriston. 2016. "Blame Zoning, Not Tech, for San Francisco's Housing Crisis." *CityLab.* Available at www.citylab.com/equity/2016/03/are-wealthy-neighborhoods-to-blame-for-gentrification-of-poorer-ones/473349/. Accessed on October 9, 2018.

Carlyle, Erin. 2016. "Bidding Wars for Homes Have Become the New Normal in Many U.S. Cities." *Forbes.* Available at www.forbes.com/sites/erincarlyle/2016/04/13/bidding-wars-for-homes-have-become-the-new-normal-in-many-u-s-cities/#1f1001e328df. Accessed on May 14, 2018.

Caro, Robert. 1974. *The Power Broker.* New York: Knopf.

Carter, Jimmy. 1980. "Housing and Community Development Act of 1980. Remarks on Signing S. 2719 Into Law." Available at www.presidency.ucsb.edu/ws/?pid=45238. Accessed on August 15, 2017.

Castro, Melissa. 2018. "Restrictive Zoning Makes Tight Charlottesville Housing Supply Even Tighter." *The Daily Progress.* Available at www.dailyprogress.com/news/business/local/restrictive-zoning-makes-tight-charlottesville-housing-supply-even-tighter/article_ef1e97fa-443b-11e8-8564-ab108fb49611.html. Accessed on July 21, 2018.

Center for Open Science. 2018. "Center for Open Science: Pre-registration Guide." Available at cos.io/prereg/. Accessed on April 10, 2019.

Chetty, Raj, Nathaniel Herdren, and Lawrence F. Katz. 2016. "The Effects of Exposure to Better Neighborhoods on Children: New Evidence from the

Moving to Opportunity Experiment." *American Economic Review* 106(4): 855–902.

City of Cambridge. 2016. "Cambridge Housing Profile." *Community Development Department*. Available at www.cambridgema.gov/~/media/Files/CDD/FactsandMaps/profiles/demo_profile_housing_2016.ashx. Accessed on May 15, 2018.

City of Lawrence. 2019. "Neighborhood Associations." Available at www.cityoflawrence.com/556/Neighborhood-Associations. Accessed on July 8, 2019.

City of Palo Alto. 2018. "Re: SB 827 (Wiener) Planning and Zoning: OPPOSE as Introduced." Available at www.cityofpaloalto.org/civicax/filebank/documents/63466. Accessed on September 14, 2018.

City of Philadelphia. 2012. "West Philadelphia Empowerment Zone Request for Proposals." Available at www.phila.gov/pdfs/2012_NFS_WPEZ_Request_for_Proposals%20May%202012.pdf. Accessed on June 28, 2018.

Clark, Zachary. 2018. "Settlement Reached Over Height of Downtown Affordable Housing." *Daily Journal*. Available at www.smdailyjournal.com/news/local/settlement-reached-over-height-of-downtown-affordable-housing/article_cda84dc6-8c9f-11e8-b02c-e33457167a8e.html. Accessed on September 17, 2018.

Climate Resolve, NRDC, and Environment California. 2018. "Re: SB 827 (Wiener) Panning and Zoning: Transit-Rich Housing Bonus – Conceptual Support." Available at www.cayimby.org/wp-content/uploads/2018/03/SB-827-Letter-3-23-18.pdf. Accessed on September 14, 2018.

Cohen, Rachel M. 2014. "The RAD-ical Shifts to Public Housing." *American Prospect*. Available at http://prospect.org/article/can-private-capital-save-public-housing-tenants-have-their-doubts. Accessed on September 14, 2018.

Commonwealth of Massachusetts. 2017. "Chapter 40A, Section 11." Available at malegislature.gov/Laws/GeneralLaws/PartI/TitleVII/Chapter40A/Section11. Accessed on August 18, 2017.

Cox, Gary W., and Jonathan N. Katz. 1996. "Why Did the Incumbency Advantage in US House Elections Grow?" *American Journal of Political Science* 20(2): 478–497.

Dahl, Robert. 1961. *Who Governs? Democracy and Power in the American City*. New Haven: Yale University Press.

Davidson, Betty. 2002. "Preserve Tree and Church." *Boston Globe*. Downloaded from Proquest.

Dawson, Michael C. 1995. *Behind the Mule: Race and Class in African-American Politics*. Princeton, NJ: Princeton University Press.

de Guzman, Dianne. 2017. "In Parts of the Bay Area, $105,350 Is 'Low Income.'" *SFGate*. Available at www.sfchronicle.com/bayarea/article/Bay-Area-low-income-105k-hud-11094978.php. Accessed on April 10, 2019.

de Kadt, Daniel. 2017. "Bringing the Polls to the People: How Increasing Electoral Access Encourages Turnout but Exacerbates Political Inequality." Working paper. Available at www.dropbox.com/s/gq787v81pq8mu53/dekadt_polls_to_the_people.pdf?dl=0. Accessed on August 15, 2017.

Dear, Michael. 1992. "Understanding and Overcoming NIMBY Syndrome." *Journal of the American Planning Association* 58(3): 288–300.

Democratic Socialists of America Los Angeles. 2018. "Statement in Opposition to SB 827 – Luxury Development for the Rich, Displacement and Dispossession for the Poor." Available at www.dsa-la.org/statement_in_opposition_to_sb_827. Accessed on September 14, 2018.

Desmond, Matthew. 2016. "Heavy Is the House: Rent Burden among the American Urban Poor." *International Journal of Urban and Regional Research* 42(1): 160–170.

Desmond, Matthew, and Rachel Tolbert Kimbro. 2015. "Inequality Is Always in the Room: Language and Power in Deliberative Democracy." *Social Forces* 94(1): 1–30.

Dillon, Liam. 2018a. "California Lawmakers Killed One of the Biggest Housing Bills in the Country." *Los Angeles Times*. Available at www.latimes.com/politics/la-pol-ca-big-housing-bill-dies-20180417-story.html. Accessed on September 14, 2018.

Dillon, Liam. 2018b. "A Major California Housing Bill Failed after Opposition from the Low-Income Residents It Aimed to Help. Here's How It Went Wrong." *LA Times*. Available at www.latimes.com/politics/la-pol-ca-housing-bill-failure-equity-groups-20180502-story.html. Accessed on July 21, 2018.

DiPasquale, Denise, and Edward L. Glaeser. 1999. "Incentives and Social Capital: Are Homeowners Better Citizens?" *Journal of Urban Economics* 45(2): 354–384.

Djankov, Simeon, Rafael La Porta, Florencio Lopez-de Silanes, and Andrei Shleifer. 2002. "The Regulation of Entry." *The Quarterly Journal of Economics* 117(1): 1–37.

Downs, Andreae. 2007. "St. Aidan's Makeover Gains Final Blessing." *Boston Globe*. Downloaded from Proquest.

Dreier, Peter, John H. Mollenkopf, and Todd Swanstrom. 2004. *Place Matters: Metropolitics for the Twenty-First Century*. Lawrence: University Press of Kansas.

Dunning, Thad. 2012. *Natural Experiments in the Social Sciences: A Design-Based Approach*. Cambridge, UK: Cambridge University Press.

Einstein, Katherine Levine, David M. Glick, and Conor LeBlanc. 2017. "2016 Menino Survey of Mayors." Available at www.bu.edu/ioc/files/2017/01/2016-Menino-Survey-of-Mayors-Final-Report.pdf. Accessed on July 8, 2019.

Einstein, Katherine Levine, David M. Glick, and Maxwell Palmer. 2018. "Menino Survey of Mayors: 2017 Results." Available at www.surveyofmayors.com/reports/MeninoReport17_011218_web.pdf. Accessed on July 8, 2019.

Einstein, Katherine Levine, David M. Glick, Maxwell Palmer, and Stacy Fox. 2019. "Menino Survey of Mayors: 2018 Results." Available at www.surveyofmayors.com/reports/Menino-Survey-of-Mayors-2018-Final-Report.pdf. Accessed on July 8, 2019.

Einstein, Katherine Levine, Maxwell Palmer, and David M. Glick. 2019. "Who Participates in Local Politics? Evidence from Meeting Minutes." *Perspectives on Politics* 17(1): 28–46.

Empower LA. 2019. "Neighborhood Councils." Available at http://empowerla.org/councils/. Accessed on June 20, 2019.

Enos, Ryan D. 2016. "What the Demolition of Public Housing Teaches Us about the Impact of Racial Threat on Political Behavior." *American Journal of Political Science* 60(1): 123–142.

Enos, Ryan D., Anthony Fowler, and Lynn Vavreck. 2014. "Increasing Inequality: The Effect of GOTV Mobilization on the Composition of the Electorate." *Journal of Politics* 76(1): 273–288. Available at https://scholar.harvard.edu/files/renos/files/enosfowlervavreck.pdf.

Environmental Protection Agency. 2017. "Smart Growth and Transportation." Available at www.epa.gov/smartgrowth/smart-growth-and-transportation. Accessed on September 21, 2017.

Epstein, David, and Sharyn O'Halloran. 1995. "A Theory of Strategic Oversight: Congress, Lobbyists, and the Bureaucracy." *Journal of Law, Economics and Organization* 11: 227.

Epstein, Paul. 2002. "Housing Is Pressing Need." *Boston Globe*. Downloaded from Proquest.

Erikson, Robert S. 1971. "The Advantage of Incumbency in Congressional Elections." *Polity* 3(3): 395–405.

Fainstein, Susan S. 2010. *The Just City*. Ithaca, NY: Cornell University Press.

Fernandez, Raquel, and Dani Rodrik. 1991. "Resistance to Reform: Status Quo Bias in the Presence of Individual-Specific Uncertainty." *The American Economic Review* 81(5): 1146–1155.

Finkel, Steven E. 1985. "Reciprocal Effects of Participation and Political Efficacy: A Panel Analysis." *American Journal of Political Science* 20(4): 891–913.

Finnegan, William. 2018. "Can Andy Byford Save the Subways." *New Yorker*. Available at www.newyorker.com/magazine/2018/07/09/can-andy-byford-save-the-subways. Accessed on July 23, 2018.

Fiorina, Morris P. 1998. "Extreme Voices: A Dark Side of Civic Engagement." In *Civic Engagement in American Democracy*, ed. Theda Skocpol and Morris P. Fiorina, 395–425. Washington, DC: Brookings Institution Press.

Fischel, William A. 2001. *The Homevoter Hypothesis: How Home Values Influence Local Government Taxation, School Finance, and Land-Use Policies*. Cambridge, MA: Harvard University Press.

Fischel, William A. 2015. *Zoning Rules! The Economics of Land Use Regulation*. Cambridge, MA: Lincoln Institute of Land Policy.

Flavin, Patrick, and William W. Franko. 2019. "Economic Segregation and Unequal Policy Responsiveness." *Political Behavior*. Available at https://doi.org/10.1007/s11109-018-09522-9. Accessed on July 8, 2019.

Florida, Richard. 2017. "Meet the 'New Urban Luddites.'" *CityLab*. Available at www.citylab.com/TheOraequity/2017/04/meet-the-new-urban-luddites/521040/. Accessed on July 21, 2018.

Fong, Christian, and Keith Krehbiel. 2018. "Limited Obstruction." *American Political Science Review* 112(1): 1–14.

Fouirnaies, Alexander, and Andrew B. Hall. 2014. "The Financial Incumbency Advantage: Causes and Consequences." *The Journal of Politics* 76(3): 711–724.

Freemark, Yonah. 2019. "Upzoning Chicago: Impacts of a Zoning Reform on Property Values and Housing Construction." *Urban Affairs Review.* Available at https://journals.sagepub.com/doi/abs/10.1177/1078087418824672?journalCode=uarb.

Frug, Gerald. 2006. "The Legal Technology of Exclusion in Metropolitan America." In *The New Suburban History*, ed. Kevin M. Kruse and Thomas J. Sugrue, 205–221. Chicago: University of Chicago Press.

Fung, Archon. 2006. *Empowered Participation: Reinventing Urban Democracy.* Princeton, NJ: Princeton University Press.

Gabbe, C. J. 2018. "Why Are Regulations Changed? A Parcel Analysis of Upzoning in Los Angeles." *Journal of Planning Education and Research* 38(3): 289–300. Available at https://journals.sagepub.com/doi/abs/10.1177/0739456X17696034b.

Gay, Claudine. 2012. "Moving to Opportunity: The Political Effects of a Housing Mobility Experiment." *Urban Affairs Review* 48(2): 147–179.

Gelman, Andrew, and Gary King. 1990. "Estimating Incumbency Advantage without Bias." *American Journal of Political Science* 34(4): 1142–1164.

Gerber, Alan S., Donald P. Green, and Christopher W. Larimer. 2008. "Social Pressure and Voter Turnout: Evidence from a Large-Scale Field Experiment." *American Political Science Review* 102(1): 33–48. Available at https://isps.yale.edu/sites/default/files/publication/2012/12/ISPS08-001.pdf.

Gerber, Elisabeth R. 1999. *The Populist Paradox: Interest Group Influence and the Promise of Direct Legislation.* Princeton, NJ: Princeton University Press.

Gerber, Elisabeth R., and Justin H. Phillips. 2004. "Direct Democracy and Land Use Policy: Exchanging Public Goods for Development Rights." *American Journal of Political Science* 41(2): 463–479.

Gilens, Martin. 2014. *Affluence and Influence: Economic Inequality and Political Power in America.* Princeton, NJ: Princeton University Press.

Giles, Michael W., and Melanie A. Buckner. 1993. "David Duke and Black Threat: An Old Hypothesis Revisited." *Journal of Politics* 55: 702–713.

Giordano, Alice. 2002. "Church's Housing Plan Draws Fire: Critics Call 74-Unit Project in Brookline Bad for Neighborhood." *Boston Globe.* Downloaded from Proquest.

Glaeser, Edward L. 2011. *Triumph of the City: How Our Greater Invention Makes Us Richer, Smarter, Greener, Healthier, and Happier.* New York: Penguin Press.

Glaeser, Edward L., and Bryce Ward. 2009. "The Causes and Consequences of Land Use Regulation: Evidence from Greater Boston." *Journal of Urban Economics* 65(3): 265–278.

Glaeser, Edward L., Joseph Gyourko, and Raven E. Saks. 2005. "Why Is Manhattan So Expensive? Regulation and the Rise in Housing Prices." *Journal of Law and Economics* 6: 71–89.

Goetz, Edward G. 2013. *New Deal Ruins: Race, Economic Justice, and Public Housing Policy.* Ithaca, NY: Cornell University Press.

Goetz, Edward Glenn. 1993. *Shelter Burden: Local Politics and Progressive Housing Policy.* Philadelphia: Temple University Press.

Goodman, Laurie, and Rolf Pendall. 2016. "Housing Supply Falls Short of Demand by 430,000 Units." *Urban Institute Blog*. Available at www.urban.org/urban-wire/housing-supply-falls-short-demand-430000-units. Accessed on April 13, 2019.

Governor Charlie Baker. 2017. "Bill H.4075." *Massachusetts House Docket*. Available at https://malegislature.gov/Bills/190/H4075.html. Accessed on July 8, 2019.

Grabar, Henry. 2018. "Why Was California's Radical Housing Bill So Unpopular." *Slate*. Available at slate.com/business/2018/04/why-sb-827-californias-radical-affordable-housing-bill-was-so-unpopular.html. Accessed on September 14, 2018.

Green, Donald P., Dara Z. Strolovitch, and Janelle S. Wong. 1998. "Defended Neighborhoods, Integration, and Racially Motivated Crime." *American Journal of Sociology* 104(2): 372–403.

Guinier, Lani. 1994. *Tyranny of the Majority: Fundamental Fairness in Representative Democracy*. New York: Free Press.

Gutmann, Amy, and Dennis Thompson. 2012. *The Spirit of Comprise: Why Governing Demands It and Campaigning Undermines It*. Princeton, NJ: Princeton University Press.

Gyourko, Joseph, Albert Saiz, and Anita A. Summers. 2008. "A New Measure of the Local Regulatory Environment for Housing Markets: The Wharton Residential Land Use Regulatory Index." *Urban Studies* 45(3): 693–721.

Gyourko, Joseph, and Raven Molloy. 2014. "Regulation and Housing Supply." NBER Working Paper 20536. DOI: 10.3386/w20536.

Hajnal, Zoltan L. 2010. *America's Uneven Democracy: Race, Turnout, and Representation in City Politics*. New York: Cambridge University Press.

Hajnal, Zoltan L., and Jessica Trounstine. 2010. "Who or What Governs?: The Effects of Economics, Politics, Institutions, and Needs on Local Spending." *American Politics Research* 38(6): 1130–1163.

Hankinson, Michael. 2018. "When Do Renters Behave Like Homeowners? High Rent, Price Anxiety, and NIMBYism." *American Political Science Review* 112(3): 473–493.

Harmon, Else. 2018. "Metro Mayors Boston: Region Must Produce 185k New Housing Units to Keep Up With Economic, Population Growth." *Metropolitan Area Planning Commission*. Available at www.mapc.org/news/metro-boston-mayors-region-must-produce-185k-new-housing-units-to-keep-up-with-economic-population-growth/. Accessed on April 13, 2019.

Harrison, Peter, and Henry Kraemer. 2019. "Homes for All: The Progressive 2020 Agenda for Housing." Available at www.dataforprogress.org/homes-for-all. Accessed on June 20, 2019.

Henderson, John A., Jasjeet S. Sekhon, and Rocio Titiunik. 2016. "Cause or Effect? Turnout in Hispanic Majority-Minority Districts." *Political Analysis* 24(3): 404–412.

Herkenhoff, Kyle F., Lee E. Ohanian, and Edward C. Prescott. 2017. "Tarnishing the Golden and Empire States: Land-Use Restrictions and the U.S. Economic Slowdown." NBER Working Paper No. 23790. Available at www.nber.org/papers/w23790. Accessed on September 21, 2017.

Hernandez, Jennifer. 2018. "California Environmental Quality Lawsuits and California's Housing Crisis." *Hastings Environmental Law Journal* 24(1): 21–71.

Hilliard, John. 2010. "After More than a Decade, St. Aidan's Conversion to Housing in Brookline Complete." *Wicked Local*. Available at www.wickedlocal.com/article/20100609/News/306099758. Accessed on June 27, 2018.

Hilliard, John. 2017. "Affordable Housing Plans Shaking Up the Suburbs." *Boston Globe*. Available at www.bostonglobe.com/metro/regionals/west/2017/09/29/affordable-housing-proposals-shaking-suburbs/8x4Jophgl7vjc8G75qXSZI/story.html. Accessed on August 1, 2018.

Hoene, Christopher, Christopher Kingsley, and Matthew Leighninger. 2013. "Bright Spots in Community Engagement." Available at www.knightfoundation.org/media/uploads/publication_pdfs/BrightSpots-final.pdf. Accessed on August 14, 2017.

Holman, Mirya. 2014. *Women in Politics in the American City*. Philadelphia, PA: Temple University Press.

Hopkins, Daniel J. 2010. "Politicized Places: Explaining Where and When Immigrants Provoke Local Opposition." *American Political Science Review* 104(1): 40–60.

Horne, Michael. 2013. "Neighbors Boiling over Boylston Plan." *Urban Milwaukee* . Available at urbanmilwaukee.com/2013/01/23/plenty-of-horne-neighbors-boiling-over-boylston-plan/. Accessed on May 15, 2018.

Hsieh, Chang-Tai, and Enrico Moretti. 2015. "Why Do Cities Matter? Local Growth and Aggregate Growth." Technical report. National Bureau of Economic Research Working Paper No. 21154. Available at https://chicagounbound.uchicago.edu/cgi/viewcontent.cgi?article=1045&context=housing_law_and_policy. Accessed on July 8, 2019.

Imai, Kosuke, and Kabir Khanna. 2016. "Improving Ecological Inference by Predicting Individual Ethnicity from Voter Registration Records." *Political Analysis* 24: 263–272.

Ioannidis, John P. A. 2005. "Why Most Published Research Findings Are False." *PLOS: Medicine* 2(8): e124. Available at www.ncbi.nlm.nih.gov/pmc/articles/PMC1182327/.

Isabella, Jeanette. 2016. "Letter: Urbanization Gone Too Far." *The Newburyport Daily News*. Available at www.newburyportnews.com/opinion/letters_to_the_editor/letter-urbanization-gone-too-far/article_98d7d97f-f31c-58c2-b21a-83334361cd29.html. Accessed on October 7, 2018.

Islas, Jason. 2018. "Los Angeles City Council Votes Unanimously to Oppose S.B. 827." *Streetsblog LA*. Available at la.streetsblog.org/2018/03/27/los-angeles-city-council-votes-unanimously-to-oppose-s-b-827/. Accessed on September 14, 2018.

Jacobus, Rick. 2017. "We Are All NIMBYs...Sometimes." *Shelterforce: The Voice of Community Development*. Available at shelterforce.org/2017/09/12/we-are-all-nimbys-sometimes/. Accessed on September 20, 2017.

Jannene, Jeramey. 2014. "Developers Slay NIMBY Objectors." *Urban Milwaukee*. Available at urbanmilwaukee.com/2014/09/01/eyes-on-milwaukee-developer-slays-nimby-objectors/. Accessed on August 21, 2017.

Judd, Dennis R., and Todd Swanstrom. 1994. *City Politics: Private Power and Public Policy*. New York: HarperCollins College Publishers.

Kagan, Robert A. 2003. *Adversarial Legalism: The American Way of Law*. Cambridge, MA: Harvard University Press.

Kahneman, Daniel, and Amos Tversky. 1979. "Prospect Theory: An Analysis of Decision Under Risk." *Econometrica* 47(2): 263–291.

Kash, Maggie. 2018. "Sierra Club Policy on Transit-Oriented Development." *Sierra Club Press Release*. Available at www.sierraclub.org/press-releases/2018/02/sierra-club-policy-transit-oriented-development. Accessed on September 14, 2018.

Katznelson, Ira. 2005. *When Affirmative Action Was White*. New York: Norton & Company.

Key, V. O. 1949. *Southern Politics*. New York: Random House.

Kiley, John. 2004. "Convert! The Adaptive Reuse of Churches." MIT masters thesis. Available at dspace.mit.edu/handle/1721.1/35692. Accessed on April 13, 2019.

Kirk, Mimi. 2017. "The NIMBY Fight That Rocked an Iowa City." *CityLab*. Available at www.citylab.com/equity/2017/09/the-nimby-fight-that-rocked-an-iowa-city/538017. Accessed on July 21, 2018.

Klapper, Leora, Luc Laeven, and Raghuram Rajan. 2006. "Entry Regulation as a Barrier to Entrepreneurship." *Journal of Financial Economics* 82(3): 591–629. Available at www.sciencedirect.com/science/article/pii/S0304405X06000936.

Knudson, Kennan. 2005. "Changes on St. Aidan's Project Trigger Unease." *Boston Globe*. Downloaded from Proquest.

Koger, Gregory. 2010. *Filibustering: A Political History of Obstruction in the House and Senate*. Chicago: University of Chicago Press.

Krogstad, Jens Manuel. 2016. "Key Facts about the Latino Vote in 2016." Pew Research Center. Available at www.pewresearch.org/fact-tank/2016/10/14/key-facts-about-the-latino-vote-in-2016/. Accessed on August 22, 2018.

Krogstad, Jens Manuel, and Mark Hugo Lopez. 2016. "Black Voter Turnout Fell in 2016, Even as a Record Number of Americans Cast Ballots." Pew Research Center. Available at www.pewresearch.org/fact-tank/2017/05/12/black-voter-turnout-fell-in-2016-even-as-a-record-number-of-americans-cast-ballots/. Accessed on August 22, 2018.

Krugman, Paul. 2005. "That Hissing Sound." *New York Times*. Available at www.nytimes.com/2005/08/08/opinion/that-hissing-sound.html. Accessed on February 22, 2018.

Kruse, Kevin. 2005. *White Flight: Atlanta and the Making of Modern Conservatism*. Princeton, NJ: Princeton University Press.

Kupferschmidt, Kai. 2018. "More and More Scientists Are Preregistering Their Studies. Should You?" *Sciencemag.org*. Available at www.sciencemag.org/news/2018/09/more-and-more-scientists-are-preregistering-their-studies-should-you. Accessed on April 13, 2019.

Lamacchia, Anthony. 2016. "Don't Get Caught Up in the Bidding War 'Hype.'" *Boston Globe*. Available at www.bostonglobe.com/lifestyle/real-estate/2016/09/16/don-get-caught-bidding-war-hype/Yp6FdOszzmxW86eCnhRnBL/story.html. Accessed on May 15, 2018.

Lassen, David Dreyer. 2005. "The Effect of Information on Voter Turnout: Evidence from a Natural Experiment." *American Journal of Political Science* 49(1): 103–118.

Lassen, David Dreyer, and Soren Serritzlew. 2011. "Jurisdiction Size and Local Democracy: Evidence on Internal Political Efficacy from Large-scale Municipal Reform." *American Political Science Review* 105(2): 238–258.

Lee, Timothy B. 2015. "How NIMBYism Is Holding Back Silicon Valley and the American Economy." *Vox Media*. Available at www.vox.com/2015/2/25/8109437/how-nimbyism-is-holding-back-silicon-valley-and-the-american-economy. Accessed on July 21, 2018.

Levine, Jeremy. 2017. "The Paradox of Community Power: Cultural Processes and Elite Authority in Participatory Governance." *Social Forces* 95(3): 1155–1179.

Lewyn, Michael. 2005. "How Overregulation Creates Sprawl (Even in a City without Zoning)." *Wayne Law Review* 50: 1171.

Logan, John R., and Harvey L. Molotch. 1987. *Urban Fortunes: The Political Economy of Place*. Berkeley: University of California Press.

Logan, Tim. 2017. "Chance to Live in New Apartments Near North Station Draws Crowd." *Boston Globe*. Available at www.bostonglobe.com/business/2017/10/25/chance-live-new-apartment-near-north-station-draws-crowd/MS0400ekGR15QZK8qnyzsJ/story.html. Accessed on May 14, 2018.

Logan, Tim. 2018. "Citing a 'Housing Emergency,' 15 Local Mayors Pledge to Boost Construction." *Boston Globe*. Available at www.bostonglobe.com/business/2018/10/02/citing-housing-emergency-local-mayors-pledge-dramatically-boost-construction/plYlzBr3OoM6W6la3L1zTL/story.html. Accessed on April 13, 2019.

Lubbell, Mark, Richard C. Feiock, and Edgar Ramirez. 2005. "Political Institutions and Conservation by Local Governments." *Urban Affairs Review* 40(6): 706–729.

Lubbell, Mark, Richard C. Feiock, and Edgar Ramirez. 2009. "Local Institutions and the Politics of Urban Growth." *American Journal of Political Science* 53(3): 649–665.

Lupia, Arthur, and Anne Norton. 2017. "Inequality Is Always in the Room: Language and Power in Deliberative Democracy." *Daedalus* 156(3): 64–76.

Mangin, John. 2014. "The New Exclusionary Zoning." *Stanford Law Review* 25: 91–120.

Mann, Thomas E., and Norman J. Ornstein. 2013. *It's Even Worse than It Looks: How the American Constitutional System Collided with the New Politics of Extremism*. New York: Basic Books.

Mannix, Andy. 2019. "In Minneapolis, a Test Case for Cities Looking to Solve Affordable Housing Crisis." *Minneapolis Star Tribune*. April 27, 2019. Available at www.startribune.com/in-minneapolis-a-test-case-for-cities-looking-to-solve-affordable-housing-crisis/509165002/. Accessed on June 20, 2019.

Mansbridge, Jane. 1980. *Beyond Adversary Democracy*. New York: Basic Books.

Marble, William, and Clayton Nall. 2017. "Beyond 'NIMBYism': Why Americans Support Affordable Housing But Oppose Local Housing Development."

Working paper. Available at www.dropbox.com/s/bdo3riekpnywgot/ MarbleNall_NIMBYPaper.pdf?dl=0. Accessed on August 15, 2017.

Martin, Emmie. 2017. "The Salary You Need to Afford a Home in 20 Major US Cities." *CNBC*.

Masuoka, Natalie. 2008. "Defining the Group: Latino Identity and Political Participation." *American Politics Research* 35(1): 33–61.

McEnery, Thornton. 2011. "The World's 15 Biggest Landowners." *Business Insider*. Available at www.businessinsider.com/worlds-biggest-landowners-2011-3. Accessed on June 27, 2018.

McKay, Amy. 2012. "Negative Lobbying and Policy Outcomes." *American Politics Research* 40(1): 116–146.

McMullen, Troy. 2016. "Cambridge, Massachusetts, Where Home Prices Are Rising by Degrees." *Financial Times*. Available at www.ft.com/content/4e9793f8-136f-11e6-91da-096d89bd2173. Accessed on May 15, 2018.

Mears, Kepler. 2002. "Keep the Church, Says Writer." *Boston Globe*. Downloaded from Proquest.

Meier, Kenneth J., Eric Gonzales Juenke, Robert D. Wrinkle, and J. L. Polinard. 2005. "Structural Choices and Representational Biases: The Post-election Color of Representation." *American Journal of Political Science* 49(4): 758–768. Available at www.jstor.org/stable/3647695.

Mettler, Suzanne. 2007. *Soldiers to Citizens: The G.I. Bill and the Making of the Greatest Generation.* New York: Oxford University Press.

Michels, Ank, and Laurens De Graaf. 2010. "Examining Citizen Participation: Local Participatory Policy Making and Democracy." *Local Government Studies* 36(4): 477–491.

Michener, Jamila. 2018. *Fragmented Democracy.* New York: Cambridge University Press.

Mullin, Megan. 2009. *Governing the Tap: Special District Governance and the New Local Politics of Water.* Cambridge, MA: MIT Press.

Murphy, Katy. 2017. "'Homes for Human Beings': Millennial-Driven Anti-NIMBY Movement Is Winning with a Simple Message." *East Bay Times*. Available at www.eastbaytimes.com/2017/11/12/homes-for-human-beings-millennial-driven-anti-nimby-movement-is-winning-with-a-simple-message/. Accessed on July 21, 2018.

National Low Income Housing Coalition. 2017. "Out of Reach." Available at nlihc.org/sites/default/files/oor/OOR_2017.pdf. Accessed on August 14, 2017.

Nodjimbadem, Katie. 2017. "The Racial Segregation of American Cities Was Anything but Accidental." *Smithsonian.com*. Available at www.smithsonianmag.com/history/how-federal-government-intentionally-racially-segregated-american-cities-180963494/. Accessed on April 17, 2018.

Oliver, J. Eric. 2001. *Democracy in Suburbia.* Princeton, NJ: Princeton University Press.

Oliver, J. Eric, Shang E. Ha, and Zachary Callen. 2012. *Local Elections and the Politics of Small-Scale Democracy.* Princeton, NJ: Princeton University Press.

O'Neil, Moira, Giulia Gualco-Nelson, and Eric Biber. 2018. "Getting It Right: Examining the Local Land Use Entitlement Process in California to Inform

Policy and Process." *Berkeley Law Report.* Available at www.law.berkeley
.edu/wp-content/uploads/2018/02/Getting_It_Right.pdf. Accessed on September 17, 2018.

Otárola, Miguel. 2018 "Minneapolis City Council Approves 2040 Comprehensive Plan on 12-1 Vote." *Minneapolis Star Tribune.* December 7, 2018. Available at www.startribune.com/minneapolis-city-council-approves-2040-comprehensive-plan-on-12-1-vote/502178121/. Accessed on June 20, 2019.

Otárola, Miguel. 2019. "After Criticism, Minneaopolis Eases Proposed Rules for Neighborhood Groups." *Minneapolis Star Tribune.* April 23, 2019. Available at www.startribune.com/after-criticism-minneapolis-eases-proposed-rules-for-neighborhood-groups/508926012/?refresh=true. Accessed on June 20, 2019.

Ouroussoff, Nicolai. 2007. "Complex, Contradictory Robert Moses." *New York Times.* Available at www.nytimes.com/2007/02/02/arts/design/02mose.html. Accessed on July 23, 2018.

Paul, Lauren Gibbons. 2015. "Not in Newton's Back Yard: Affordable Housing in Newton." *Boston Magazine.* Available at www.bostonmagazine .com/property/article/2015/02/24/affordable-housing-in-newton/. Accessed on August 24, 2017.

Paulson, Michael. 2001. "Real Estate Boom Leaves Churches Worth Millions." *Boston Globe.* Downloaded from Proquest.

Paulson, Michael. 2004. "Diocesan Headquarters Sold to BC." *Boston Globe.* Available at archive.boston.com/globe/spotlight/abuse/stories5/042104_ sale.htm. Accessed on August 16, 2018.

Pendall, Rolf. 1999. "Opposition to Housing: NIMBY and Beyond." *Urban Affairs Review* 34(1): 112–136.

Peterson, Paul E. 1981. *City Limits.* Chicago: University of Chicago Press.

Petrishen, Brad. 2014. "Officials, Residents Ponder Worcester's Problems, Potential." *Telegram.com.* Available at www.telegram.com/article/20140921/ NEWS/309219882. Accessed on May 17, 2018.

Pioneer Institute for Public Policy Research and Rappaport Institute for Greater Boston. 2005. "Massachusetts Housing Regulation Database." Prepared by Amy Dain and Jenny Schuetz. Available at www.masshousingregulations.com/ dataandreports.asp. Accessed on March 2, 2017.

Popkin, Susan J. 2017. "Proposed Cuts to Public Housing Threaten a Repeat of the 1980s Housing Crisis." *Urban Institute Blog.* Available at www.urban.org/urban-wire/proposed-cuts-public-housing-threaten-repeat-1980s-housing-crisis. Accessed on September 14, 2018.

Putnam, Robert D. 2007. "E pluribus Unum: Diversity and Community in the TwentyFirst Century (the 2006 Johan Skytte Prize Lecture)." *Scandinavian Political Studies* 30(2): 137–174.

Quigley, John M., and Larry Rosenthal. 2005. "The Effects of Land Use Regulation on the Price of Housing: What Do We Know? What Can We Learn?" *Cityscape* 81(1): 69–137.

Rae, Douglas- W. 2004. *City: Urbanism and Its End.* New Haven, CT: Yale University Press.

Rich, Michael J., and Robert P. Stoker. 2014. *Collaborative Governance for Urban Revitalization: Lessons from Empowerment Zones*. Ithaca, NY: Cornell University Press.

Robitaille, Jeremy, and Rachel G. Bratt. 2012. "Fear of Affordable Housing: Perception vs. Reality." *Shelterforce: The Voice of Community Development*. Available at shelterforce.org/2012/10/10/fear_of_affordable_housing_perception_vs-_reality/. Accessed on August 1, 2018.

Rodriguez, Joe Fitzgerald. 2018. "SB 827 Rallies End with YIMBys Shouting Down Protestors of Color." *San Francisco Examiner*. Available at www.sfexaminer.com/sb-827-rallies-end-yimbys-shouting-protesters-color/. Accessed on September 14, 2018.

Rogers, Dave. 2017. "Former Mr. India Site Sold, Condos Planned." *Newburyport Daily News*. Available at www.newburyportnews.com/news/local_news/former-mr-india-site-sold-condos-planned/article_87ec9bfa-9768-5316-850d-58e63861c440.html. Accessed on October 5, 2018.

Rothstein, Richard. 2017. *The Color of Law*. New York: W.W. Norton.

Rothwell, Jonathan. 2018. "Housing Costs, Zoning, and Access to High Scoring Schools." *Brookings Institution*. Available at www.brookings.edu/wp-content/uploads/2016/06/0419_school_inequality_rothwell.pdf. Accessed on April 15, 2019.

Rothwell, Jonathan T., and Douglas S. Massey. 2013. "Density Zoning and Class Segregation in U.S. Metropolitan America." *Social Science Quarterly* 91(5): 1123–1143.

Roy, Anamika. 2014. "Neighbors in Ashland Call Proposed 40B Site Plans an 'Insult.'" *Metrowest Daily News* . Available at www.metrowestdailynews.com/article/20140718/news/140716579. Accessed on August 1, 2018.

Sabatini, Joshua. 2018. "SF Supes Vote 8-3 to Oppose Wiener Legislation Changing City Zoning." *San Francisco Examiner*. Available at www.sfexaminer.com/sf-supes-vote-oppose-wieners-sb-827-housing-proposal/. Accessed on September 14, 2018.

Samburg, Bridget. 2004. "Two Trees Grow." *Boston Globe*. Downloaded from Proquest.

Sampson, Robert J. 2012. *Great American City: Chicago and the Enduring Neighborhood Effect*. Chicago: University of Chicago Press.

Sances, Michael W., and Hye Young You. 2017. "Who Pays for Government? Descriptive Representation and Exploitative Revenue Sources." *Journal of Politics* 79(3): 1090–1094.

Sandel, Megan, Richard Sheward, Stephanie Ettinger de Cuba et al. 2018. "Unstable Housing and Caregiver and Child Health in Renter Families." *Pediatrics* 94(2): 1–10.

Schaerlaeckens, Leander. 2013. "Senior Living and Retirement: Best, Most Affordable Places for Senior Housing in the Hudson Valley in 2013." *Hudson Valley Magazine*. Available at www.hvmag.com/Hudson-Valley-Magazine/February-2013/Senior-Living-and-Retirement-Best-Most-Affordable-Places-for-Senior-Housing-in-the-Hudson-Valley-in-2013/. Accessed on February 22, 2018.

Scharfenberg, David. 2001*a*. "Brookline Tries a Balancing Act: Goals of Two Housing Groups Are at Odds." *Boston Globe*. Downloaded from Proquest.

Scharfenberg, David. 2001*b*. "A Closed Church Sets Off Hostilities in Brookline: Neighbors Urge Saving St. Aidan's Facade, but Church Frets About Cost." *Boston Globe*. Downloaded From Proquest.

Schiffman, Betsy. 2002. "Holy Real Estate." *Forbes Magazine*. Available at www .forbes.com/2002/12/06/cx_bs_1206home.html#1482a4ae35eb. Accessed on June 27, 2018.

Schleicher, David. 2013. "City Unplanning." *Yale Law Journal* 122: 1672–1736.

Schlozman, Kay, Sidney Verba, and Henry E. Brady. 2012. *The Unheavenly Chorus: Unequal Political Voice and the Broken Promise of American Democracy*. Princeton, NJ: Princeton University Press.

Schneider, Benjamin. 2018. "Meet the PHIMBYs." *CityLab*. Available at www .citylab.com/equity/2018/04/nimbys-yimbys-and-phimbys-oh-my/557927/. Accessed on September 14, 2018.

Schuetz, Jenny. 2009. "Guarding the Town Walls: Mechanisms and Motives for Restricting Multifamily Housing in Massachusetts." *Real Estate Economics* 36(3): 555–586.

Self, Robert O. 2003. *American Babylon: Race and the Struggle for Postward Oakland*. Princeton, NJ: Princeton University Press.

Sharkey, Patrick. 2013. *Urban Neighborhoods and the End of Progress Toward Racial Equality*. Chicago: University of Chicago Press.

Shaw, Randy. 2018. "Special Report: Why SB 827 Failed." *Beyond Chron: The Voice of the Rest*. Available at www.beyondchron.org/special-report-sb-827-failed/. Accessed on September 14, 2018.

Sherman Oaks HA. 2018. "SOHA Says No to Wiener's SB827 . . . Here's Why." *Los Angeles Times*. Available at www.citywatchla.com/index.php/375-voices/15202-soha-says-no-to-wiener-s-sb827-here-s-why. Accessed on September 14, 2018.

Shingles, Richard D. 1981. "Black Consciousness and Political Participation: The Missing Link." *American Political Science Review* 75(1): 76–91.

Silver, Christopher. 1997. "The Racial Origins of Zoning in America." In *Urban Planning and the African American Community: In the Shadows*, ed. June Manning Thomas and Martha Ritzdorf. Thousand Oaks, CA: Safe Publications.

Simmons, Joseph P., Leif D. Nelson, and Uri Simonsohn. 2011. "False-Positive Psychology: Undisclosed Flexibility in Data Collection and Analysis Allows Presenting Anything as Significant." *Psychological Science* 22(11): 1359–1366.

Soss, Joe, and Vesla Weaver. 2017. "Police Are Our Government: Politics, Political Science, and the Policing of Race-Subjugated Communities." *Annual Review of Political Science* 20: 565–91.

Starr, Terrell Jermaine. 2018. "Washington, DC, Is Being Sued for Gentrification." *The Root*. Available at www.theroot.com/washington-d-c-is-being-sued-for-gentrification-1826899679. Accessed on September 14, 2018.

State of California. 1872. "Chapter 2: Obligations of Owners [840-848]." Available at leginfo.legislature.ca.gov/faces/codes_displaySection.xhtml?lawCode=CIV&sectionNum=841. Accessed on September 14, 2018.

State of Massachusetts. 1872. "Chapter 131: Section 140: Removal, Fill, Dredging or Altering of Land Bordering Waters." Available at malegislature.gov/Laws/GeneralLaws/PartI/TitleXIX/Chapter131/Section40. Accessed on September 14, 2018.

Stickgold, Emma. 2006. "Reaching Peace at St. Aidan's: Board Backs Resolution." *Boston Globe*. Downloaded from Proquest.

Stone, Clarence N., and Robert P. Stoker. 2015. *Urban Neighborhoods in a New Era*. Chicago: University of Chicago Press.

Stone, Clarence Nathan. 1989. *Regime Politics: Governing Atlanta, 1946–1988*. Lawrence: University Press of Kansas.

Sugrue, Thomas J. 1996. *The Origins of the Urban Crisis: Race and Inequality in Postwar Detroit*. Princeton, NJ: Princeton University Press.

Talbot, Victoria. 2018. "Beverly Hills City Council Resolves to Fight Transit-Rich Housing Bill SB 827." *Beverly Hills Courier*. Available at http://bhcourier.com/2018/01/11/beverly-hills-city-council-resolves-to-fight-transit-rich-housing-bill-sb-827/. Accessed on September 14, 2018.

Tighe, J. Rosie. 2010. "Public Opinion and Affordable Housing: A Review of the Literature." *Journal of Planning Literature* 25(1): 3–17.

Town of Lawrence. 2018. "Planning Board." Available at www.cityoflawrence.com/572/Planning-Board. Accessed on August 22, 2018.

Trounstine, Jessica. 2008. *Political Monopolies in American Cities: The Rise and Fall of Bosses and Reformers*. Chicago: University of Chicago Press.

Trounstine, Jessica. 2013. "Turnout and Incumbency in Local Elections." *Urban Affairs Review* 49(2): 167–189.

Trounstine, Jessica. 2016. "Segregation and Inequality in Public Goods." *American Journal of Political Science* 60(3): 709–725.

Trounstine, Jessica. 2018. *Segregation by Design*. New York: Cambridge University Press.

Trounstine, Jessica, and Melodie Valdini. 2008. "The Context Matters: The Effects of SingleMember versus At-Large Districts on City Council Diversity." *American Journal of Political Science* 52(3): 554–569. Available at https://onlinelibrary.wiley.com/doi/abs/10.1111/j.1540-5907.2008.00329.x.

Tversky, Amos, and Daniel Kahneman. 1973. "Availability: A Heuristic for Judging Frequency and Probability." *Cognitive Psychology* 5: 207–232. Available at https://msu.edu/ema/803/Ch11-JDM/2/TverskyKahneman73.pdf.

Verba, Sidney, Kay Lehman Schlozman, and Henry E. Brady. 1995. *Voice and Equality*. Cambridge, MA: Harvard University Press.

Wang, Jenna. 2018. "Residents Sue Washington D.C. for Racist Gentrification Practices." *Forbes*. Available at www.forbes.com/sites/jennawang/2018/06/28/residents-sue-washington-d-c-over-1-billion-for-racist-gentrification-practices/#780c6fa13e8f. Accessed on September 14, 2018.

Warner, Joel. 2001. "To Develop or Preserve? St. Aidan's Case Frames Larger Townwide Debate." *Boston Globe*. Downloaded from Proquest.

Warner, Joel. 2002a. "Devotedly Theirs." *Boston Globe*. Downloaded from Proquest.

Warner, Joel. 2002b. "Oy Vey to Church." *Boston Globe*. Downloaded from Proquest.

Warner, Joel. 2002c. "Taking Church Fight to Rome, St. Aidan's Group Hires Canon Lawyer." *Boston Globe* . Downloaded from Proquest.

Weaver, Vesla M., and Amy E. Lerman. 2010. "Political Consequences of the Carceral State." *American Political Science* Review 104(4): 817–833.

Wei, Iris I., Beth A. Virnig, Dolly A. John, and Robert O'Morgan. 2006. "Using a Spanish Surname Match to Improve Identification of Hispanic Women in Medicare Administrative Data." *Health Services Research* 41: 1469–1481.

Welch, Susan. 1990. "The Impact of At-Large Elections on the Representation of Blacks and Hispanics." *Journal of Politics* 52(4): 1050–1076. Available at www.jstor.org/stable/2131682.

Welch, Susan, and Timothy Bledsoe. 1988. *Urban Reform and Its Consequences.* Chicago: University of Chicago Press.

Wenger, Yvonne. 2014. "Nearly 74,000 Sign Up for Baltimore's Section 8 Wait List." *Baltimore Sun*. Available at www.baltimoresun.com/news/maryland/baltimore-city/bs-md-ci-section-8-20141031-story.html. Accessed on May 14, 2018.

White, Ariel. 2019. "Misdemeanor Disenfrachisement? The Demobilizing Effects of Brief Jail Spells on Potential Voters." *American Political Science Review* 113(2): 311–324.

The White House. 2011. "The White House Neighborhood Revitalization Initiative." Available at www.hud.gov/sites/documents/NEIGHBOR-REV.PDF. Accessed on August 16, 2018.

White House. 2016. "Housing Development Toolkit." Available at www .whitehouse.gov/sites/whitehouse.gov/files/images/Housing_Development_ Toolkit%2of.2.pdf. Accessed on March 2, 2017.

Wiener, Scott. 2018. "SB-827 Planning and Zoning: Transit-Rich Housing Bonus." California Legislature 2017–2018 Regular Session. Available at leg info.legislature.ca.gov/faces/billTextClient.xhtml?bill_id=201720180SB827. Accessed on September 14, 2018.

Winkler, Elizabeth. 2017. "'Snob Zoning' Is Racial Housing Segregation by Another Name." *Washington Post*. Available at www.washingtonpost.com/news/wonk/wp/2017/09/25/snob-zoning-is-racial-housing-segregation-by-another-name/?utm_term=.67d178c8a2b5. Accessed on April 17, 2018.

Word, David L., Charles D. Coleman, Robert Nunziata, and Robert Kominski. 2000. "Demographic Aspects of Surnames from Census 2000." Available at www2.census.gov/topics/genealogy/2000surnames/surnames.pdf.

Yglesias, Matthew. 2013. "My Five-Point Plan for Fixing Everything." *Slate*. Available at www.slate.com/blogs/moneybox/2013/10/23/how_to_ fix_everything.html. Accessed on July 21, 2018.

Zahniser, David, Liam Dillon, and Jon Schleuss. 2018. "Plan to Dramatically Increase Development Would Transform Some L.A. Neighborhoods." *Los Angeles Times*. Available at www.latimes.com/local/lanow/la-me-ln-housing-bill-transit-20180325-htmlstory.html. Accessed on September 14, 2018.

Zillow. 2017. "Zillow Research." Available at www.zillow.com/research/data/. Accessed on July 8, 2019.

# Index

216 *Index*

vs. land use regulations, 42*fig*
Neighborhood Revitalization Initiative, 30
neighborhood-level empowerment, 4, 15, 22–23, 28–32, 46
neighborhood-level institutions, *see* participatory institutions
Nelson, Leif, 164
NIMBY (Not in My Backyard), 4, 13–14, 34–35, 121
Nolan, Hamilton, 148
nonprofits, 163
Norton, Anne, 121
Not in My Backyard, *see* NIMBY

O'Malley, Sean (cardinal), 24
Obama administration, 9, 30

Parriott, Jed, 155
participatory inequality
  addressing at city- and town-level, 166–169
  addressing at local level, 159–163
  comprehensive reform of, 171–172
  difficulties addressing, 157–159
  in housing politics, 13–14, 42–43, 56, 128, 157–159
participatory institutions, *see also* land use institutions
  as tool to delay construction, 26–27
  neighborhood empowerment by, 4, 28–32
participatory politics, *see* political participation
permits, *see* building permits; special permits
Peterson, Paul, 170
Phoenix, AZ, 54
PHIMBY (Public Housing in My Backyard), 154
Pioneer Institute for Public Policy Research, 54, 60
planning board meetings
  attendee comments, 1–3, 16–18, 89, 96–97, 112, 117–121, 130, 131, 139–143
  attendee demographics, 99–101
  commenter characteristics, 101*table*, 101–103
  construction opponents vs. supporters, 36–37, 97, 107*fig*, 109*table*, 106–111

Latino participation in, 39, 100, 104, 105
  local participation in, 1–3, 13, 24, 80–82
  participation as political activism, 134
  racism in comments, 137–139, 155
  reforming, 163–165
  resident concerns vs. meeting focus, 87–88, 115
  underrepresentation of Latinos, 133
planning boards, 26
  Acton Zoning Board, 119
  Amesbury, MA Planning Board, 131
  Brookline Zoning Board, 120, 121
  building permitting process, 26–27
  Cambridge Planning Board, 1, 80, 95
  Charlottesville Planning Commission, 12
  Duxbury Planning Board, 122
  LA Department of City Planning, 152
  LaGrange, NY Planning Board, 16
  Lawrence Planning Board, 105
  Lowell Zoning Board, 143
  Worcester Zoning Board, 139, 142
political activism
  planning meeting participation as, 134
political inequality, *see also* participatory inequality
  in land use institutions, 15
political participation
  impact of carceral state on, 41
  in housing policy, 1–4, 13, 16–19, 22–23, 95–97, 112–113, 116–118
  of housing policy, 131
  St. Aidan's as example of, 44–51
political tools
  CEQA lawsuits, 125–126
  delay, 4, 21, 25, 27–28, 128
  expert testimony, 120–122
  homeownership, 38–39, 114
  incumbency, 21
  litigation, 122–125
  neighborhood associations, 130–134
  participatory institutions, 26–27
Pollard, H.L., 40
Portney, Kent E., 132
private deed restrictions, 12
pro-housing interest groups
  to address participatory inequality, 161–163
property redevelopment
  natural experiment, 71–73, 75*fig*, 77, 78*fig*

Made in United States
North Haven, CT
14 April 2023

35430844R00146